Charles Kuralt's America

Also by Charles Kuralt

A Life on the Road
On the Road with Charles Kuralt
North Carolina Is My Home
Dateline: America
To the Top of the World

Charles Kuralt's
America

Charles Kuralt

ANCHOR BOOKS
DOUBLEDAY
New York   London   Toronto   Sydney   Auckland

AN ANCHOR BOOK
PUBLISHED BY DOUBLEDAY
a division of Bantam Doubleday Dell Publishing Group, Inc.
1540 Broadway, New York, New York 10036

ANCHOR BOOKS, DOUBLEDAY, and the portrayal of an anchor
are trademarks of Doubleday, a division of Bantam Doubleday Dell
Publishing Group, Inc.

Charles Kuralt's America was originally published
in hardcover by G. P. Putnam's Sons in 1995.
The Anchor Books edition published
by arrangement with G. P. Putnam's Sons.

Library of Congress Cataloging-in-Publication Data

Kuralt, Charles, 1934–
Charles Kuralt's America / Charles Kuralt. — 1st Anchor Books
trade pbk. ed.
p.   cm.
1. United States—Description and travel.   2. United States—
Social life and customs—1971–   3. Kuralt, Charles, 1934–
—Journeys—United States.   I. Title.
[E169.04.K87   1996b]
973.92—dc20   96-18992

ISBN 0-385-48510-7
First Anchor Books Trade Paperback Edition: October 1996

1   3   5   7   9   10   8   6   4   2

FOR CATHERINE,
WITH LOVE.

Contents

Acknowledgments

I wish to express my thanks to Karen Beckers, my friend and associate of many years, for her unfailing aid and encouragement. I am grateful to Joseph and Greg Bellon for proposing a book along these lines in the first place, and for ably representing me in this and other undertakings. I thank Neil Nyren, publisher and editor in chief at G. P. Putnam's Sons, for awaiting yet another overdue manuscript with his customary mannerliness.

I am grateful to Phil Johnson, Granville Hall, Hugh Morton, Catherine Morton, Mike and Julie Hillman, Wallace McRae, and Phil Norton for reading portions of this story and calling errors to my attention. Errors may remain; if you write enough words, one or two of them may jump up and bite you. I hope I have made it through this volume unbitten, and if I haven't, I apologize.

I thank Cryder Bankes for knowing everything, or at least knowing where to look it up. I am grateful to Alan H. Goldberg of Modernage Photographic Services for his careful handling of my efforts at photography. I thank Katherine Powis of the Horticultural Society of New York for answering a number of questions about growing things.

As for all the good people I met along the way, old friends and new, who took time to indulge my curiosity about their lives, I can only say they made this the most memorable year of my own life. I am grateful to them.

And most of all, to Petie, for keeping a light in the window.

Foreword

It was a long, happy affair, and I was faithful. I loved CBS News ardently at first, as a boy loves a girl. (At first, I *was* a boy, only twenty-two when I came to work in the newsroom on Madison Avenue.) My passion tempered outwardly as the years went by, but inside the old flame burned.

We gave each other gifts. CBS News gave me travel and excitement and a reason for living, and eventually a measure of fame and fortune. I gave her most of my waking hours, and most of my thoughts and energy, and nearly all my dreams of the future. I took crazy chances for her, especially in the beginning, often sleeping too little, working too hard, driving too fast, risking too much in places too dangerous, all to prove my love. I was ever constant. She took notice. We were consumed in each other. We were content.

Then I woke up one morning and realized I didn't love her anymore.

Time had passed, and we had changed. We no longer suited each other. An inner voice spoke to me. It said you are going to have to give up your big salary and your corner office and leave that Sunday morning program of yours to somebody else.

The voice said you haven't a world of time left to do all those things you promised yourself you'd do someday. For now, your lungs are still strong enough to let you walk through a mountain meadow and your legs will still support you in the current of a trout stream. You have plenty of curiosity left, and energy and love of life. You have at least one good long trip in you yet. If that's what you really want, you'd better be about it.

When I was younger, I thrived on the chatter and commotion of television. Suddenly, I found I'd had enough of it. A desire for substance and reality came over me. Maybe, sooner or later, this craving hits everybody. It hit me hard.

Go away, the voice said. Go be free.

I had worked at CBS for thirty-seven years. Without a single misgiving, I sat down at my desk at home and typed a short letter to my boss:

"Dear Eric, I feel it is time to resign from CBS News. Accordingly, I ask that you find a replacement for me on *Sunday Morning* as soon as possible—by the end of this month, I hope. . . ."

I delivered this letter that same day. The second it was out of my hand, I felt a wave of giddy release. I felt like singing. The thing was done, and I was on my own.

CBS announced my departure as my "retirement," and Dan Rather read the announcement so solemnly on the air that many people, upon hearing it, assumed at first that I had died. It wasn't an obituary notice I had meant to hand in; it was a Declaration of Independence. I wanted Roman candles, not funeral wreaths. Even the word "retirement" suggested a withdrawal I was nowhere near ready for. I knew I might retire somewhere down the road, but I desired an adventurous passage from here to there.

I planned a trip. I had spent nearly all my life traveling in the United States, but there was one more fanciful journey I had always wanted to make. Now I had the chance, and the prospect thrilled me: I would revisit my favorite American places at just the right time of year—the Florida Keys before it got too hot, the Minnesota canoe country before it got too cold, Charleston in azalea season, Montana in fishing season, Vermont when the oaks and maples turn crimson and gold. I would go to New Orleans and Alaska and the Blue Ridge Mountains and old New Mexico and the coast of Maine. I would go alone and without a plan and without a budget—I'd saved enough to live on for a while—and I wouldn't do anything that felt very much like work. I had never been any good at doing nothing; I thought I would try to learn.

I would drift with the current of life. I'd be footloose and a little irresponsible, and I'd have a perfect year in America.

One day I said goodbye to all my old friends at the office. The next day, I left.

Charles Kuralt's America

JANUARY

New Orleans

It's not a long taxi ride from the airport to the hotel where I like to stay in the French Quarter, twenty minutes or so if there's no traffic. That was plenty of time for John Laine, the cab driver, to discourse on the main themes of the city: family, music, and food.

"My great-grandfather was one of the first white jazzmen, 'Papa' Jack Laine. You must have heard of him. He played with Kid Ory and Leon Rappolo and those guys around the turn of the century. His drums are in the Jazz Museum. You can see 'em there.

"Of course, what I remember him for is not his drumming. He used to work with mules down beside the old molasses factory, and he'd stick his whole arm into a mule's rectum to lubricate up in there. I was just a little boy, and I'll tell you, that impressed the hell out of me!"

I could have closed my eyes in the backseat of the taxi and known where I was purely by the pungent accent washing over me from up front. The authentic dialect of New Orleans has been compared to Brooklynese, but really it is like no other in the world. From the first time I heard those sweet New Orleans intonations, they have been music to my ears.

"My grandfather Alfred played the trumpet. He came up with Louis Armstrong. He loved that man, and I did, too, especially when he sang 'What a Wonderful World.' Louis Armstrong should have been a U.S. ambassador. Everybody loved him."

John paused just long enough for me to murmur agreement and moved on to another subject, the truly universal one of spices and sauces and sustenance.

"I don't know where you're going to eat tonight, but you can't go wrong in New Orleans, you already know that, right? I got relatives in Spokane, Washington. I can't believe it, these people from Spokane just eat plain food!"

"Papa" Laine's great-grandson turned into Toulouse Street and stopped in front of the Maison de Ville. "Here we are," he said. "Life is short, now, so have a good time while you're here."

The next noon, I heard those exact words from Ella Brennan. I was sitting at a second-floor table in Commander's Palace, her Garden District restaurant, arguably the best eating place of all in this city devoted to eating. I had finished a good lunch of sautéed trout crusted with pecans, and was surreptitiously sopping up the last of the brown sauce with a crust of bread. Just then, of course, the grande dame of New Orleans cooking dropped by to catch me eating with my fingers. I think she forgave me; we have known each other since we were in our twenties.

We fell to talking about the city's chronic problems: poor people and crooked politicians.

"I wish we didn't have the poverty and corruption," Ella said, "but a friend of mine asked me, 'Do you like Italy?' I said of course, everybody likes Italy. My friend said, 'Well, think Italy.'

"I guess it's true. New Orleans is a Mediterranean city. It has certain habits, like good food, good times, families, friendship, poverty, sin . . . We're not going to change it."

Her gaze shifted to the rows of great gray tombs in the old Lafayette Cemetery across the street. "Just look over there," she said, and when I did, I knew right away what she meant.

She gave my hand a little squeeze as she got up to go. She said, "Have a good time while you're here."

Unless you're broke or sick or blue-nosed, I don't see how you could have anything but a good time in New Orleans. "Unique" is a word that cannot be qualified. It does not mean rare or uncommon; it means alone in the universe. By the standards of grammar and by the grace of God, New Orleans is the unique American place.

This would still be so if all the city had to offer were the flickering gas lamps in the soft nights, or the delicate tracery of the iron work on the galleries of the French Quarter (in New Orleans, they are *galleries,* not balconies, and they hang above *banquettes,* not sidewalks), or the open doors of the Dionysian dives bellowing loud music into Bourbon Street. But there is also the all-important matter of grillades and grits, of red beans and rice, of crawfish *étouffée* and filé gumbo and *pompano en papillote.*

"If you understand New Orleans food, you understand New Orleans life."

This is Joe Cahn talking, standing in the bountiful herbs and spices aisle of his Louisiana General Store in the old Jax Brewery building on Decatur Street.

"Most of the United States was settled by Anglo-Saxons and Puritan types. The work ethic prevailed, and all the pleasures of life were frowned on. It's real simple: work ethic equals bland food.

"But New Orleans, on the other hand—oh, man, New Orleans didn't know what the work ethic is, still doesn't! We were settled by Catholics from Spain and France who thought work should never interfere with the enjoyment of life. And that's what makes this place different from the rest of America. People in New Orleans believe in living in the present, and skimming off as much pleasure as they can today and eating as well as they can tonight. That goes for everybody. If you go to confession and say to the priest, 'I overate, Father,' you'll have his interest right away. He'll probably ask you, 'Where did you eat?' "

Joe Cahn has become a ruminative philosopher of food, maybe because he grew up in New Orleans gastronomically deprived. His father was not Cajun or Creole. He was Jewish, the southern representative of B'nai B'rith. Joe's mother couldn't cook. But Joe liked to eat. It didn't take long for the city's pervasive cooking culture to draw him in.

"I worked in restaurants, always in the front of the house. I was never a chef. I appreciate chefs, but waiters are almost as important. The best food in the world served with arrogance is no good at all."

Anyway, the real New Orleans cuisine, Joe Cahn says, isn't in the restaurants.

"It's in the kitchens, where the people who do the cooking only have so much to spend on food. One way to learn to cook is to go to the supermarket and hang around the greens counter or the meat counter. When you see someone buy a cheap cut of meat, ask 'What are you going to do with it?' "

In the back of the store, Joe Cahn operates the New Orleans School of Cooking. His tenured professor is an enormous and congenial man named Kevin Belton, six-foot-nine and 360 pounds, who moves about the kitchen classroom with the gladness and grace of a dancer. With many generations of New Orleans in his lineage, Chef Belton had the kind of upbringing Joe can only dream about.

"I always realized I was eating really well," he told me. "I imagine when I was about two weeks old, I thought, well, this nursing milk is fine, but let's get to the fish and crabs and shrimp, all that good stuff!

"I'd come home from school and say, 'What's for dinner, Ma?' She'd be looking in the pantry and she'd say, 'I don't know yet. Give me a minute.' She was a real New Orleans cook. She could make great meals out of whatever there was in the house.

"I was always in the kitchen with my mother. She was a teacher, and if she had to speak to a student on the phone while she was cooking, she'd say, 'Kevin, do this' or 'Kevin, do that.' So I learned to do it all.

"Now my sons do their homework in the kitchen with me, and they're learning to cook the same way I did. Getting together in the kitchen is so much better than getting together in the TV room. If you go to a party, it's always two parties, the one in the living room and the one in the kitchen, and the one in the kitchen is the best."

In a three-hour class, Kevin Belton cooks for a roomful of adoring out-of-towners, mostly women making notes. The day I was there the women hailed from Massachusetts, Pennsylvania, Arizona, England, and Japan. They were cultivated folk and probably pretty good at cooking the food of wherever they came from, but Kevin, a missionary possessing Holy Orders, approached them all as aborigines in mortal need of enlightenment. He wound himself up and started preaching the true gospel, beginning with the Louisiana Trinity—onion, celery, and green pepper. His sermon was so fervent that I started making notes myself.

"Jambalaya!" he exclaimed. "Jambalaya! The basic dish of rich man and poor man! Couldn't be simpler! One cup of rice, two cups of Trinity, two cups of liquid!"

He made the women repeat after him in unison: "One cup of rice, two cups of Trinity, two cups of liquid!"

"Right!" Kevin said. "And your two cups of liquid should include three-quarters of a cup of liquid from your cooked Trinity. The other cup-and-a-quarter is seasoned water if you're poor, fine stock if you're rich, whatever you've got!"

A mental image came to me of Kevin's mother looking around in the pantry for the dinner ingredients.

"Now," he asked, "shall we use butter or margarine in this recipe?"

The women were catching on. They recited, "Whatever you've got!"

"Right!" Kevin boomed. "Shall we add some chicken or some sausage?"

"Whatever you've got!"

"Right! And if you're cooking in big pots for a crowd the way my mother did—whole households of relatives would come over to our house on the weekends—you just have to be able to multiply: twenty cups of rice, forty cups of Trinity, forty cups of liquid!"

He set the jambalaya on the stove to simmer and moved on to the next recipe. When class was over, he served the students heaping dishes of jambalaya and bowls of gumbo, and for dessert, bread pudding with whiskey sauce. He set a place for me, too, and I can certify that a happier lunch was not consumed in New Orleans that day. One of the women at my table asked Kevin, "Could I substitute rum for the bourbon in the bread pudding sauce?"

Kevin beamed her a wide and silent smile.

"Oh, right!" she said. "Whatever I've got."

My purpose in revisiting New Orleans was to eat my way through a whole month of contented days and nights. This might be considered gluttonous any place else, but New Orleans is not any place else. I had a collaborator, Phil Johnson, writer, musician, comrade, cook, and connoisseur, who has a busy schedule but is always ready to drop everything to go to dinner. We have been going to dinner in New Orleans for thirty years, Phil and I, and I have yet to pay for a meal. I guess I am going to have to put Phil Johnson in my will to pay him back, for this is his town and these are his restaurants. He is proud of them, and when he sits down at their tables, it is always as host, not guest.

Phil grew up in the third ward, a blue-collar neighborhood bounded by Canal Street, the river, and the cemeteries, among immigrants' children who learned to appreciate good food at home. One of Phil's childhood friends was Warren Leruth. While Phil worked his way up in journalism—starting on the roof of the Pelicans' baseball park collecting foul balls for seventy-five cents a night, getting to know the sports writer for the New Orleans *Item,* and becoming, in time, a writer for the *Item* himself—Warren was making a similarly modest start as an apprentice chef. Both of them eventually became famous in town, Phil as the nightly editorialist on WWL-TV, Warren as the proprietor of the city's most celebrated restaurant, LeRuth's. (He thought the capital *R* gave a little class to the name.)

Well, technically, LeRuth's wasn't in the city. It was across the river in Gretna, where Warren could afford the rent. Before he opened the restaurant thirty years ago, unpaid carpenters and tinsmiths were banging on the door with Warren barricaded inside hollering, "Mr. Leruth's not here! Come back tomorrow!"

Not long after LeRuth's opened, however, Warren's ingenious and original cooking brought people streaming over the bridge to have a meal—including his old friend Phil Johnson. My first dinner there with Phil one night in the Sixties was a mouth-watering and eye-opening experience which I have remembered all these years. Warren Leruth's artichoke and oyster soup shook up the old Galatoire's and Antoine's world of New Orleans cuisine the way Paul Prudhomme's blackened redfish was to do a generation later.

There's no LeRuth's any more—the daily pursuit of perfection finally wore down the chef and he closed the place rather than diminish it—but Phil and I had a reunion with the great man at the annual Chef's Charity at the Fairmont Hotel one afternoon. The chefs in the kitchen, many of them illustrious in their own right, crowded around to shake hands with a living legend. I thought I caught Warren, a modest man, blushing. I was touched to see that chefs really are venerated in New Orleans the way movie stars are in Hollywood—even by one another.

In retirement, Warren has become a "taste doctor" for the big food companies, showing them how to make their salad dressing more palatable or inventing a better over-the-counter chicken sandwich or precisely copying a competitor's food, if that's what they want. His son, Larry, told me Warren recently copied all the Pepperidge Farm cookies, just to prove to himself that he could.

Starting, I suppose, with Warren Leruth, Phil Johnson long ago became friendly with every great chef in town. He is welcome to enter their restaurants through the kitchen to see what's cooking before ordering his meal.

With Phil's wife, Freida, we drove through a biblical thunderstorm one night, thirty miles across Lake Pontchartrain to the beautiful country inn, La Provence, near Mandeville, where Chris Kerageorgiou creates sauces that would make cardboard taste delicious. It is a trip I have made many times. I think those sauces alone make La Provence one of the best restaurants in the world.

Chris's friend and foil—"I am the sexy one, he is the old one"—is Goffredo Fraccaro, founder and chef emeritus of La Riviera in Metairie. Phil used to take me to lunch there (in the days before the restaurant was open for lunch) with a friend from the third ward days, A. J. Capritto, a lawyer given to sage pronouncements about New Orleans. ("The poor ye have with ye always, but the rich go away in the summertime.")

Chef Goffredo is a master of veal and pasta, but his supreme accomplishment, the one that guarantees his immortality, is his Scampi La Riviera, still on the menu years after his so-called retirement. I stood over his shoulder one day and watched every move as he prepared this dish. He gave the world a cunningly abridged version of the recipe in a popular cookbook, but here is the real thing. If you care anything about good cooking, you will thank me for this:

Scampi La Riviera

2 lbs. large shrimp	1/2 cup butter
6 cloves garlic, chopped	1/2 cup red vinegar
2 Tablespoons olive oil	8 mint leaves
1/4 cup parsley, chopped	3 Tablespoons lemon juice
1 Tablespoon paprika	pinch of oregano
salt	

Preheat oven to 400 degrees. Shell the shrimp, leaving only the tail shell. De-vein and rinse the shrimp and place them in a large cast-iron skillet atop a thin layer of olive oil. Season them with salt and sprinkle them with paprika. Bake in the oven for 7 minutes.

Remove the skillet from the oven and add lemon juice, chopped mint, garlic, vinegar, and parsley. Sprinkle on a little more olive oil.

Place the skillet on a medium flame.

Add a bit of water and the butter and oregano. Cover the skillet and cook for 2 minutes, or until the flavor is concentrated and the sauce is smooth and thick enough to coat a spoon.

Top with parsley and serve.

After I first tasted this dish from Goffredo Fraccaro's stove, I have never seen any reason to order scampi anywhere else.

Oh, the dinners I had in that fabled January!

I remember braised duck with duck crackling, andouille sausage and sweet potatoes at Brigtsen's in the River Bend section. Frank Brigtsen studied Fine Arts at Louisiana State University, then came back home to apprentice under Paul Prudhomme, first in the kitchen at Commander's Palace, then at Prudhomme's vastly popular K-Paul's on Chartres Street. Now Frank practices the Finest Art of all in his own restaurant, full every night of admiring local folk.

Emeril Lagasse, another Commander's Palace graduate, opened his own place in the Warehouse District in the spring of 1990. By the end of that year, *Esquire* magazine had anointed Emeril's Best New Restaurant in America. His is an open kitchen, so I was able to sit at the table and watch the artist at work.

Gunter Preuss of the Versailles served snails in a brioche, then scallops wrapped in fish on a plate with three sauces. I ordered a terrific, expensive bottle of cabernet. Phil paid, as always.

Tom Weaver gave us a haute Creole masterpiece of a dinner at Christian's, in a converted church.

A wry young Frenchman, Gerard Crozier, served us the best quail I've ever tasted, at Crozier's.

I remember a dish of oysters, spinach, and leeks in phyllo pastry (a variation, come to think of it, of Oysters Rockefeller) at Susan Spicer's Bayona Restaurant on Dauphine Street.

And I had several good meals at the popular tourist bar and cafe named "Olde N'Awlins Cookery" on Conti Street. The place is owned by Mike Lala, a long-time television cameraman in New Orleans who, after all those years of hanging out in bars, decided to open one. He has made his fortune serving the same four appetizers, four soups, and eight entrées year after year. It's a successful formula with the out-of-towners. "I don't change anything," Mike told me. "I don't even like to change the lightbulbs." Phil has known Mike Lala even longer than I have, but I always went to Olde N'Awlins alone. Phil says he isn't going there until Mike starts using tablecloths.

It is perfectly possible, I suppose, to have a bad meal in New Orleans; "What a pity," Orleanians would say about such a disappointment, and "Ain't that a shame!" But I got an early start in the better oyster bars and po' boy sandwich joints of the city. I have been a frequent visitor since I was a young reporter in the late Fifties covering the integration struggles and astounding politics of Louisiana. This beginning, and the informed culinary prejudices of my friend Phil, led me to a lifelong passion for New Orleans cooking. I have been overfed in this city, Lord knows, but I cannot remember ever being poorly fed, and I return frequently to New Orleans, always in anticipation, my eyes, as my mother used to say, always bigger than my stomach. I can't swear that all these recollections of New Orleans meals and New Orleans events date to my one January sojourn. Some of them may go back to the January before, or the January before that. My memories of New Orleans are glazed with remoulade sauce, and happily converge.

I admit that in this January it felt peculiar at first to have no assignments, no duties, nothing to do for a change but enjoy myself. I am a product of the Puritan work ethic Joe Cahn was talking about, and it seemed wrong not to be working. I kept these misgivings under control, and after a while they began to go away.

Most mornings, I was out early while the shop keepers were hosing down their sidewalks and the residents of the floors above were still opening their shutters to see what sort of day it was going to be. I was purely pleasure-bound, and I followed this route: down Toulouse toward the river, pausing at the newspaper boxes on the Bourbon Street corner for a *Times-Picayune* and a *New York Times,* left on Royal, right on St. Peter, and diagonally across Jackson Square, scattering the pigeons on an unswerving course for the Cafe du Monde in the French Market. There, I usually was able to settle myself at the same curbside table for my beignets and coffee.

You can buy beignet mix and cans of distinctive chicory-flavored Louisiana coffee and take them home, but the sugary square doughnuts and the café au lait never taste the same as when they are brought hot to your table and served in the open air beside the crossword puzzle and the basketball scores there at the corner of Decatur and St. Ann. There is never an hour of day or night when beignets and coffee are not tendered at the Cafe du Monde, but even if you have to keep your jacket buttoned against the cool fog rolling over the levee into the market squares, the hour after sunrise is best. Then, late revelers and early risers meet. Once I was among the former, but in my old age I have discovered that the coffee, the best in the world, tastes even better after a little bit of sleep.

My early walks to the Cafe were mostly uneventful, but not always. One morning, I followed a trail of bubbles hanging in the air. The bubbles led me around a couple of corners before I spied their source: three tipsy college girls carrying rum drinks and bubble wands. (The Cafe du Monde is not the only place open all night; so are most of the bars.) These young women were lost. They stopped me as I passed to ask where they could find a taxi to the Bourbon Orleans Hotel. When I pointed out that they were standing, at the moment, squarely in front of the hotel, they giggled, blew me some bubbles of thanks, and wobbled through the door.

New Orleans
. . . .
11

Hack Bartholomew

Roselyn Lionhart
and David Leonard

Chef Kevin Belton

*Chef Chris Kerageorgiou
and Phil Johnson*

Ellis Marsalis

This also happened: At the corner of Dauphine and St. Louis, a bottle broke with a loud crash. Scruffy young men poured out of a bar. An unmarked car with two plainclothesmen in it roared up and screeched to a stop. Somebody hollered, "He's the one with no shirt!" A guy in a clown suit shouted that he'd been robbed. One cop jumped out of the car and ran down St. Louis Street, the other circled the block fast with siren and lights going. By the time I had walked to Bourbon Street, a man with no shirt was lying on the corner out cold. Blood was coming from his head. He was handcuffed. The clown raced back down Bourbon past me as fast as he could run. Police cars arrived from all over, then an ambulance. All these things happened, and I walked on without knowing exactly what happened. My reporter's instinct failed me. I didn't even ask. I am a retired reporter.

By mid-morning in the French Quarter, after breakfast is done, a parade of familiar characters begins to appear. After a few days, as I met them or they became known to me, I could identify Ruthie the Duck Lady, who used to walk with a live duck and now carries a stuffed one; Willie the Dancer; George the Street Cleaner; the Chimney Sweep advertising himself with his top hat; the Clothes Pole Man selling forked poles to hold your clothesline up; and a changing cast of peddlers, shoeshine guys, mimes, painters, caricaturists, and musicians, all seeking a living in the street.

I met Mike the Banjo Player, who plays and sings old songs on the Moon Walk above the river, a nice guy with weepy drinker's eyes. The hat at his feet had only three dollars in it, though he had been singing for an hour. "Just trying to get enough money—not for a drink," he said, "though I do drink—but for lunch at my girlfriend's cafe down there." He waved vaguely toward Decatur Street. Mike said he could play in clubs but prefers the street. "We're a family out here," he said. "We're closer than some families that live in houses together."

I ran into Hack Bartholomew, who has been playing his horn at the French Market for years, and singing, soulfully, old marches and ballads, and hymns like "Amazing Grace." His grandfather was Reverend Hack, the preacher at Mahalia

Jackson's church, Mt. Maria. Hack remembered me and wanted to know if I am a Christian.

"More or less," I said.

Hack said, "More is better."

Some of the street performers are precocious beginners, like Joseph Urby, nine years old, who tap-dances on Royal Street in sneakers with bottle caps tacked to the soles.

Some are old pros, like David Leonard and Roselyn Lionhart. She plays guitar, mandolin, and several African instruments—kalimba, morimbula, and the like—and he plays guitar, cornet, and harmonica. They both sing. They are very good, and their open guitar case fills quickly with cash whenever a crowd gathers.

Here is Roselyn explaining New Orleans jazz funerals to a knot of tourists:

"You're not supposed to cry at a funeral. Did you know that? You're supposed to rejoice that another poor soul has escaped this vale of tears. And if you can't rejoice that another poor soul has escaped this vale of tears, at the very least you can be glad it wasn't you!"

At that point, the two of them launch into a fine, swinging "Saints Go Marching In." Since the audience never tires of the song, neither do they. When the weather gets too hot in New Orleans, David and Roselyn said, they go off to play in the streets of Paris or Perugia.

The French Quarter street scene offers livelier sounds than most of its indoor music clubs these days. Sad to say in the city of Buddy Bolden, King Oliver, and Louis Armstrong, there is no single place a visitor can go to hear consistently superior traditional jazz.

"The good jazz clubs were mostly mob-owned," Banu Gibson told me. She ought to know. She used to sing in them.

"I don't know whether those guys liked the music, or whether it was a matter of mob pride—'My club is nicer than your club!'—or whether it was just a way to launder money, or what. But when they cleaned the mob out in the Eighties, the clubs all folded one by one."

Banu is a bright, pretty, grown-up woman who thinks and walks and talks music and dancing and records with her own "New Orleans Hot Jazz Band." She came to lunch with me at the Bistro on Toulouse Street and brought along a copy of her itinerary for the coming spring: Spokane; Kansas City; New York; Chattanooga; Little Rock; Vienna, Austria . . . There's a place for her and her New Orleans band everywhere but New Orleans.

But she's not leaving. "I was born in Dayton, and I lived in Florida and New York, and when I moved to New Orleans, I wasn't ready for this place. I was in the supermarket checkout line and the woman behind me said, 'Do you have a car?' I started thinking New York thoughts. She wants a ride, or worse. She's trying to pull some kind of scam. Then she said, ''Cause I hope you don't have to carry those bags all the way home on foot.' She was worried about me! I was not ready for the friendliness of New Orleans, or the heat or the hedonism. But now that I'm used to it all, I can't imagine living any place else. I hope to find a regular gig, maybe open a jazz club of my own in one of the new hotels.

"However it works out," she said, "I'll say this for music: It's a business that doesn't hurt people. You go through your whole life singing and dancing, and you do no residual harm."

The remark endeared Banu to me. Thinking about it later, I realized she had put her finger on the reason I have always liked musicians so much, though I can't even carry a tune myself.

I made the rounds: Preservation Hall, the Famous Door, Pete Fountain's nightclub at the Hilton, the jazz brunch at the Court of the Two Sisters. All good tourist fun, but the best music seems to have drifted out of the Quarter downriver into precincts where tourists rarely venture. I took a long walk across Esplanade along Frenchmen Street one night and heard some first-class musical improvising at places with the unlikely names of Cafe Brasil, Cafe Istanbul, and Snug Harbor.

I heard rumors of late Thursday night jam sessions at a neighborhood place out near the Naval Base where self-taught young brass players show up to show off, but the directions I got weren't good enough to get me there. This was just as well, because it forced me into my one encounter with true greatness. I returned to the Quarter to hear Percy Humphrey play a set of his legendary trumpet solos at the Palm Court on Decatur Street. He plays only on Thursday, and maybe not for too much longer; Percy Humphrey is ninety years old. I concluded that jazz is hanging on in New Orleans, if not exactly flourishing.

This frustrates Ellis Marsalis, Jr., father of the celebrated Branford Marsalis (saxophone), Wynton (foremost trumpeter of our time, I say), Delfeayo (trombone), and Jason (drums), and a fine pianist himself, who plays at Snug Harbor Saturday nights. I found Marsalis *père* in his office at New Orleans University, where he heads the jazz faculty.

"Louisiana doesn't care a thing about its own music," Ellis Marsalis said. "Nobody encourages the young musicians. One year the state budgeted zero dollars for all the arts, less than any other place, less than Guam! There's just no support."

I asked him where he got his own jazz education. He laughed.

"I started out playing clarinet at Xavier School," he said. "If you were taught by the nuns, you didn't play jazz, I guarantee you. And my dad was the manager of an ESSO station. There was no music in the family. I learned mostly by listening to records, Charlie Parker, Art Tatum. I did hear Dizzy Gillespie in person one time, and that was an education right there. I just picked music up. I played for strippers, played for shuffles, played for comedians . . . If genes account for my sons' ability, they're genes from their mother's side. She's related to Alphonse Picou and some other great early musicians."

However that may be, as a pianist with a famous saxophone player and trumpeter in the family, and a fine trombonist and promising young drummer coming along, all Ellis Marsalis needs is a bass player and he'd have a band. I couldn't help suggesting to him that it might be one of the greatest jazz bands of all time.

"Well, maybe," he said, "but I never wanted a family band. You shouldn't ever stifle your children, and that's what a band would do if it was a bread-winning thing. An opportunity would come along for one of them, and he'd feel he'd have to turn it down to keep from deserting the family. I told each of them to look over his options and do what was best for himself. That's the only way a person should live his life."

A procession of young students came and went in the hall outside Ellis Marsalis's office as we talked. As Professor Marsalis, he is helping them perfect their art and find their own opportunities in music, as he helped his sons. Most of them are going to find their opportunities outside New Orleans, which doesn't encourage them to stay. What a pity, as they say. Ain't that a shame?

I tramped all the streets of the French Quarter in the cool January afternoons, in love with the arcades and shaded courtyards, the ferns in hanging baskets, the glitter of old silver in the shop windows, the faded pink patina of brick walls in the sun. I made one extravagant purchase, at Waldhorn's on Royal Street, the oldest antique shop in town. I meant only to walk in and look around. Before I knew it I'd bought an eighteenth-century English partner's desk, an old leather armchair, a stylish architect's table, and a library ladder to equip the small office I planned for myself back in New York. That's what happens to a man suddenly liberated from the sheltering bosom of a big corporation. He gets drunk with freedom. Temptation overcomes prudence.

New Orleans is a city teeming with temptations, of course, and always thinking of new ones. They are building a world-class casino for organized gambling, which strikes me as a world-class mistake. Las Vegas is one kind of city, New Orleans is another, and I'd hate to see the two become confused. But New Orleans is not without greed. They are already selling potions for gambling success in the voodoo shops on the side streets.

If you are comfortably situated in a French Quarter courtyard, as I was, with a fountain murmuring, the greatest temptation of all is to settle for the fascinations just outside your door. This is a local attitude of long standing. When the Americans flocked to New Orleans early in the last century to settle the city uptown (that is upriver, on the other side of Canal Street), the original French and Creole residents saw little reason to cross the dividing line and mingle with the uncouth newcomers. New Orleans is still a city devoted to staying put. People live distinct lives in distinct neighborhoods, with precious little coming and going between them. Joe Cahn told me about an old woman, a friend of his, who moved from Chartres Street to Royal, a distance of one block. She came moping into his store one day, obviously feeling a little down.

"You all right?" he asked.

"Yes, yes," she said, "but I miss my old neighborhood."

A visitor really shouldn't succumb to such constraints, so as the days went by, by a force of will, I directed myself from the Quarter into the other 350 square miles of the sprawling reclaimed swamp of a city (two hundred of which square miles are said to be more or less on dry land).

I took a rickety seventy-year-old streetcar out St. Charles Avenue, *ding-a-ling, ding-a-ling, clickety clack,* a satisfying slow, stately way to travel through the quiet precinct of live oaks and crape myrtles and great antebellum houses. This other New Orleans was put here by the Protestant planters and entrepreneurs who floated down the river from the East after the Louisiana Purchase. The Garden District stands in elegant contrast to the crowded Creole city only a mile or two away, and it reflects an entirely different view of what life should be: serene and sumptuous, not brazen and exciting. I admire the mansions the newcomers built, but I think I would have preferred the more stimulating company of the Creoles. Look at the names of the streets where the Americans built their most beautiful dwellings: First, Second, Third, and Fourth. These people were long on orthodoxy and short on imagination.

Streets in such a whimsical metropolis should have better names than First, Second, Third, and Fourth. Luckily, a more creative class of street namers was also at work. Half a dozen blocks away, the stroller seeking more felicitous streets, comes, sure enough, to Felicity, and then to the Greek Muses in turn, Polymnia, Euterpe, and Terpsichore, pronounced Terpsy-core. Never mind pronunciation. Who wouldn't rather live on a street named for Thalia, the muse of comedy, than on First or Second or Third? Erato, who inspired love poems, has her street, and so does Clio, goddess of history, almost under the Pontchartrain Expressway. Melpomene Street, after it crosses St. Charles, becomes Martin Luther King Boulevard. I wonder whether somebody in City Hall, looking for a street to rename for the martyred Dr. King, remembered that Melpomene was the goddess of tragedy.

After you get over the disappointment of the few numbered blocks, it slowly dawns on you that New Orleans rejoices in the most lyrical street names in the world. Where else can you take a walk down Narcissus Street, or Venus, Adonis, or Bacchus? Not only are the gods so honored, but also all the best human impulses, Community, Concord, and Compromise. On my way to the Pontchartrain lakefront one day, riding with a cab driver who blessed himself with the sign of the cross as we passed each Catholic church (but not the other churches), I took note of the names of the streets we crossed: Abundance, Treasure, Pleasure, Benefit, and Humanity. Then I remembered the name of the wide thoroughfare on which we were traveling, a boulevard so familiar that nobody thinks any more about the meaning of its name—Elysian Fields! The paradisiacal home of the blessed after death is best known, in temporal New Orleans, as the fastest way to get from the river to the lake.

Weakness of the flesh is recognized in the street names too. Everybody knows the name of one such street by the tram that used to run along it, the Streetcar Named Desire. Just for the mainly reverent record of the New Orleans street-namers: the street one block over from Desire is Piety.

Some of the street names are too much for present-day Orleanians to handle. The correct way to pronounce them is exactly the way it's done locally; when in the Big Easy, do as the Easies do. Chartres has become Charters, for example, and if you try to give it the pronunciation of the French cathedral city, nobody will know which street you are talking about.

Other street names defy proper spelling. Phil Johnson told me about a police officer who encountered a dead mule on Tchoupitoulas. Having to write a report, he dragged the animal to Camp.

One rainy afternoon, almost one hundred and eighty years to the day after Andy Jackson fought the British in the Battle of New Orleans, I took the sternwheeler *Creole Queen* down the river to Chalmette, where the battle was fought. When the boat got there, I turned my raincoat collar up and took a walk across the field. Because of the rain, I had the place pretty much to myself.

It was easy to imagine the brilliant array of British soldiers, scarlet-coated dragoons, proud Highlanders in their regimental tartan—thousands of them, under the command of the chivalrous and debonair General Sir Edward Pakenham—charging across that field with drums rolling and pipes playing. Waiting for them, behind a wall of mud, was a genuine American conglomeration, if not exactly what you'd call an army: Kentucky long-riflemen, Tennessee volunteers, Mississippi irregulars, Louisiana militiamen, free black men, Choctaw Indians, a regiment of Irish, a collection of Creoles, and a band of pirates under Jean Lafitte.

It was the last battle of the last war between the British and the Americans. It lasted half an hour. When it was over, Pakenham was dead. Most of his senior officers were dead. Two thousand British soldiers were dead, wounded, or captured, and the rest were in flight. The American casualties numbered thirteen. That must have been some half hour.

The body of General Sir Edward Pakenham went back to England preserved in a keg of rum. Andrew Jackson went back to New Orleans in triumph. They rang the bells of the Cathedral and placed a laurel wreath on Jackson's shaggy head. Eighteen pretty girls in white gowns with silver stars on their foreheads, representing the eighteen states, cast flowers in his path as he strode through the public square. There's a majestic statue of him in the middle of the square now, the conquering hero astride a rearing horse. They don't make them like that any more, either statues or heroes.

The Americans supplied the pluck of New Orleans, the Creoles supplied the rapture, the Africans provided the cadence. But that still doesn't account for a certain spice in the life of the city. The spice was the gift of the Cajuns.

The Cajuns came here in the first place because they didn't have any place else to go. More than two hundred years ago, the British expelled them from Nova Scotia, which the French called Acadia. Families were torn apart by the banishment. Thousands died at sea. Three or four thousand found their way to New Orleans, but not being city people, they moved on to the embracing safety of the swamp grass between the Mississippi and the Gulf. Here the Acadians became, in the lingo of their neighbors, Cajuns, and here many of them still live a sort of preindustrial agrarian life, farming and fishing and hunting in the bayous and letting the good times roll.

I have spent many contented hours in Cajun country, which is south and west of New Orleans in the once-unpopulated countryside. One day years ago, I pulled a chair up to an outdoor table at Harvey's Cypress Inn on the Bayou Chevreuil shortly after noon. When the sun went down, I was still there, still working at a meal of boiled crawfish, lightly seasoned, still tossing the shells overboard into the black water, still drinking beer and listening to Cajun fiddle tunes. It had to be a long meal because there is no way to eat crawfish in a hurry, and even if there were, it would be wrong to rush through such a pleasure. I don't have very many regrets about my life, but one of them is that I haven't spent more afternoons like that one.

I wouldn't want you to think the Cajuns are only eaters and drinkers and singers of songs. They have close, strong families. They support one another in time of trouble. They are devout Roman Catholics, up to a point. Cajuns believe in God, but they also believe God winks at a lot of little things.

I fell to wondering how Cajun habits and music and language are prospering these days, so I drove down through the swamps to Houma to see an acquaintance, Lenn Naquin. He and his brother, L.J., took me to lunch at Savoie's Restaurant, where Jimmy and Sandra Savoie, mistaking me for a celebrity, couldn't be stopped from preparing seafood gumbo, stuffed bell peppers, jambalaya, sautéed oysters, shrimp and fried perch, and serving all these dishes at once while Lenn and L.J. talked about Cajun life and how it has changed.

"It's the hunting and fishing life that appeals to me," L.J. said, "and I'd say that hasn't changed at all. I go deer hunting and duck hunting—mallards, wigeons, pintails, ringnecks. And I go fishing for red drum and speckled trout and bass and *sac-à-lait*—that's our Cajun spotted perch. The hunting and fishing right here in Terrebone Parish is the best I've heard of in the world. I went to Colorado one time with my son and asked at a sporting goods store where we could go trout fishing, and the guy took out a map and showed me a spot. He said, 'One man had a real good day here yesterday. He had three strikes and caught one fish.' I thought, good God, one fish is a good day? See, I'm used to catching a hundred fish before lunch."

"There's always something happening," Lenn said. "Gator season is September. Everybody tries to get an alligator tag and get 'em a gator. Well you can see why. I think this year, a gator was worth forty dollars a foot at the tanning company. You get you a twelve-foot gator and that's pretty good money.

"Shrimping is closed right now, so all the shrimpers are out trapping—nutria, otter, muskrat, some mink. That's until February, and then pretty soon the shrimping starts up again."

Jim Savoie, who had pulled up a chair, said, "Don't forget the crawfish."

Lenn said, "Oh, yes, the crawfish are just coming in, and they'll be good until about the first of June. During Lent, I still don't eat meat on Friday. Most people don't. It's not a sin anymore, people just don't do it, and the peak of crawfish season is during Lent. On Good Friday, every crawfish in the parish better fear for his life!"

"Ain't that the truth?" Jim Savoie said.

As our talk meandered on, though, I inferred that aside from the sporting aspects, Cajun life is being watered down by the influences from the world outside.

"We were brought up on the bayou," Lenn said. "It's Bayou Dularge, and we were probably the last generation to remember going out in our pirogues and playing in the bayou all day, and then sitting out on the porch and talking all night. Traffic? You could hear a car coming for five miles in the silence of that place.

"We always went barefoot to school. We weren't poor—Daddy had the grocery store and the shrimpers would take whatever they needed and come back and pay their bill after they went shrimping. It was just that nobody wanted to wear shoes to school.

"Our father spoke French—well, his customers, that's *all* they spoke. Out the end of the bayou where the road stops, the old families still speak French. But my generation was the first to have to speak English in school, that was the new rule. It was in the Fifties, I guess, all the school books came out in English.

"Now there's a big effort to teach the children French again to keep the heritage from dying. But they'd rather watch TV. It's too late, see."

"Ain't that the truth?" Jim Savoie said.

"I wish you could meet one old woman I know," Jim said. "She lives back in the swamp. She knows every bird and animal. She calls the alligators up to be fed. There are still some old folks like that, but not as many as there used to be."

"Ain't that the truth?" It was Lenn's turn to say it.

I asked about Cajun music, which is infectious and full of joy, and seems to be thriving at places like Prejean's in Lafayette and Fred's Lounge in Mamou. Fred's is the place you didn't think existed any more, the place your mama told you to stay away from when you were a kid, and you grew up and didn't and were never sorry.

"I love that music," Lenn agreed. "Daddy had a saloon beside the store. Friday was Crab Boil Night, and Sunday was Music Night, accordion and fiddle, I can hear it yet. But right around here, there's not much French music anymore, not even on the radio. Maybe the oil-field workers who came from outside never got into it, and our people died off. Maybe there were never as many Cajun musicians as we thought."

Was the day coming, then, when Cajun country would be like every other place?

"Well, the day may be coming when Cajun country isn't here at all," Lenn said. "Terrebone is the largest parish in Louisiana, but it gets smaller with every storm. The erosion is terrific. The Gulf is taking the land and we'll never get it back again."

He sat for a minute shaking his head over that sobering fact. "The Lord giveth," he said, "and the Lord taketh away."

Then he brightened and smiled. "But here we still are," he said. "Everybody's friendly, you go around and see. Everybody will talk to you like they know you. That's the Cajun way, and most people here are still Cajuns. You can tell by their names. Just go down the road and read the names. All you'll see are Boudreaus, Heberts, Dupres, LeBlancs . . .

"And here we are eating at Savoie's. How do you like your food?"

That night, back in New Orleans, a woman customer at the bar where I went for a late-night beer was bantering with some boisterous male conventioneers adorned with necklaces of Carnival beads.

"Give me some beads!" she said.

"Show us something!" they said.

She pulled up her sweater, undid her bra, and gave them a flash of her breasts.

They cheered and gave her all their beads. I knew it was time to get out of town.

New Orleans looks forward to Mardi Gras, but after a month, I was feeling spiritual about the city. I felt I'd had my darling to myself, and I was in no mood to share her with others at a raucous party.

A night or two later, I had dinner alone at Antoine's, the one-hundred-fifty-year-old restaurant that is one of the abiding charms of the French Quarter. It was just before closing time, but Mr. Guste let me in. (He is identified on the back page of the unchanging menu: *"Bernard R. Guste, Propriétaire Cinquième*

Génération.") I ordered six Oysters Bienville, baked in white wine sauce flavored with onions, pimiento, and peppers, a dish created at Antoine's sometime in the last century—six oysters, nothing more. I ordered a noble bottle of white Burgundy, Meursault *Les Charmes.* I ate slowly, thinking about the taste of the oysters. I drank a silent toast in the emptying dining room to good food and drink, to all things traditional and enduring, and to a month without care in one of the last places on earth that cares about such things.

The mist was coming in off the river as I walked back to my room. The next morning, John Laine came by in his taxi to drive me to the airport.

Key West

It is a speck of rock in a pastel sea. Palms whisper. Songbirds sing. The place has never known a frost. People spend their days at rest in wicker chairs on gingerbread verandas. Flowers bloom all year and love is free. Without a hint of irony, everybody calls it Paradise.

Key West seduced me and changed me. I arrived wearing a blue blazer, gray trousers, and polished black shoes. The first day, I shed the jacket. The second day, I changed to canvas boat shoes. The third day, still feeling overdressed, I dug around in my duffle bag and found my shorts and a polo shirt. A day or two later, except for excursions into town, I gave up the shorts for a bathing suit and took off the shirt.

And the shoes.

And stopped shaving.

My little house was provided with a lighted blue pool behind a high wooden

fence. The fence was banked with flowering bougainvillea and hibiscus. A co-
conut palm stirred beside the pool. There, at night, under the stars, I took off
the bathing suit, too, and swam naked. Padding across the patio back into the
house following those midnight swims with nothing but a towel over one shoulder, I finally felt properly dressed for Key West.

The place has no dignity, but much style. I came upon this observation in a
perceptive history and guide written by a Keys novelist, Joy Williams, and before I left, I saw the truth of it. Key West is the greatest of all the end-of-the-road
towns. This assures its lack of decorum. The island is full of dreamers, drifters
and dropouts, spongers and idlers and barflies, writers and fishermen, islanders
from the Caribbean and gays from the big cities, painters and pensioners, treasure hunters, real estate speculators, smugglers, runaways, old Conchs and young
lovers. The residents are all elaborately tolerant of one another, and that is where
the style comes in. If you wish to be known by your first name only, everybody
understands. It's simpler that way and—who knows?—it may offer a little protection against some warrant or grievance from another time and place.

Key West calls itself the Conch Republic. In 1982, the Border Patrol set up
a roadblock and started searching all cars on the only highway north for illegal
drugs and aliens. Lines of fuming cars and drivers stretched halfway back to town.
Citizens of Key West were genuinely annoyed, and finally, in a spirited rally on
the waterfront, declared their secession from the United States. Now they have
a prime minister, a flag and a flagship, and honorary consuls in selected cities.
With a big sign at the airport, they welcome you to the Conch Republic. They
are only partly kidding. Dangling there at the bottom of the map, Key West is
connected to the United States, but the better you get to know the place, the more
tenuous the connection seems.

While Puritanism enjoys a rebirth elsewhere in America and virtuous re-
formers filled with moral certainty spring up everywhere to instruct others how
to live, Key West shrugs. "Human beings are made to hang out," Clyde Hensley said to me, "not to be weighted down with cares."

Clyde was my affable and offhand host, proprietor with his wife, Brigid, of the Travelers Palm on Catherine Street in Old Town. There, hidden away on an unpromising, dusty street, they created a small Eden behind a sturdy gate with a few eclectic accommodations scattered here and there along brick walkways. Walking through the gate, Clyde said, gives him the same sense of coziness and security he had as a kid when he climbed into a big cardboard box. Embraced there by foliage and silence and shade, with the ceiling fan turning lazily in my bedroom, I felt the same.

I was late the night I arrived after the long drive down the Keys, so Clyde and Brigid just included me in the family steak dinner at the outdoor table under a banana tree. (This table also serves as the reception desk, but I never did check in. Come to think of it, I never checked out, either. I just came, and when it came time to go, I went.)

Travelers palm, the tree, a big example of which shades the courtyard, nourishes travelers with an accumulation of water at the base. Travelers Palm, the inn, leans toward beer, or at least it did that night as Clyde and Brigid and I sat around after dinner and talked, while Marina, their seven-year-old daughter, practiced her piano lesson inside, and Scooter, their border terrier, chewed my shoe laces under the table.

"Human beings were made to hang out," Clyde said again. "Simplicity is bliss. I keep learning that and then forgetting it."

He said he and Brigid had enjoyed creating the Travelers Palm but now aimed to rid themselves of their earthly possessions, including the inn. They were feeling tied down and antsy and ready to resume an odyssey that had taken them from Key West to Tuscany, where they built boats for a while, then to the North Carolina mountains, where they bottled spring water for a while, then to the Dominican Republic, where they made a movie about humpback whales. I may have missed a few of their other stops in the course of the conversation.

Before he had met his Boston-Irish wife, I learned as the days went by, Clyde made a living as a merchant seaman, bagpiper, carpenter, fisherman, diver, whatever seemed a good idea at the time. He was at sea, literally and figuratively, until he washed up on the shore at Key West.

"Ninety-nine percent of the old-timers you run into here arrived by boat. That's the way I arrived twenty years ago."

We were idling around the harbor in Clyde's center console Pursuit, using maybe one one-hundredth of the potential of the twin 200-horsepower Mariner outboards, sufficient to zip the Pursuit past pretty nearly anything else that floats.

"I saw a National Geographic special on television about how they were finding gold on the Spanish shipwrecks. I sold everything I had in Norfolk and came down in my 40-footer with my two dogs, an Irish wolfhound and a border collie. Came right down that channel over there, low on fuel. When I tied up at the dock, I had thirty-six cents. I was never happier in my life."

Clyde caught on as a contract treasure diver and found work as a charter captain. He may have made a few high-risk, high-reward dashes to Cuba to smuggle paying customers off lonely beaches. What with one thing and another, he achieved prosperity, which he was now good and ready to turn his back on.

"Marina is only seven, but she's a certified diver," he said. "She has her own scuba gear. Brigid's ready to go. So I'm all set to disencumber myself and start looking for a boat we can live on."

Where was he going?

"Wherever," he said. "You don't always have to know where you're going in life. On the ocean, you don't even need a clock. The ocean has its own clock, the tides and the weather. You don't have any middleman between you and nature. No taxes out there, minimum hassles."

He glanced out toward the horizon.

"No big rush," he said, "but it'll soon be time to go."

Clyde and Brigid and Marina and Scooter haven't left yet. In fact, they are expanding the Travelers Palm to embrace the lots next door. This will make room for more visitors looking for laid-back accommodations, and give Scooter more shoe laces to chew under the table by the pool. But I am guessing that the sea's horizon still beckons to Clyde and Brigid, and that they will not remain innkeepers in Key West forever. Stability is contrary to the nature of the place.

Key West was founded by pirates, notoriously shifty characters by nature of their occupation, and settled by an assortment of transient rogues and wreckers. The town has been burned down by fires and blown away by storms and depopulated by epidemics and devastated by economic collapse. The sponge harvesters, the cigar makers, the turtle hunters, all had their tremendous booms and busts.

The turtles were the last to go. After the green turtle became nearly extinct and the turtle trade was outlawed in the 1970s, the decrepit Turtle Kraals on the waterfront were run as a tourist attraction for a while, featuring Big George, an ancient loggerhead the size of a Volkswagen. He starred in a B-movie in which he ate the bad guy. I had been truly impressed by Big George before and went back this time to see him again, but he's gone—not to his reward, I take it, which may not come for another hundred years—but gone to an aquarium someplace. The old cannery has become a bar and George's pen is empty. Nobody stays in Key West forever.

This was a Navy town for years, but now the Navy's going too. Sailors are becoming an endangered species like the turtles.

A huge shrimp fleet used to moor in the inner harbor, but the sweet, pink, nocturnal shrimp are disappearing in their turn. Shrimp have not been declared endangered yet, but the pollution of Florida Bay by agricultural fertilizer washing down from the mainland has created a summer algae bloom that probably will do them in pretty soon.

In the meantime, the shrimp boats have been banished north to Stock Island to make room for development. There's one remaining stretch of seedy and attractive waterfront, Key West Bight, where schooners still tie up and local folk still meet, a remnant of the little seaport that used to be. The city fathers—the "Bubbas," they are called—seem determined to lease this last unspoiled harbor to the hotel builders and restaurant franchisers who are hot to turn Key West into Fort Lauderdale. This makes everybody sick, but under the thatched roof of the venerable Schooner Wharf Bar ("I always thought the less teeth the women have, the better the bar," Clyde said about the Schooner Wharf) the regulars are drinking their Mother's Milks fast and looking over their shoulders for the bull-dozers.

Of course, I see the city fathers' point, up to a point. With no more sponges, cigars, turtles, sailors, or shrimp to count on, Key West has to count on tourists. In February, the tourists oblige by crowding into town, taking all the parking places, and milling along Duval Street in unruly herds. They wear tacky halters and T-shirts bearing vulgar aphorisms. Most of them are young and a little drunk, or late at night, drunker than a little. This is a condition easy to attain; there are more than one hundred saloons on an island one mile wide. If you get drunk and fall down in any direction on Duval Street, somebody said, you fall into another bar.

I am the last guy in the world to mock tourists: I have been one most of my life. But in Key West, I found myself ducking into alleys to sidestep boozy youths in raucous packs. The loud, crowded bars of Barefoot Bob's, the Hog's Breath, the Ugly Rooster, and Sloppy Joe's were there to be bellied up to, but I would rather have spent an hour in hell. This is a generational thing, as they say. I know Sloppy Joe's was "Hemingway's Favorite Bar," but it was around the corner in a quieter street in Hemingway's day, and they hadn't invented heavy metal music yet, or six-foot stereo speakers.

A playful, tipsy lass who said she was from Chicago recognized me from my television days—"Hi, Cholly, I'm Molly!" she recited at the top of her lungs—and dragged me into Sloppy Joe's one night. It was too noisy in there to hear anything else she said. I bought her a Barbancourt Rum, the genuine Haitian item just off the embargo list, which she had done nothing to deserve, and the minute her back was turned, I fled. Nothing against you, Molly. We just have different ideas of what's fun.

By the same kind of fancy footwork, I avoided Mallory Square at sunset. I suppose everybody who visits Key West should squeeze into the six-o'clock throng there once, piña colada in hand, mingle with the stilt walkers and break dancers, watch the cat jump through the flaming hoop, buy a cookie from the Cookie Lady, and applaud as the sun sinks behind all those other people on the pier. I did it once, a long time ago. The sunset can be truly melodramatic at Key West, depending on the presence of high clouds and air pollution, both of which make it better. But it is best watched in peace from anywhere but Mallory Square.

The quality of a visit to Key West probably can be defined by the things you don't do. To list a few items at random: I didn't have my picture made at the big red and yellow buoy set in concrete and inscribed "Southernmost Point in the USA"; I did not buy a shell necklace; I did not have my bottom tattooed at the Paradise, "The Best Place to Get Stuck"; I did not have a public ten-dollar massage on the porch of the massage place on Front Street; I did not buy a "See the Lower Keys on Your Hands and Knees" T-shirt at the Green Parrot Bar, or any other T-shirt at any other place. ("How can all these T-shirt shops make a profit?" I asked a local, who rolled his eyes at the question. I finally got it. They don't all have to make a profit, having already fulfilled their intended function, laundering drug money.) I did not have my fortune told or a ring placed in my navel; I did not enter the porn video store, Raincoat Willie's, though I admired the classy name; I did not visit Hemingway's House, having discovered on a previous visit that Hemingway is no longer at home, any more than he is down at Sloppy's having a drink; I did not ride the glass-bottomed boat; I did not smoke any marijuana or purchase any wind chimes.

It was enough, following Clyde's advice, just to hang out and feel my cares slipping away. Even after the month in New Orleans, I had brought a lot of cares to Paradise—like my clothes, more than I really needed. All my life, I have been a great one for planning ahead. In Key West, I gradually stopped worrying about the next day and eventually even about the next hour. I left my doors open at night to let the soft breezes blow through the house. Every morning just before dawn, I heard a rooster crow somewhere in the block. A dignified black and white neighborhood cat often jumped down from the fence, padded through my bedroom and out through the front door on a shortcut to wherever he was going. A car without a muffler rumbled by in the muffled distance, an old "Conch Cruiser" driven by somebody unlucky enough to have to be going to work. I lay there listening to the sounds of those early mornings, and then did something I hadn't been in the habit of doing for years: I rolled over and went back to sleep.

Sometimes it was eight or nine o'clock before I got up and put the coffee on and moseyed down to Mr. Valladares's for the morning papers.

A good newsstand is an ornament to any city, and in L. Valladares & Son on upper Duval, Key West rejoices in one of the great newsstands of the world. It's a vast store filled with the newspapers of the Americas and Europe, racks of magazines to suit every taste—gardening, embroidery, bondage fantasies—and aisle after aisle of paperbacks, with front-row preference given to Key West authors of past and present. Just walking through the door of L. Valladares & Son every morning and gazing over that sea of words on paper got my day off to a good start.

Arthur Leonte Valladares, the "Son" in the name of the place, is a gentlemanly third-generation Conch, or Key West native. When I asked him about his family one morning, he began at the beginning:

"My grandfather Leonte came from the Canary Islands. There were thousands of cigar makers here at that time, but he was known as the best cigar maker in Key West. My grandmother was from Cuba, of French descent, and a woman of beauty.

"My father, also Leonte, started a book store and pharmacy in 1927. Ernest Hemingway was a customer, and one day he asked my father to get the New York papers, the *Times,* the *World,* the *Herald-Tribune,* all of them. So that's how the news business really started, as a service to Hemingway. The papers came two days late by train until the train was blown away by the hurricane in 1935. But my father was a very strong man. By then, he had a good business going and he wouldn't give up. He found a way to get the newspapers here, and I learned from him: Do everything to keep the regular customers coming back.

"Ask the old-timers who Leonte Valladares was, they'll tell you. He would fight at the drop of a hat. Tennessee Williams always sent his valet in here to get a *New York Times,* but he wouldn't pay for it a week in advance like everybody else who really wanted it. He was Tennessee Williams and felt he didn't have to. So one day my father told the valet, 'I'm sorry, we're sold out.' Tennessee himself got out of his car and came in and said, 'Come on, I know you have the papers there behind the counter.' My father said, 'They're bought and paid for, and we're sold out.' Tennessee said, 'I'm Tennessee Williams.' Of course, my father knew who he was. He said, 'If you were Jesus Christ, I'd tell you the same. We're sold out.' I saw all this. He was a very strong man, my father."

I asked Mr. Valladares if he remembered Hemingway himself.

"Sure," he said. "The Hemingways had a pool and I used to go swimming over there. I knew John and Patrick as teenagers. Patrick comes back to Key West, but he doesn't come around. That's okay. The great thing about Key West is that prominent people can come here and relax and do exactly as they wish."

Mr. Valladares thinks the newsstand is the second-oldest business in town, after only Fausto's Food Palace, the grocery. His store has existed for nearly seventy years, which in ephemeral Key West amounts to an epoch.

"They've changed everything but the weather," he said. "We're not a small town any more. You used to be able to go to the beach and leave your bike and come back a day later—*two* days later—and the bike would still be there. In the last two years, I've had five bikes stolen from in front of the store. But anyway, we're still here." He nodded toward his son, Anthony, busy in a far corner unwrapping a shipment of magazines. "And I guess we're here to stay," Mr. Valladares said.

"I've seen a lot of history and I've known a lot of good people. John Hersey, Elizabeth Bishop, Richard Wilbur, they've all been customers of mine."

"If they want *The New York Times,*" I asked him, "do people like that have to pay a week in advance?"

He nodded gravely. "They do," he said.

I suppose Mr. Valladares was the steadiest citizen I met in Key West. Nearly everybody else had a less tangible history and a hazier occupation. I don't mean they were not perfectly admirable people.

I met Diver Doug, for example, a lean and always shirtless man weathered to the shade of fine old morocco leather. He is famous for free-diving for stone crabs and catching them barehanded. A stone crab can take a man's finger off, but Diver Doug has all his fingers.

I met Trey, no last name, who after our first acquaintance kindly presented me with a hat he had woven of fresh palm fronds, a beautiful piece of work constructed so as to allow for alterations as it dries out. After a few early sailing adventures as a kid, Trey left the Keys to join a carnival. I ventured to ask him what his job had been.

"I was a thief," he said. "I ran a rigged game. I didn't mind it, because I was always bilking smart guys and showoffs, but then in some little town in North Carolina a nice, quiet man and his wife showed up with their child. He obviously needed a big win to pay a debt or buy something they needed. He was taking their rent money out of a bank envelope. I told him to go away, the game was closed, and I went down to the office and quit. Now I'm back here weaving hats and doing whatever I can do."

I met a couple with no names at all, or none they wanted to volunteer, who lived aboard a battered wooden boat anchored in the harbor. Whenever they needed food, they went fishing for yellowtail and grouper. When they needed money, which wasn't often, they said, they fished a little longer and sold their catch on the Key West dock. When they craved company, they sought it on Christmas Tree Island, a few hundred yards offshore, where an assortment of free spirits can usually be found camping out and smoking pot, sharing whatever they have in the way of food and shelter. They are mostly gentle people who take care of one another and live rent-free, until the owner shows up once or twice a year to run them all off. By comparison to their Christmas Tree Island neighbors, the easy-living couple on the boat are industrious and hard-working.

Best of all, I met Dave Wegman. He is a soft-spoken nomad with kind eyes, a bald head, and a beard down to the middle of his chest. First, I thought of him as a seafarer, because I heard he lives most of the time in Borneo, having sailed his schooner across the Pacific alone.

Then he showed me some of his paintings of maritime scenes and South Sea islanders, and I began to think of him as an artist.

Then one night he bicycled over to Clyde and Brigit's, with a turkey cooking on a flaming charcoal grill in the basket of his bike. A slice of that turkey was the best meal I had in Key West. "Use Kraft salad dressing as your marinade," Dave said. I saw that he was a chef.

He broke out his fiddle that night. His pretty wife, Halley, sang the old ballads and hymns with him, the two of them in perfect harmony. Their three-year-old, Aurora, waded in the pool ("Aurora's been through a typhoon in the Pacific; she was potty-trained on the Tasman Sea"), and their six-week-old baby, Crescent, slept in Halley's arms. Somebody picked up a guitar and played soft accompaniment to Dave and Halley. It was a perfect evening of music and rapport.

"It was my great-grandfather's violin," Dave said. "Sometimes my great-grandfather talks to me when I'm playing it. If everybody's in tune and I'm playing well, he says to me, 'That's right, that's right.' " I discovered Dave is a musician.

All this was before I saw him restoring a sailboat and found that he's really a boat builder.

The boat was a derelict 35-foot Hereshoff yawl, which Dave was converting into a typical Key West sponge boat to be put on display at the Wrecker's Museum. Working under a shade tree behind a chandlery, Dave had cut off the old cabin trunk and installed a Key West cabin with a live well and a cargo hatch. While I watched, he created the long boom of a sponge-fisherman by splicing two timbers with the prettiest baling-wire splice any sailor could ever ask. Magically, the pleasure yawl was taking on the lines and rigging of a working sloop.

Properly dressed for Key West

Mel Fisher

Clyde Hensley

Dink Bruce, captain of the Conch

Dave Wegman and Isaiah Alford

Dave even soaked 300 feet of nylon rope in ebony stain to age it, and created "rust" along the gunwales with deftly applied rust-colored paint.

"The only thing wrong is this teak deck," he said, regarding the beautiful deck thoughtfully. "No sponge boat ever had a teak deck."

"Oh, no!" said his helper, Isaiah Alford, a Jamaican who spent his life aboard fishing boats off the African coast until arthritis got him in his hands. "Oh, no! If you thinking about replanking this deck, mon, you got to count me out!"

Dave laughed. "We'll let it go," he said. "I'm probably the only one who will ever care."

It seemed to me that Dave Wegman cared about every little detail of life, and was letting very few details pass him by.

He told me about his first sailing trip out of sight of land, back when he was twenty-five. It was meant to be a seventy-five-mile jaunt from Key West to the Dry Tortugas. He took along a Texaco roadmap, a compass, and a transistor radio. A few hours out at sea, he heard on the radio that a big low pressure system had formed off Honduras and was headed north. He knew that wasn't good but thought he might as well sail on. The hurricane hit him at dawn, almost before he could get his sails down. He spent the next ten days bailing for his life, with the boat frequently on its side, the mast nearly in the water. "I'd see a can of corn float up from the galley, and I'd grab it and open it and wolf it down and go back to bailing." When the storm ended, he didn't know where he was. He sailed one hundred fifty miles due east, spotted land, and drove the boat right up on the beach. A man stood there watching him.

"Where am I?" Dave asked.

"Naples, Florida," the man said.

After finishing that first trip a few hundred miles off course, nothing about being on the ocean worried Dave any more. He said he figured it never could be that bad again.

Dave Wegman is the man you'd choose to be stranded with on a desert island. He could amuse you with paintings and songs and stories while you were on the island. Then he could build you a boat to get off.

I was having a drink with Dave and Clyde at the Schooner Wharf one night, when a man wandered over wearing a flowered shirt and a gold chain with a big emerald-encrusted gold medallion hanging from it. The man had a soft smile, as if he knew something nobody else knew.

Clyde said, "What's happening, Mel?"

The man said, "Well, I'm up to my ass in emeralds. You don't know where I can find some good emerald cutters, do you?"

I suddenly realized I was face to face with Mel Fisher, the most famous citizen of the Florida Keys. Books have been written about him. Cliff Robertson played him in the movies. The gold chain around his neck didn't come from some glitzy jewelry store. It came from the ocean bottom, a trifle among 400 million dollars' worth of riches he found down there in the wreck of the 1622 Spanish treasure ship *Atocha*. He wore a smile because the treasure was all his, and there was a lot more where that came from.

"This week we've been vacuuming up emeralds," he said. "I had a big one appraised uncut at two hundred thousand dollars, and after it was cut, it was worth eight hundred thousand. I figure the emeralds I'm finding now might be worth two billion or so, but maybe three or four times that when cut. So you see why I'm looking for good emerald cutters."

Mel Fisher said all this in the tone of a man discussing another day at the office.

Mel read *Treasure Island,* as other kids do, and dreamed of finding fabulous piles of gold. Unlike other kids, he never got over it. He told me that when he was eleven, growing up in Indiana, he made a diving helmet out of a five-gallon paint can, melted down his lead soldiers to give it weight, and stuck the valve stem from his bicycle tire on top. He went down in a gravel pit with a buddy pumping air down to him by jumping up and down on the inner tube of a truck.

There was no gold down there, of course, but plenty of bluegills and catfish to see. He always hated it when the inner tube ran out of air and he had to come up.

Mel pursued life as a saxophone player in Indiana and a chicken farmer in California, but all the time, he was thinking about underwater piles of gold. He and his wife, Deo, honeymooned by diving on wrecks in Florida. They bought a couple of Jacques Cousteau's original scuba outfits and opened the world's first dive shop. In 1963, the two of them turned to treasure-diving full time. The next summer, poking around a 1715 shipwreck, Mel looked down and saw more than a thousand gold coins lying in the sand. It was just the way he'd imagined it in the gravel pit back home—the ocean bottom paved with gold.

That did it, of course. Mel Fisher spent the next thirty years combing the archives of the Spanish Main, finding bigger and better shipwrecks, investing in more and more sophisticated gear—infrared sensors, ocean-probing radar, satellite location finders—and successfully fighting off the claims of those, including the state of Florida and the United States of America, who maintained the booty should rightfully be theirs. The Supreme Court finally said it's not theirs, it's his—the gold bars from the *Atocha,* the gold coins, the gold chains, the gold plates and bowls and jewelry, not to mention the 150,000 silver coins and thirty-two tons of silver bars, the precious gems and all the artifacts from cannons to candlesticks. All his.

The treasure did not come without cost. Dirk Fisher, one of Mel's sons, and two other divers lost their lives in the quest, a loss that still gives Mel and Deo considerable anguish. But Mel has become the best-known treasure hunter in the world now. He knows where piles of Spanish gold are waiting to be picked up, and he couldn't just leave the treasure where it is even if he wanted to. The museums and archaeologists and auction houses, the television networks and moviemakers are all watching and waiting, and Mel's substantial army of divers and mappers and curators and lawyers have come to depend on him for a living. Rivals are always in the wings. He knows he has a shark by the tail.

"I think the *Santa Margarita* is going to be a much bigger find than the *Atocha*," Mel said, when I went to see him in his office overlooking the waterfront. The *Santa Margarita* was a sister ship that went down in the same 1622 storm, almost within sight of Key West.

"There's no end to the emeralds we're finding now," he said. "And there's forty tons of gold we're close to finding. I was out there on the *Santa Margarita* this week looking for it."

I did the arithmetic later. Forty tons of gold is worth 500 million dollars at current bullion prices, perhaps many times that when marketed as romantic treasure fetched from the deep.

Mel runs a museum and gift shop in his waterfront building to show off a portion of the treasure already recovered. For a hefty price, you can buy a gleaming Spanish coin made into a pendant or ring. You get the impression that the coins in the showcase are the last ones remaining and you'd better act quickly. What visitors don't see are the three laboratory floors upstairs where tens of thousands of silver *reales* embossed with the Castillian seal are soaking in electrolysis tanks alongside corroded swords and padlocks and cannon balls and cooking pots, just waiting until demand well exceeds supply. If they want to, Mel Fisher's children will be able to sell Spanish gold and silver until the end of their lives. It happens that a considerable part of the fortune of the Spanish Empire has fallen into the hands of a former chicken farmer from Indiana, their old man.

When I stopped by to say goodbye to Mel, he had charts spread out all over his desk. They weren't charts of the Florida Keys but of the Rio de la Plata in Uruguay. He was poring over the charts and talking to himself.

"The researcher thinks it went down on this sandbar," he said, "but I'd say it's over *here* in twenty-two feet of water."

"What is?" I asked him.

"Why, the ship," he said, looking up. "Maybe I didn't mention it. In the eighteenth century, there was a Jesuit gold foundry at Iguassu Falls. They made wonderful stuff there. One of the shipments to Spain was on a ship that sank in the river. I'm going down to Montevideo tomorrow to start looking for it. I'm pretty sure I'll be able to find the Virgin."

"The Virgin?"

"The life-sized solid-gold Virgin Mary," Mel said.

He went back to the charts. I saw he had things on his mind, so I left.

On the way from Mel's place, I stopped by Fausto's for some groceries. Something happened there, a little thing, but it has stayed with me. Ahead of me in the checkout line was a girl of thirteen or fourteen with matted hair and a sad face, carrying a ratty backpack over her arm. She was a runaway from somewhere, buying an ice cream on a stick. She paid for it with food stamps, went outside, and squatted down in front of a newspaper box on the curb. While she ate the ice cream, she read the top half of the front page, the part that showed through the plastic window.

I thought, two blocks away there's a man so successful that he is about to acquire a life-sized solid-gold Virgin Mary he doesn't even need, and here are you, kid, your life such a mess that you can't afford a quarter for a newspaper. She caught my eye as I passed.

"Hi," she said.

"Hi," I said.

I stopped. I found myself saying, "Can I help you with anything?"

"Nope," she said. "I'm fine."

She smiled a little smile and went back to reading the paper through the window in the box.

I walked on. She was somebody's lost little girl and she was not fine. Afterwards, I could imagine her face on one of those missing children milk cartons in Michigan or Ohio. I wished I had offered to buy her a plane ticket home, or staked her to a warm bath and a good meal. What could I have done? At least, even if she put me down as a busybody, I could have thrust the bag of groceries into her hands. I didn't do anything, and I didn't see her again. I'm sure she was not the only vulnerable kid who needed help in Key West that month, but she was the one I ran into. I hope somebody was kinder to her than I was.

Considering that I had fallen into a routine of doing hardly anything during my days in Paradise, the days went by in a hurry. On a balmy Sunday morning when a February snowstorm was said to be hitting New York, I went for a walk on Roosevelt Boulevard along Houseboat Row. There is special pleasure, of course, in hearing northern weather reports in Key West in February, where the houseboats are protected even from most Key West weather. They are tethered on the leeward side of the island. The morning I visited, the wind was blowing hard a mile away. All the flags were standing straight out in the main harbor and all the halyards clanking, but Houseboat Row was tranquil. One of the residents was out on deck tending his tomato plants. A woman in a bathing suit sat with the Sunday paper in her lap looking across the water. The pretty sound of a flute floated through an open companionway. These homey craft had names: *Fiasco, Serenity, Sea Dog. Chance to Dance in France,* one of them was called. They had gardens on their patios, pots and planters of seagrapes, hibiscus, roses, and aloe. (Aloe makes great sense in a boat garden, come to think of it; if you get sunburned, you just reach over and slice off a leaf or two for instant medication.) This neighborhood of floating bungalows and split-level ranch houses is raffish and conventional at the same time, the perfect place for a hippy who decides he wants to live in the suburbs.

Newcomers have always been welcome, with one famous historic exception. Back in the Sixties, a houseboat named *Proud Mary* was occupied by a group of sullen bikers who didn't fit in. When some of the people in town found out that their daughters were paying visits to this vessel, the bikers were appealed to. They refused to vacate. One morning, a city crane arrived, fastened a sling under *Proud Mary,* plucked the craft out of the water, and hauled her away to the city dump. Things have been nice and quiet on Houseboat Row ever since.

The mostly black section of town, tucked in behind the Naval Base, struck me as an even more neighborly place to live. There, people sit on the front steps talking from early morning until late at night. I was in the neighborhood often at both times of day, to have supper at a funky cafe called Blue Heaven and sometimes to come back the next morning for breakfast. Good as the evening meal is in the Blue Heaven garden—I remember a terrific dish of pork loin and sweet potatoes—breakfast is better, with chickens running around underfoot. The place is run by Rick Hatch, a young man who left the University of North Carolina, the same place I went to school a generation earlier (Blue Heaven is what they call the basketball arena at Chapel Hill), and came to Key West to make it as a free-lance journalist. His magazine pieces didn't pay the bills, I take it, but you have to stand in line to get into his restaurant. It may be the only eating establishment in town that doesn't serve conch chowder, conch salad, or conch fritters, which made it stand out right from the start.

(A word about conchs. They are the symbol of Key West, as noted, and so well-loved that they have become endangered in the Keys, like the turtles and the sponges. The conch offered on the menus and the conch shells for sale on the street come from the Bahamas. As a food, the conch is okay by me, a chewy morsel with a taste of the sea, and possible other properties. There used to be a Bahamian vendor who rode his bicycle around Key West crying, "Conch salad, make you horny! Conch salad, make you horny!" But as a shell, the conch is unexcelled. It can be held to the ear, where it produces the sound of the surf, as every island child knows. It can be sawed off at the tip and played as a horn. I can play a conch shell myself, not as well as the late Reverend Thurlow Weed of the Key West Presbyterian Church, who could play the march from *Aida* and the "Ode to Joy," but given time to practice, I can toot out a perfectly serviceable "Little Brown Jug." The conch shell is also widely used as a room decoration and receptacle for keys, safety pins and pocket change. Since the ban on conchs went into effect in Keys waters, the creatures have made a considerable comeback and are now easy to find in the shallows. Many a Conch considers it his sovereign right to come home from a day on the water with a contraband conch or two hidden in his beer cooler.)

In the course of my strolls through the Key West neighborhoods, I found a little street nobody notices, Free School Lane, which leads to a beautiful place nobody knows about, Nancy's Secret Garden. Nancy sits inside the gate half hoping for visitors, but the place is so well hidden that hardly anybody ever comes. It's Nancy's own fault. She's shy, and not very willing to let it be known that she's there.

She is Nancy Forrester, an artist who wanted a retreat from the world. Twenty-five years ago, she bought a dump right in the middle of Key West.

"Well, a dump is what it was, literally," she said to me in her shy voice. "It was full of bed springs and old refrigerators and broken glass. Winos used to sleep in the weeds."

Now it's a beautiful little rain forest of an acre or more with narrow paths circling in on one another in a wondrous setting of palms and ferns and flowers. It would be easy to get lost in the beauty of the place.

"There is nothing growing here now that was here back then," Nancy said, "except that big gumbo-limbo tree there in the middle."

We went for a walk around.

"I planted this Royal Palm in 1980," she said, "a little four-foot stick of a thing no bigger around than my finger. Just stuck it in the ground, didn't fertilize it, and went off on a trip. How tall do you think it is now? Sixty or seventy feet, I'd say. You can see it from the harbor."

Nancy could live on the fruit of the trees she has planted, mangos and guavas and a big sapodilla ("It's like a pear but better than a pear, with a slight cinnamon taste") and oranges and limes and papayas. She showed me 125 varieties of palms and 200 varieties of orchids—I had to ask her to refrain from naming every one—and pointed out vines and ferns and lilies in lush profusion. "This is a breadfruit tree," she said. "It kept Fletcher Christian alive, you know." She showed me exotic flowering plants, Bishop's Cloak and Angel's Trumpet and Dutchman's-pipe. When we paused in a clearing, she said, "I had a botany professor say that he could teach two semesters on the plants we can see from where we're standing."

Nancy's garden is a hideaway to her, and a paradise, and a life's work. To the City Commissioners, it is a high-density residential lot which would support thirteen housing units and twenty-three parking spaces. They tax it accordingly, which is a terrible discouragement of beauty, if not a civic crime. Occasional visitors who hear about the garden and search it out leave contributions, but nowhere near enough. Nancy, who works in the garden by day, has to work in a T-shirt shop at night to pay the taxes. Shy she is, but also determined. I could see that there will be thirteen housing units and twenty-three parking places on that acre over Nancy Forrester's dead body. It will remain a garden, and while she really doesn't want strangers strolling through her sanctuary, she has to have them and really needs more of them.

"Perhaps I could put a table in a clearing," she said, "and serve watercress sandwiches without the crust, and tea . . ." Her voice trailed off.

She walked me to the gate.

"Goodbye," she said. "Come again."

She waved shyly, and sat down again by the entrance in case any visitors came.

Key West bred such lethargy in me that I must have assumed all of Paradise was passive. It came as a surprise to meet a zealot, but I did meet one, the genuine item with fire in his eyes. Richard O'Barry spent much of his life capturing and training dolphins for the *Flipper* TV series. After he found one of his retired Flippers dying in a dirty tank at a circus, he experienced a revelation. Now he burns with the ambition to hijack dolphins from every aquarium and movie set in the world and set them free in the ocean. He has been through hunger strikes and gone to jail to press his cause.

Clyde and I drove up to Sugarloaf Key to a secluded lagoon where O'Barry was teaching six captive dolphins to ignore human beings and fend for themselves in the wild.

"Three of these animals were trained by the Navy to guard a submarine base," O'Barry said. "They had lethal needles on their snouts and devices to shoot a .45-caliber bullet into a swimmer. The Navy called them Advanced Biological Weapons Systems. Now I'm trying to show them how to be dolphins again." A couple of his charges rolled through the lagoon in unison, as if to show they were learning.

Richard O'Barry travels in an old school bus with slogans painted on it: "No Whale Jails" and "Stop Dolphin Slavery." He takes pleasure in parking this vehicle prominently at ocean theme parks. He said, "Sea World calls it 'the bus from hell.'"

I said I'd always thought dolphins enjoyed showing off for human beings.

"Look," Richard O'Barry said, "these are not companionable animals. They are wild animals. Children go to the dolphin shows and get the idea that human dominance is good, human dominance is natural. That is the wrong idea. Teaching a child not to step on a caterpillar is just as important to the child as to the caterpillar. It's wrong to exploit the lives of animals for our entertainment."

He said his Dolphin Project was planning to release the first three dolphins at Marathon Key sometime in the spring. Why Marathon Key? "Because," he said, "that's where they were captured."

And after that?

Richard O'Barry turned his fierce eyes on me. "Well," he said, "there are about a thousand dolphins in captivity. I'm going after them all."

If I ran an ocean amusement park, I think I'd be worried about this guy.

With my time in Paradise running out, one thing I hadn't done that I'd meant to do was go fishing offshore. I like fly-fishing for trout in mountain streams and thought it might be fun to try saltwater fly-casting for tarpon or permit. I even got an invitation from the Key West writer, Dan Gerber. But then he gave me a story he'd written for *Sports Afield* about his own six-year quest for a permit on a fly.

"It requires a knowledge of tides," he wrote, "and currents, winds, temperature, the behavior of birds and rays, vigilance, instinct, muscular and delicate casting—maybe out to ninety feet in a bothering wind—timing and sensitivity in setting the hook, a lot of luck in clearing the line to the reel, and from there on, the strength of your arms, understanding of the fish, dexterity, readiness of wit, and, if it all works out, the grace not to gloat about it."

I decided I might not be quite good enough to go fishing with Dan Gerber.

I did have a day on the water, though, and I still put myself to sleep at night thinking about it. I owe it to the persistence of a couple of friends of friends, Dink Bruce and Nance Frank. Dink is a slight and cultured young fifth-generation Conch whose tin-roofed bungalow seems always filled with pals who have dropped in from the ends of the earth. Nance is a blue-water sailor who once captained an all-woman crew in the Whitbread Round-the-World race and hungers to do so again. We had a couple of meals together. They kidded me about my Key West languor and urged me to snap out of it long enough to accompany them for a few hours on the bounding main. "It's beautiful out there," Nance said.

The main was not bounding on the morning we set out. The sea was as flat and reflective as a mirror. Our vessel was Dink's resplendent little outboard-powered pontoon boat *Conch,* an eye-catching, flag-flying homemade affair with an oaken superstructure strong enough to clamber around on. But I did not clamber. I reclined in a lawn chair up front while Nance poured champagne and Dink steered from the stern. I began to see that this trip was not going to be as arduous as I had feared.

The good ship *Conch* proceeded at a stately pace to an area of widely spaced mangrove islands about fifteen miles at sea. There we dropped anchor in the flats and waded to a sandbar for lunch. Nance sweetly rigged a towel and visor over my bald head to take the place of the cap I'd neglected to bring along. The two of us walked to the end of the sandbar and sat down to study the incoming tide.

"Spiny lobster," Nance said. "Sea urchin. Whelk."

I saw that she was naming the creatures she could make out in the waters at our feet.

"Starfish." She leaned into the water and picked it up. "Beautiful, isn't it?"

A dozen silver needles hurtled through the air a few yards away. "Gar," Nance said.

We sat and watched. "Blowfish," Nance said. "Sea cucumber. Horse conch."

A gray shadow emerged and vanished. "Nurse shark," Nance said.

Gulls and terns flew over. An osprey flapped slowly from the mangroves and circled out to sea. Sandpipers arrived a little way up our sandbar and went piping and skittering along the tide line.

Looking away to the south out over the Atlantic, I counted seven distinct shades of blue in the layers of water and sky and could not tell which was the horizon. I began to feel suspended in air, hypnotized, not present in a place at all, but in a state of enchantment I'd never experienced before.

I sat there silent for an hour or longer, perhaps much longer. To have said anything to Nance would have been to break the spell. The tension of life, which I had been trying to escape on shore, finally flew away over the ocean and disappeared. Peace came over me, a mood so meditative that I felt an instant of resentment when Dink called from the boat to say it was time to go home.

On the way back, a big manta ray swam beside us for a distance, and a school of shining jacks boiled on the surface, and a lovely fog bank rolled in. There must have been other things to see, but I was still back there on the sandbar.

All I could say to Nance was, "My God!"

All she could say to me was, "I told you so."

That was the best day in Paradise.

MARCH

Charleston, South Carolina

~

I'll remember March for a mockingbird singing in the moonlight. I am not conjuring up a romantic image of the Old South here. I am talking about a real mockingbird in a real magnolia tree on a real moonlit night on Montagu Street in Charleston.

I had a magnificent month admiring Charleston's houses and gardens, which are the most harmonious in America. I met many Charlestonians, who are the most genteel of Americans. But my steadiest companion was that cocky mockingbird perched in the next-door garden. He sang not only in the moonlight but also in the first light of morning, in the blaze of noon, and in the dusk of evening. He mimicked other birds. He mimicked the cats and the crickets and the squeak of my screen door. From time to time he sang what seemed to be pure mockingbird songs, of which he had an amazing repertoire. He varied his rhythm and volume and pitch, but he almost never shut up. I thought him charming at first;

later on, late at night when I was trying to sleep, I could have wrung his neck. But, as every southerner knows, it's a sin to kill a mockingbird.

Only Charleston natives count for very much among Charlestonians, and the mockingbird qualifies. He was discovered here in 1713 by Mark Catesby, an English naturalist who called him the "Carolina Mock-Bird" and noted that the Indians credited him with four hundred songs. Make that four hundred and one. One morning when I whistled to him the first four notes of Beethoven's Fifth Symphony, he whistled them right back to me.

The mockingbird and I resided together in style, he in his tree, I in a rented three-story "carriage house" (that's what Charlestonians call small dwellings that used to be dependencies of a nearby larger house; they may or may not have held carriages) with a "garden room" (screened porch) opening onto the "courtyard" (back yard). Above my garden wall hung the graceful second-floor piazza of the people next door, owners of the magnolia and landlords to the mockingbird, but I tried not to glance that way. I was intent on obeying the Charleston tradition called "north side manners," which, as explained to me by my friend David Kludt, goes this way:

"The city appears dense from the street because its houses come up to the sidewalk. What that means is that space, air, sunlight, landscaping, fountains, trees, and grass are behind the house or next to the house where they ought to be for privacy. Only midwesterners are dumb enough to put the yard and porch out front. Everybody's piazza is on the south or west side of the house to shade it from the sun. You don't look out your windows overlooking your next-door neighbor's piazza and courtyard. That's *their* space, and what they do out there is none of your business."

So I didn't spy. I felt lucky to be living for a while like an elegant Charlestonian and did my best to observe all the niceties. My little house was described to me in advance as "pure Charleston," which turned out to mean jam-packed. The house was full. I mean there was no more surface space for another item of decoration, no floor space for another piece of furniture, no wall space for another painting. The decorator followed the Victorian principle of furnishing: "Too much is just right." Even the landings of the staircase were embellished, one by a sculpture of ten-penny nails hanging in the window and spelling out an adage: "You Can't Plow a Field by Turning It Over in Your Mind." I was so taken by the adornment of the little house that one night when the mockingbird was keeping me awake, I made a partial inventory of the contents of my 12' × 12' second-floor bedroom:

One blanket chest supporting a world globe, an antique cash register, a tin rooster, and a marble obelisk. Five floor lamps and a tall table lamp on the plaster base of a Corinthian column. Two upholstered wing chairs with embroidered pillows. A captain's chair. A six-foot Chippendale chest of drawers topped by an ornate candelabrum. A pine secretary. A four-poster bed, a luggage rack, a bedside table with a clock radio. A fireplace with brass andirons, fireplace tools, and screen. On the mantel, two gilt candlesticks and the model of a square-rigger, *Fragata 'Española' Año 1780*. On the wall above the mantel, four sailing prints ("Yacht *Sappho* Leaving Sandy Hook, New York, Bound for Europe," for example). On the other walls: a nineteenth-century watercolor of an old black man, hat in hand, waiting upon two formally dressed young ladies seated in rocking chairs; pressed violets in an oval frame; the *New Yorker* cover showing Manhattan as four-fifths of America; three prints of shore birds; six framed miniatures of island scenes; a medal from Victoria Day in Windsor, Ontario, 1901; and a *Vogue* poster of a veiled model astride a rearing zebra. On the door: a coat hook atop a full-length mirror. On the floor: two threadbare Oriental rugs. On the windowsills: a mallard decoy; a bronze steam iron; a wooden grain scoop; two painted wooden boxes, one containing a neatly curled girl's pigtail; a piece of petrified wood; seashells in a ceramic plate; a telephone; and twenty-four books including novels by Colette, plays by Eugene O'Neill, *The Pocket Book of Great Operas,* and Aldo Leopold's *A Sand County Almanac.* On the secretary: eighteen leather-bound volumes of *The World's Famous Orations* and a collection of the prose, poems, plays, novels, and fairy tales of Oscar Wilde; an inlaid wooden pillbox; three candlesticks; a matching inkwell and blotter; a black-and-white television set; a silver trivet; alabaster carvings of two elephants, two dogs and a porpoise; a leather box containing a dozen tokens inscribed "Liberty's Last Chance" on one side and "God Bless America" on the other; and a basket of paper flowers. Each of the four windows in the room was draped with heavy damask curtains. Hanging from the ceiling was a six-armed brass chandelier with a pineapple motif.

The effect was charming in its way. But when I took off my pants to go to bed at night, there was no place in the room to lay them down.

I didn't spend much time in my cloister anyway. Spring in Charleston is a great show. I didn't want to miss the yellowing of the forsythia or the deepening blue of the wisteria or the first burst of white dogwood blossoms or, most brilliant of all, the psychedelic azalea explosion which begins in the middle of the month. So I walked about the streets peeking into gardens through wrought-iron fences (I don't think "north side manners" counts if you're on the sidewalk) and inhaling the fragrance of Charleston's finest season. The spring came on stronger every day. At the Harris-Teeter supermarket on East Bay Street (which sells fresh, hot apple fritters in the morning and offers thirty-six kinds of coffee beans and hundreds of varieties of wine, and where you can also find fresher flowers than in most florist shops) I bought two fistfuls of tightly closed daffodils on a Saturday morning and stuck them in a glass of water on my kitchen table. On Saturday night, there was a single open flower; on Sunday morning, six; and while I had my breakfast, by very careful observation, I could see some of the other buds actually moving, squirming slightly in the water glass, straining to open. They sat in the light of the window that day, and when I returned after dark, two dozen brilliant yellow blooms were there to give me back the Sunday sun.

When spring comes to Charleston, it comes in a showy rush. Visitors clopping along in horse-drawn carriages crane their necks to take it all in. Old Charlestonians, however, seem to accept the season as their birthright, just another perfect spring in an unbroken line going back to 1670. It would not be suitable for Charlestonians to be caught oohing and aahing. That is for the ordinary run of people, namely those from "away," those unlucky enough to have been born somewhere else. Charlestonians genuinely feel sorry for such people.

The Rutledges and Ravenels, the Pinckneys and Middletons put a premium on equanimity. The old families are undisturbed by the rich newcomers who have been buying the fine houses south of Broad and moving in as if they belonged here. They do not belong here. They never will.

"But you are not impolite to the new people?" I asked a blueblood acquaintance.

"Certainly not," she said. "We wave to them on the street."

But they do not invite them to join the South Carolina Society, for membership there is inherited; or the St. Cecilia, where members are drummed out if divorced or the children of divorce, and where women may not attend the annual ball if more than two months pregnant; or the St. Andrews Society, or the Yacht Club or the Charleston Club or the Carolina Assembly. The offspring of the "new people" will not be invited to the Children's Cotillions at the South Carolina Hall on Wednesday afternoons, the little girls in their party dresses and the little boys in their Sunday suits; nor, upon attaining young womanhood, will their daughters be introduced at the Debutante Ball in Hibernian Hall. I realize there is still such a thing as "Society" in Boston and Philadelphia, but for sheer disdainful exclusion, Charleston Society wins all the blue ribbons.

A Charlestonian I met, a dilettante direct descendant of Rene Ravenel (arrived 1686), grew up in a house on South Battery that had a cook, caretaker and gardener, and a maid for each floor. Describing old Charleston's habits, he said, "We do not do these things to impress others. We do them because they have always been done."

To which I reply: nonsense. What is the point of Society but to impress those who can't belong? Charleston was founded by lords and ladies as the home of the only American nobility. It was meant to be a reflection of the English Restoration across the sea. Only here can barons, landgraves, and caciques live on, minus their titles and perhaps their land holdings, but secure in their lineage. They believe in their hearts that theirs is the Holy City, set aside for their ancestors and themselves. Nothing like the Charleston aristocracy exists elsewhere in the United States. It ought to be preserved in amber. I suppose, in a way, it is.

Not that all the early settlers of Charleston were refined and respectable. My favorite of them all is Anne Bonny, illegitimate daughter of a merchant and planter from Ireland. When she was only fifteen, a Charleston boy tried to wrestle her into the bushes; she broke the would-be lover's jaw with an uppercut. A year or so later, she ran away to the Bahamas with a ne'er-do-well fortune hunter, James Bonny; left him for one sea dog after another, ending with a pirate captain, Calico Jack Rackham; and, dressed as a man, bristling with pistols and knives, led Rackham's crew in looting dozens of merchant ships. A witness testified she "cursed and swore with the best of men and never cringed from murder." When one of Rackham's sailors pinched her, she shot him dead. When she and her pirate mates fell into a British Navy trap, Anne resisted with guns and a cutlass while Rackham meekly surrendered. As he was about to be executed, she sweetly remarked, "If you had fought like a man, you would not now be about to be hanged like a dog." Anne, who was pregnant, was given a reprieve from the gallows, and eventually released from prison. She took up with the ship's doctor of one of the vessels she had plundered, moved back to Charleston as a reputable surgeon's wife, and lived to a ripe old age in the Low Country as the patrician Mrs. Radcliffe. Daniel Defoe tells Anne's gaudy story in his *General History of Pirates*. Present-day Charleston Radcliffes never mention Anne.

Aristocrats are generally associated with wealth, but in Charleston, not these days, not necessarily. Charleston has suffered more affliction than any other American place. Fires, hurricanes, and earthquakes brought many a family to financial ruin. The British looted the city during the Revolutionary War, hauling away, so it is said, five hundred rice barrels of silver from the town houses and surrounding plantations. And just as one generation of Charlestonians had recovered from the Revolution, the next generation was indiscreet enough to start the Civil War—the "War of Northern Aggression" you can still hear it called here—and the Yankees and carpetbaggers plundered the city all over again. For decades, the old Charlestonians were left huddled in their crumbling mansions "too poor to paint and too proud to whitewash." I can remember visiting Charleston with my parents in the Depression years, and looking upon its Georgian houses and Greek temples as a vast classical ruin.

I grew up only half a day's drive away in North Carolina, but that is a different sort of state with an entirely different state of mind. Regarding the cavalier Virginians and the haughty South Carolinians, we say North Carolina is "a vale of humility between two mountains of conceit." Everybody has to have something to be proud of, and we North Carolinians always have been mighty proud of being humble. Our state motto is *Esse Quam Videri,* "To be, rather than to seem." Nobody back home ever would have dreamed of putting on airs the way they do in Charleston, whose motto is *Aedes Mores Juraque Curat,* "She guards her customs, buildings, and laws." This is perfect for a place that has always assumed its superiority, the place where, as Charlestonians remark, "the Ashley and Cooper rivers flow together to form the Atlantic Ocean."

But, in fact, Charleston deserves our thanks for guarding her historic buildings. No glass and steel skyscrapers interrupt the perfect architectural balance created here in the eighteenth and nineteenth centuries (it's understood that no new building may be taller than the steeple of St. Philip's Church), and today nearly every house in town is restored to gleaming perfection.

There is a double irony in this. Hurricane Hugo helped by striking the city head-on in 1989; that is irony number one. Billions of insurance dollars rebuilt the community to a historical standard tastefully enforced by its powerful Board of Architectural Review. Irony number two is this: insurance rates and property taxes immediately climbed to the sky, and For Sale signs now adorn glorious houses whose owners can no longer afford to live in them.

One of these antebellum mansions dominates the corner of Rutledge and Montagu, a block or two from my over-furnished bedroom and my tireless mockingbird. It is more a palace than a home, set in a formal garden of boxwoods and fountains, with six great columns topped by ornate ram's-head capitals supporting a massive classical facade. The house was built by one Isaac Jenkins Mikell for his third wife; the first two wives, if still living, must have been green-eyed at the sight of a dwelling more stately than most courthouses or capitols. I imagined myself living there every time I passed and even memorized the realtor's name from the sign out front: Disher, Hamrick & Myers. I considered posing as a buyer in order to have a look at the majestic spiral staircase and lavish rooms I heard were inside but thought better of it, fearing Disher, Hamrick & Myers would know a gawker when they saw one. The place will be bought by some outsider with a couple million dollars in his pocket and another million or two for fix-up costs, just the sort of person old Charlestonians will wave to on the street.

The newcomers don't understand the ways of the Charleston patricians, and vice versa. David Hoffman, who has restored many fine houses, told me about a dowager he knows who was forced to let her servants go, move to her country home, and rent out the old family mansion on Church Street. The new tenant called her to say, "It's a wonderful house, but really, the kitchen is a wreck. We have to do something about the kitchen."

The owner took a while to absorb this remark.

She said, "You went *into* the kitchen?"

Thus, slowly, like everything in Charleston, the old order changes.

If you're going to get to know Charleston, what you need are introductions. Most of mine were provided by Jane Kiser, a tour guide who came to seem like an old friend. She said there was really nothing to her job but "chattin' and grinnin' " but I discovered that she knows everybody and everything. For a born and bred southerner, she lives her life at a disconcertingly fast pace. Thinking back on Jane, I see a blur of blonde hair and hear a sugar-coated southern accent I accused her of attaining by daily practice before a mirror.

"Chahlz, dawlin'," the voice on the telephone would say, while I was still wiping the sleep out of my eyes, "this is Jane Kizah." She hardly needed to say her name; she couldn't be anybody else.

"Chahlz," she would say, "I have a mahvelous idea fouah youah mawnin'!"

Even if I had a plan of my own for my morning, I always abandoned it when Jane called.

"There is just a mahvelous puhs'n ah want you to meet," she would say, and that's how I met, among others, Gedney Howe III.

He is the best-known criminal lawyer in Charleston, successor to his legendary father. Generations of Charlestonians who have been caught in one felonious circumstance or another have known to take their troubles immediately to one Gedney Howe or the other. But as famous as Gedney Howe III may be around the courthouse, it's what he did at the Calhoun house that staggered the town.

The Calhoun mansion at 16 Meeting Street, largest in the city at twenty-four-thousand square feet, actually was condemned as a hazardous wreck in 1975. Its portico was caving in and its porches were falling off. Gedney Howe III, less than two years out of the University of South Carolina Law School, took a deep breath, found $30,000 for a down payment, and set out to save the building. His father said he wasn't sure he wanted to practice law with a son that crazy.

Gedney lived in one room, cooking on a hot plate, for the two years it took to patch the roof and shore up the porches. He'd rush down to the court, defend some miscreant, collect a fat fee, and return to pour his earnings into the house on Meeting Street.

"The first three years were all damage control," he said as he showed Jane and me around. "Then I rewired the whole place. That may not sound very exciting, but it was the first affirmative step. When we got it rewired, I opened a bottle of champagne!

"The whole house was too much to think about," he said, "so I approached it like the truck driver. Somebody said the truck driver drives to Los Angeles, and he said, 'No, I drive to Birmingham. Then I drive to Cincinnati. Then I drive to Oklahoma City. Then Albuquerque, then Las Vegas, then from there to Los

Gedney Howe's Calhoun mansion

John Drayton Hastie

Jane Kiser

Carriageful of people from Away

Philip Simmons (photo by Ron Anton Rocz) and his valentine gate

Angeles. Los Angeles is too far to drive to.' The house was too much to restore. I couldn't handle it emotionally. I did one room at a time, without thinking about the next room."

That way, room by room, year by year, he brought the five floors of the great old house back to life, uncovered the fabulous satinwood entryway inlaid with walnut, restored the fourteen-foot ceilings and the intricate plaster moldings, rebuilt the seventy-five-foot stairwell which ascends to a dome of etched glass, refurnished the dining room to seat twenty-six in splendor, restocked the library with nineteenth-century volumes, provided the lavish music room with a gilded harp and piano, combed the world for suitable furniture, gigantic oil paintings, weighty curtain fabrics and marble statues, and, year by year, room by room, created one of the most magnificent houses in America.

Being the sharpest criminal lawyer in town helped, at least once. One of his best carpenters shot and killed a relative. Gedney got him acquitted with a plea of self-defense. Then, during a layoff at the house, the same man shot and wounded a policeman in another county. That was a little tougher. Gedney pleaded him insane. The verdict worked out fine. The jury found that the carpenter *was* insane, but not *so* insane that he couldn't come back to Charleston and work on the house.

After another layoff, Gedney called the man and said, "Okay, we're ready to start on the front bedroom."

"I'm sorry, Mr. Howe," the man said, "I'm doing some work for Mr. Johnson."

"Come on," Gedney said, "I need you to work on the bedroom."

"No, I'm busy with Mr. Johnson right now."

"Well, next time you shoot somebody, tell Mr. Johnson to get you off."

Pause.

"Okay, Mr. Howe, I'll be there Monday."

The twenty-year Calhoun mansion revival is sublimely complete now, except for a few pieces of statuary its owner still wants to place here and there, and I got the impression that something has gone out of Gedney Howe's life. He doesn't live there—"It's no place to bring up children," he said—so it serves as Charleston's gleaming Victorian showplace, the one landmark visitors who see it never forget.

"I showed Prince Charles through a couple of years ago," Gedney Howe said as he and Jane and I climbed to the rooftop for a look out over the city.

"I bet he was knocked out," I said.

Gedney paused on the stairs and looked me straight in the eye.

"He was," he said. "He was knocked out."

Gedney Howe III offered to let me move into the house for a night or two so as to look around the thirty-five rooms at leisure. I imagined myself spilling coffee on the spotless carpet or leaving a cigarette burn on a priceless sidetable. Once, at Washington and Lee University, I was permitted to sleep in Robert E. Lee's bed in a similarly unoccupied mansion, silent except for the resounding ticking of Lee's own grandfather clock in the bedroom and the reverberation of its chimes on the quarter hour. I took it as long as I could. Then I climbed out of bed and *stopped General Lee's clock!* I had a devil of a time getting the thing reset and going again in the morning before my affront could be found out. That was enough of sleeping in museums. I declined Mr. Howe's invitation as politely as I could and went back to my modest carriage house and my mockingbird.

I confess to a fascination with other people's houses, though. It's lucky I don't live in Charleston, where houses, one's own and everybody else's, amount to an obsession. While strolling on East Battery one day, I met a retired dentist, Dr. Joe Sam Palmer, who lives in the thirty-room house at No. 5. He must feel lost in there among thirteen bedrooms, ten bathrooms, ten fireplaces, and twenty-five telephones, but he loves the pink color of the house—"the color of healthy gums!" he is said to have exclaimed—and its spacious piazzas looking out to sea. The builder of the house, John Ravenel, a rich planter, served celebratory drinks to his neighbors on one of those porches, so they could all have a cheerful view of the shelling of Fort Sumter. Two years later came a shelling they enjoyed considerably less; this time, they were not spectators but, by specific command of President Abraham Lincoln, targets. I heard that there are Charlestonians who still won't ride in a Lincoln car.

With Jane Kiser, my energetic blonde shadow, I had a tour of the Rodgers Mansion, built after the Civil War by a corner grocer who took to brokering—buying cotton and tobacco cheaply before it was harvested—and then found a European market for his cheap cotton and tobacco and started a shipping company, and, during the depths of Reconstruction, profiting partly from the misfortune of his neighbors, became the wealthiest man in the impoverished city. His house is headquarters of an insurance company now, but it's clear from the Tiffany windows how well Rodgers lived—Tiffany musical notes above the door to the music room, Tiffany vegetables around the entrance to the dining room, Tiffany flowers, floor to ceiling, at the door to the garden. Leaving aside the house they're in, those windows alone are an irreplaceable treasure of Charleston.

Are you tiring of wandering through mansions? Eventually, I did, too. The House and Garden tours were coming up, an annual chance to gape into the settings of private lives. Jane Kiser told me she thought she could acquire one of the coveted tickets for me, but by then I was in a mood to strike out on my own. Charleston's peninsula is small enough that you can almost cover the historic lower end on foot, and I almost did.

I noticed that wherever I walked, I was never out of sight of a church steeple. Charleston's original constitution, written by John Locke, provided for freedom of religion, and I would say the old city has taken full advantage of it. It contains 188 churches of 36 denominations, which makes for a wonderful cacophony of bells on Sunday mornings. All other steeples, however, are overshadowed by those of St. Philip's and St. Michael's, once outposts of the Church of England where Tories and patriots worshipped in neighboring pews. Though there is no established church, these are still the churches of the establishment. I inspected the pew at St. Michael's where Washington and Lafayette once sat.

The purest and most beautiful Greek Revival house of worship in town is not a church at all. It's a synagogue, Beth Elohim, with a congregation that came together here twenty-five years before the Declaration of Independence. This is the birthplace of Reform Judaism in America. I've always been a little unclear on the differences among Orthodox, Conservative, and Reform Jews, and I didn't ask the friendly rabbi, Dr. William A. Rosenthall, to explain. It must have something to do with a lack of pretentiousness. I noticed "Shalom, Y'all" T-shirts for sale in the Reform gift shop.

The pleasure of the old city is in the details—the cobblestone lanes so cherished that when the power company had to dig one up, the city required that each cobblestone be numbered for replacement just where it had been; the earthquake bolts that were used to squeeze old buildings back into shape after the quake of 1886; the "single houses" whose street doors open onto airy piazzas; the docking posts on Water Street dating from the time when the street was a canal; the jasmine and crabapple blooms poking through the iron fences above the Tradd Street sidewalk; the sweetgrass basket ladies displaying their woven wares in the shade of the Post Office on Meeting Street; the statue of John C. Calhoun, that haggard, bitter, fanatical man, defender of slavery, towering on a monumental pedestal above Marion Square.

" 'John C. KILL-hoon,' that's what we call old John."

I was in the company of Alphonso Brown, band director at Rivers Middle School, black historian and speaker of Gullah, the rich black patois of the Carolina Low Country.

"White people remember history here," Alphonso said. "Well, we remember it, too. He was KILL-hoon back then, and he'll be KILL-hoon a hundred years from now." Alphonso told me that as a statue, Calhoun used to be at ground level, but he was so regularly vandalized by black Charlestonians that the Daughters of the Confederacy had to put him up in the sky out of reach. Alphonso chuckled to think about it.

From Alphonso Brown, you get a little different perspective on Charleston history. Down at the Battery, gesturing toward Sullivan's Island in the harbor, he said, "That was our Ellis Island. Slaves from Africa spent two weeks in quarantine in the Sullivan's Island pesthouse. Then they were brought into the Customs House and sold."

Alphonso on the Reconstruction years: "The freed slaves were promised forty acres and a mule. Some got twenty acres and a mule. Some got twenty acres and no mule. Some got a mule and no acres. Most got nothing. Life was hard for everybody."

Alphonso on the sweetgrass basket sellers in their bonnets and long dresses: "They dress poor but they live rich. Those women make a lot of money. One of them has a husband who comes to collect her at the end of the day in a big Mercedes-Benz."

Alphonso on Low Country speech: "The linguists say Gullah is a dying language. Ain't nothing dyin' about Gullah. Just last night, I heard a woman say, 'Dat food cookin' smell s' good mak' my jaw leak.' " He said this so fast and musically that he had to repeat it a couple times before I could understand it. He laughed. "You ain't necessarily *supposed* to understand it," he said.

Alphonso on black craftsmen: "Nearly everything you see around here was built by blacks—the houses, the walls, the streets and sidewalks—and not just by slaves, either. In 1850, there were thousands of free black artisans and business people in Charleston."

Or, as he put it in a guide he wrote to Gullah Charleston: *"Dem cyaapentas, boat mekkah, brick maysar, cook, iyon wukkah, net mekkah, en pleny mo', is wu'k dat de Black people bin doin' ya fuh shree hunnad odd yea' . . . Roll unuh eye 'bout! Yenna ain' kno' who mek dese place ya? De Black han', dat who!"*

At least one celebrated blacksmith is still around, Philip Simmons. "If you see a beautiful iron gate with meticulous curves," Alphonso Brown said, "it was made by one of the master blacksmiths of two hundred years ago—or it was made by Philip Simmons." We went to see some Philip Simmons gates—a valentine gate he made for his church, St. John's, for that is where he says his heart is; an egret gate at 2 St. Michael's Alley; a snake gate at 329 East Bay, once the house of Christopher Gadsden, who designed the Revolutionary War serpent flag with the legend "Don't Tread On Me."

Then we went to see Philip Simmons. He is a kindly man of eighty-two whose forge is in a ramshackle tin building behind his house on Blake Street. It doesn't look like the workshop of a National Treasure, but that's what Mr. Simmons is, officially certified by the Smithsonian Institution.

I asked him how he got started.

"When I was thirteen," he said, "I used to stand in the door of the blacksmith shop and see the red-hot fire and see the sparks flying, and I liked that. The blacksmith let me help out, hold the horse while he was putting the shoe on, turn the hand forge, clean up the shop. After a while, he learned me the names of everything. If he said, 'Boy, hand me that three-inch swage,' I had to know what he wanted. I learned that way.

"There were blacksmiths all over Charleston. I had many competitors. I was shoeing horses and fixing wagons, but people kept coming to tell me this company was going to trucks, that company was going to trucks, no more horses, no more wagons, blacksmiths going out of business, see? I had to start studying what I was going to do."

He turned to gates and fences and window guards.

"I've made more than two hundred gates and other ornamental iron works since then. Made gates for the Smithsonian in Washington and the South Carolina State Museum in Columbia, and this Charleston Visitor Center down here. The doctor says don't do any heavy work, but I may make some more gates yet. You know who my competitor is now?"

He gave me a soft smile.

"Father Time," he said.

There is an old saying among blacksmiths that the two ways a blacksmith can go to hell are by hammering cold iron and not charging enough. It appeared to me from his modest living conditions that Mr. Simmons hadn't charged enough.

"Well, I put my children through school," he said. "I gave money to my church. I have everything I want. And I am rich in friends."

After we said goodbye to Mr. Simmons and headed back downtown, Alphonso Brown said, "Some of these homeowners leave Charleston sometimes. I have noticed one thing. When they leave, they take their Philip Simmons gates with them."

Historically, Charleston was a special hell for black people. As slaves, even more brutally than in most of the rest of the South, they were publicly whipped, branded, and hanged (occasionally gaining a little momentary revenge by poison or arson, which always lead, of course, to a new round of frightened white repression). As "free" citizens, within my own memory, blacks were harassed, segregated, disfranchised, imprisoned without cause, discriminated against in every way the white imagination could devise.

A white Charlestonian, U.S. District Judge J. Waties Waring, helped end all that. A member of one of Charleston's oldest and most tradition-bound families, he nevertheless ruled in 1947 that South Carolina's all-white Democratic primary was unconstitutional, and later, well before the U.S. Supreme Court got around to agreeing with him, that racial segregation in the schools was inherently unequal. A cross was burned in front of Judge Waring's house on Meeting Street and a brick crashed through his window. A former friend, Charleston's Congressman L. Mendel Rivers, called Judge Waring a "monster" on the floor of the House. The judge was shunned by his own relatives. He was forced to resign from his clubs and even from his church, and finally, from the federal bench. He and his wife fled to New York for their safety.

I knew Judge Waring during his long exile from his native city and once asked him how, considering his background, he had ever arrived at his landmark decisions in the first place.

"By being a judge," he said, "I gradually became judicious."

He returned to Charleston only to be buried. I was there as a reporter at the Magnolia Cemetery on January 17, 1969, when the funeral cortege arrived at the grave site. I remember no more than six or eight white faces in the crowd; white Charlestonians, including most members of his family, stayed home that day to show their contempt for him. Hundreds of black people stood there shoulder to shoulder to show their respect.

I thought then, and think now, that the judge was an unsung American hero. Perfect racial justice hasn't arrived in Charleston yet, of course, but for what it's worth, a bronze sculpture of J. Waties Waring now stands in the corner of the City Council meeting room at City Hall.

Things have changed. Charleston has a successful black middle class and fair political representation. The police chief, Reuben Greenberg, is black (and Jewish!) and highly visible as he makes his rounds—sometimes in a squad car, sometimes on rollerskates or on horseback. Black deference to whites, once taken for granted, exists only in the memory of old folks. A black woman friend of Jane Kiser's said, "I'm not picking any more cotton, honey. I don't even pick the cotton out of the aspirin bottle!"

Before I left Charleston, I had occasion to remember part of a poem from my school days:

> Britons, you stay too long;
> Quickly abroad bestow you,
> And with a merry gale
> Swell your stretch'd sail,
> With vows as strong
> As the winds that blow you.

The poet was Michael Drayton, friend of Shakespeare, who is buried in Westminster Abbey. The verse is from his poem "To the Virginia Voyage," a salute to the heroism of the first English colonists in the New World. Drayton never made the trip himself, but some of his grandchildren did, "bestowing" themselves on Charleston in 1676. There is a picture of the poet in my encyclopedia. Except for the Elizabethan collar he is wearing, he looks exactly like John Drayton Hastie, his eleventh- or twelfth-generation descendant, who showed me around Magnolia Gardens. Mr. Hastie wore a tie and a fine tweed jacket and strolled the grounds as master of the manor, with two dogs on a leash.

"This formal garden," he said, "was planted by my great-great-great-great-great-grandmother, Ann Fox Drayton, in 1676."

He walked on a few steps before adding, matter-of-factly, "which makes this the oldest garden in the Western hemisphere."

Today, the formal plot is merely the smallest part of a vast and wondrous pleasuring ground a dozen miles up the Ashley River from Charleston, uplands and rolling fields and stream banks and marshes, all in bloom in March. A thousand breathtaking sights waited to be seen. Mr. Hastie, pushing eighty, wanted me to see them all, and I had to walk fast to keep up with him.

"The original garden survived nicely," he said. "I can't say the same for the buildings. The first house was burned down by accident. The second house was burned down by Sherman. This is the third, where my wife and I lived until recently, just a cottage, really."

The house was under construction.

"I'm having columns added to it," Mr. Hastie said, "because the visitors expect columns."

The plantation gardens were opened to the public after the Civil War by the Reverend John Grimke Drayton in order to save the place. He sold his Sea Island farmstead and his magnificent house on South Battery in Charleston and much of the acreage of Magnolia Plantation itself in an effort to keep his former slaves employed and his gardens blooming. The slaves, educated by Drayton in violation of the law, were mostly loyal and saw the gardens, as their former master did, as the only potential source of income in the ruined postwar countryside.

So Magnolia Plantation, once dedicated to rice growing, became Magnolia

Gardens, dedicated to beauty. Excursion steamboats brought visitors up the river from Charleston. The Reverend Mr. Drayton is the gardener who introduced azaleas to America (250 varieties were blooming the day I visited) and was among the first to plant camellias out-of-doors (900 varieties now thrive along the miles of garden paths).

By 1900, the Baedeker guide to the United States listed three must-see attractions: the Grand Canyon, Niagara Falls, and Magnolia Gardens. Maybe because I am a sucker for three-hundred-year-old live oak trees hung with Spanish moss, and for azaleas and camellias and dogwoods, and for Cherokee roses growing on fences, I think I'd put Magnolia Gardens first on that list.

I am a sucker for eccentrics, too, and Drayton Hastie enjoys this distinction. He barred bulldozers from his grounds after the havoc of Hurricane Hugo and, instead, to the incredulity of his neighbors, hired a helicopter for six months at $1,000 an hour to lift trees back into place and haul away wreckage.

After hunting birds and animals for the first sixty years of his life, he suddenly turned anti-hunting. "I started thinking what it would be like to be hunted," he said. He now gives 20 percent of Magnolia Gardens' income to animal organizations and has arranged his affairs so as to continue this endowment for eighty-five years after his death.

The population of his lawns, woodlands, and marshes include such diverse creatures as miniature horses, peacocks, pileated woodpeckers, egrets, and alligators. He delights in them all, except perhaps for the doves in his indoor tropical garden. "They are here to coo," he said. "They don't coo. They eat the plants and leave their droppings all over the place." He is undecided about the doves, but he leaves catfood along the trails for the foxes.

Like his Civil War-period ancestor, he has disposed of his house in town. "I don't have much to do with Charleston people," he said. "They all talk about this place, but they never come out here. I get along very well without them."

I found Mr. Hastie's antisocial streak appealing. It started early. He nodded toward a tall cypress tree growing in the middle of his swamp. "I built a treehouse in that cypress seventy years ago," he said. "I used to paddle my little boat over there and get away from it all. The treehouse is gone, as you can see. I often wish it were still there."

The family tomb, established in the 1600s, stands on a knoll above the river. Out of curiosity, Mr. Hastie once found the hidden entrance and entered. He found the caskets disintegrated, and such a jumble of skulls and bones littering the floor that he started trying to think of a more seemly resting place for his own ashes. One day, it came to him—the treehouse solution! He pointed to a neat hole drilled about fifty feet overhead in the trunk of a spreading live oak. "That's where I'm going," he said.

Drayton Hastie's gardens were my greatest Charleston pleasure, except for Drayton Hastie's company. I think he enjoyed my company, too. He wrote me a note and had it delivered to my little house on Montagu Street: "Sorry we had so little time with you; but perhaps you will return."

Perhaps I will. I hope so. I hope it is in March, when Charleston is in her glory. I hope things will not have changed too much. I hope the hole in that live oak at Magnolia Gardens is still unfilled. I hope a mockingbird is singing.

A Change of Plans

~

A butterfly changed my plans for April.

I didn't even see the butterfly. He was in New Zealand, to begin with, a place I've never been. And it was in November 1983—a long time before I had any plans for April twelve years later—that this faraway butterfly changed them.

That's the way life goes, of course. A breeze comes up in Rhode Island on a morning in March during the Civil War, and a Union soldier home on leave goes into a park in Providence to fly a kite, and a young woman sees the kite in the sky from her front stoop a block away and wanders into the park, where she meets the soldier and likes him, and they write letters to each other after he goes back to his outfit, and they are married after the war, and they have a son, who grows up and has a son, who grows up and has a son, who is named Charles after the soldier. And here I am. But I wouldn't be, if a Rhode Island day in 1864 had turned out calm, rather than breezy. I owe everything to the wind and to Providence.

I had planned to go to California in April, and except for that New Zealand butterfly, I would have. I had it all figured out: I was going to drive up the coast road to Big Sur, and park myself in a hideaway room at the Ventana Inn with a fireplace and a balcony and a fifty-mile view of the mountains and the ocean, and stay there until my money ran out, which, at the Ventana, wouldn't have taken long at all.

Then I was going to Point Lobos and walk through the gnarled and twisted Monterey cypresses, through the wind-blown grasses, to the continent's most majestic meeting place of land and sea. There I was going to sit, maybe for days, and watch the waves boil into fantastic eddies of blue and white and green in the recesses of the rocky shore. I was going to watch the pelicans and the sea lions. I was going to watch the whales go by.

Then I was going to the place on the steep hill above the curving beach which Father Junipero Serra chose for the most important of the California missions— San Carlos Borromeo del Rio Carmelo. The Mexican fishermen eventually took over from the friars, and then the artists and writers took over from the Mexicans, and then the corporation presidents and rich retired folk took over from the artists, and the spot became a town too pretty to be true. The name was shortened to Carmel. I'd have had my breakfasts at Katy's and my lunches outdoors at the Clam Box down the block, and I'd have walked around to all the art galleries of Carmel, trying, and failing, to look as if I belonged there.

Then I was planning to buy a dozen golf balls, and try really hard not to leave them all in the ocean on that scary par-three seventh hole at Pebble Beach. I had been looking forward to this, making perfect five-iron shots to the sunlit green of my dreams. Golf is on a long list of diversions I greatly enjoy and am no good at. I much prefer it to tennis or poker or chess, because by careful prearrangement, golf can be played alone, with nobody watching.

After my birdie on the seventh, I was going to dawdle along the rest of the

Seventeen-Mile Drive, to gawk at the manicured grounds of the mansions, and check up on the famous Lone Cypress on its knob above the sea, and walk on the white sand beach at Spanish Bay.

I had planned to visit John Steinbeck's Cannery Row in Monterey. The canneries are gone from the waterfront, because the sardines that used to be canned there are gone from the sea. It's Restaurant and Boutique Row now. But there is a fabulous new consolation prize. The Packards of Hewlett-Packard, David and Lucile, have given more than two hundred million dollars to create an aquarium and underwater research institution dedicated to the rich marine life of Monterey Bay. Dead sardines have been replaced by live sharks on Cannery Row. The aquarium is new since I've been to Monterey, and I'd love to have seen it. I hear they have the world's largest jellyfish collection, and a sting ray, minus his stinger, in a petting tank. I know I could have spent hours in that place watching the sharks and petting the ray.

I'd have gone to Pacific Grove, too. April is when the monarch butterflies, a couple of million of them, take flight from Pacific Grove. I once saw thousands of monarchs rise into the air there, flutter for a moment to get their bearings, and form into a bright, wavering, golden thread a mile long, northward bound across the blue waters of Monterey Bay.

The monarchs are the greatest mystery of nature, if you ask me. They spend the winter in Pacific Grove, then fly as far as two thousand miles into Canada to spend the summer. There, they breed and die. But their offspring return to Pacific Grove each fall, to the same forest, to the very same trees. The migration of salmon and geese and hummingbirds is amazing enough, but at least we can imagine their being guided along familiar paths by the ocean currents or the terrain or the stars. Monarch butterflies also know exactly where they are going. However, it is to a place *they've never been!*

How do they do it? Human beings have no idea. We outweigh monarchs, but they outsmart us. They know something we don't.

But I didn't see the Pacific Grove monarchs, because that other butterfly, the New Zealand one, changed my plans. This is going to require a little expla-nation, and I need to make a running start:

I have a friend, Granville Hall, who raises daffodils in Gloucester, Virginia. I feel lucky if I see him once every ten years, but he is the sort of man who doesn't let time and distance impede friendship. Nearly every summer he sends me a box of daffodil bulbs, old standbys and new hybrids, and I dutifully plant them in the fall in a grove of Connecticut maple trees, which I've come to think of as Granville's Woods.

I look forward to the October ritual. I take a sturdy bulb planter and a big bag of the right kind of fertilizer from the shed, and twist the twelve-month stiff-ness out of my gardening gloves, and spend a day or two filling in patches of ground where I haven't planted Granville's bulbs in years past. There is satis-faction in this. The bulbs don't need much attention from year to year, and that forest floor has become a pretty good daffodil show in the spring.

But I have not always been able to be there in the spring to enjoy it. One year, CBS News sent me off to Moscow in April for a summit conference, and another year to Beijing in the peak daffodil weeks. One of the frustrations of my job was not being able to say, "I'm sorry, I can't cover this cosmic event on the other side of the world, because I have to go watch my daffodils bloom."

Well, now I didn't have a job anymore. I was free to go watch my daffodils bloom, which, come to think of it, is everybody's reason for retiring—to take time to smell the flowers. And here I was, still driven by this immutable, ram-bling habit of mine, planning—on my own!—to be on the other side of the con-tinent in daffodil season. Suddenly, the Monterey Peninsula didn't seem quite so crucial to my perfect year. In a perfect year, you ought to be free to change your mind.

Besides, Granville Hall had paid me a considerable compliment the previ-ous fall. Into his annual shipment of daffodil bulbs—large yellow trumpets and double whites and tazetta hybrids, each labeled by name—he had tucked a paper bag sealed with staples containing two bulbs he obviously meant to be special.

When I opened the bag, a label fell out. It said, *"Narcissus* Charles Kuralt." It took me a few minutes to realize it wasn't a joke. Granville had named a daffodil for me.

In a letter which came later, he said that in all his years breeding daffodils, this was the first cultivar he had ever registered. He sent along the certificate from the Royal Horticultural Society. He said he had raised the bulb from seed and had named it in honor of my impending retirement. In all the world, he said, there now existed just three "Charles Kuralt" daffodil bulbs. He wanted me to have two of them.

I had planted those two bulbs with special care in a pretty place, on a slope above a mill pond. They had been there gathering strength all winter. I calculated that their first shoots would appear toward the end of March, and that they should bloom in the third or fourth week of April. Narcissus, you know, was a youth who pined away in love for his own image in a pool of water and was turned into a flower. Now that Granville Hall had turned me into a flower, a wave of narcissism washed over me. I wanted to see myself as a daffodil. I decided Monterey Bay would still be there next year.

It was a lovely April in New York. I had acquired a writing room atop a building in midtown Manhattan and fixed it up with mahogany shelves and cabinets, shutters at the windows, and Oriental rugs on the floor. I installed the desk and chair I'd bought in New Orleans and arranged everything to resemble the library of a very small and down-at-the-heels men's club, just the effect I wanted. Now I went there to comport myself as a gentleman of leisure, to read at my desk when I wanted, and to type up my travel notes at an outdoor table on the planted terrace. I thought of this as reflection and meditation; once upon a time, I would have called it goofing off. I realized I was playing a role, but it was a role I was beginning to enjoy.

All the time, I was waiting for my daffodil to bloom. I knew a lot of hard work and good luck went into breeding a new daffodil, but I had no idea how much time and patience went into it, until I asked Granville Hall to tell me the details, and he responded with a letter from Gloucester. That's when I found out about the New Zealand butterfly.

Most of the daffodil varieties on file with the International Daffodil Registrar in London are the result of careful hybridizing—applying the pollen of one show-stopper bloom to the stigma of another—and keeping careful records of this cross-pollination for the five or six years it takes for a tiny seed to become a blooming bulb. But, as a flower, my own birth was unplanned. As we used to say down home in North Carolina, I was a love child.

Granville wrote, "I wish I could tell you that *n.* Charles Kuralt is the product of years of brilliant and strategic cross-pollination by a master of the trade. 'Tain't so.

"Your lovely namesake was conceived by a butterfly (or by an ant or spider or naive bee, or by the wind) among the plantings of "Phil" Phillips at Otorohanga, New Zealand. The happy accident occurred in November of 1983.

"Phil Phillips, now deceased, was a world-famous hybridizer of 'Down Under' daffodils, and a generous man, to boot. Each spring (which ends in December down there), he would gather open (naturally) pollinated seeds from his faded blooms and send them to Dr. William Bender of Chambersburg, Pennsylvania. Dr. Bender nicknamed these shiny little black birdshots "POPS"—Phillips Open Pollinated Seed—and, equally generously, offered them to others . . . *Narcissus* Charles Kuralt was among some 1,500 POPS I acquired from Dr. Bender and planted in the spring of 1984.

"(Incidentally, you will find that *n.* C. K. looks a great deal like "Pop's Legacy," with which Dr. Bender won "Best Bloom in Show" at the National Show in King of Prussia, Pennsylvania. No small potato, that.)

"After they'd been two years in the seed bed, I transplanted all surviving seed (some don't germinate) of the POPS group to a regular row in my production field, where *n.* C. K. first bloomed in 1990. It caught my eye in the spring of '92, whereupon I dug it in June, and planted it in the fall in a T.L.C. bed in my side

*Goofing off on the terrace
(photo by
Karen Beckers)*

Narcissus *"Charles Kuralt"*

yard. An enthusiastic comment last March by my neighbor and resident expert inspired me to register it."

So, as a flower, I was the child of an unnamed mother and an unknown father, conceived in New Zealand, bred in tidewater Virginia, and now a resident of Connecticut. I was dying to know what I looked like. The possibilities, of course, were astronomical. Granville had told me that professional breeders who cross daffodil genes don't always, or even usually, obtain a pretty flower. So what could a butterfly (or ant or bee or spider) have accomplished by chance?

All I had to go on was a copy of Granville's application to the Royal Horticultural Society: "Seed parent: unknown. Pollen parent: unknown. Perianth: white, 53 mm. length, flat, spade-shaped, good overlap, good uniformity of shape. Corona: yellow, 53 mm. length, moderate funnel shape, flange concentric at 51 mm., notched about 5 mm. deep at 3 mm. intervals. Flowering season: early. Attributes: increases well, free flowering, good garden plant."

This sounded promising. I let my imagination wander. There was a new flower in the world! Perhaps all who saw it would be awe-struck and wish to have it for themselves. I didn't expect daffodil-mania to sweep the world like the tulip speculation of 1634; that year, a Dutch collector traded twelve sheep, eight pigs, four oxen, a bed, a suit of clothes, and a thousand pounds of cheese for a single Viceroy tulip bulb. But I had heard of high prices for daffodils. Three bulbs of a new variety, Will Scarlet, changed hands in 1899 for nearly a thousand dollars; a now-abundant daffodil named Fortune sold for seventy-five dollars a bulb when it was first introduced in 1923; and even King Alfred, which is now sold by the hundreds of tons each year and is the only daffodil name most people recognize, brought twenty or thirty dollars a bulb when it was a new variety. Maybe my namesake daffodil, which I was about to see for the first time, would become internationally coveted and make Granville Hall a rich man! Then I learned from Granville that there are more than twenty thousand named daffodils, and that another couple of hundred are added to the International Registry each year. This fact dimmed my dreams of fortune.

But it didn't dim the romance. It pleased me to think of those two bulbs in Connecticut giving forth their first pale green spikes to the sunshine. They were descendants of the first daffodil bulbs to make their way to Europe from Turkey in the Middle Ages, and of Wordsworth's daffodils in that poem I had to memorize in the sixth grade:

> *Ten thousand saw I at a glance,*
> *Tossing their heads in sprightly dance.*

Granville Hall told me those were very rudimentary daffodils Wordsworth saw in the English Lake Country. He wrote, "I wonder what he would compose if I took him to the Richmond show next spring?"

For modern breeding has changed the shapes and colors of daffodils and given the gardens and meadows of the world a variety beyond anything the old poet could have imagined two hundred years ago. The old, well-remembered flowers have contributed some of their finest qualities to hundreds of variations. Granville wrote, "All of the red, orange, and primrose in any daffodil anywhere in this world came from that little ring of red in the eye of n. Poeticus Recurvus (Old Pheasant's Eye)."

So I didn't go to California. I did some reading and writing and relaxing, and then I went to Connecticut. I was there on the morning the first *Narcissus Charles Kuralt* opened to the world. Some daffodils are showy and assertive. Some are pert. This one was delicate and refined. From the midst of its creamy white petals arose a trumpet of pale yellow with a feathery lemon-yellow fringe. The flower faced the sun demurely, but with what I thought was a certain confidence. Well, it seemed to say, here I am. What do you think? I thought it was beautiful, and not quite like any other daffodil I'd ever seen.

Each bulb yielded two blooms. Each of the four flowers was perfect. Several times each day, I walked to the knoll where they were growing to make sure they were all right. When I had to return to New York, I cut them and drove them home with me. They rode in a glass of water wedged into the passenger seat. I stopped for gas at a place where they still clean your windshield, and the guy said, "Nice flowers." I wanted to tell him the whole story, of course. But all I said was, "Thanks."

When you leave your job after a long time in the public eye, everybody wants to have a dinner and give you a plaque or a scroll. Such dinners were given for me during the year by organizations I admire: the Anti-Defamation League and People for the American Way. The old pros of the Radio-Television News Directors Association gave me their highest award at a black-tie dinner. The Television Critics Association invited me to Los Angeles for their annual Career Achievement Award, and the National Press Club had me to Washington for their annual Fourth Estate Award, with amusing speeches by old friends, Bill Moyers and Ed Yoder and Calvin Trillin and Andy Rooney. Tom Brokaw handed me the DuPont Columbia Award in New York, and Allen Neuharth gave me the Allen Neuharth Award in South Dakota, and I got to sit with Jane Alexander and William and Rose Styron and Sarah and Jim Brady at the Common Wealth Awards in Wilmington, Delaware. My old university put my name on a building. This was all very heady stuff.

But I didn't know what narcissism was until I beheld my own narcissus.

Plaques tarnish. Scrolls fade. But those daffodil bulbs will divide and multiply. Within a year or two, I'll be able to give a couple of bulbs to each of my daughters. If they plant them and care for them, those will divide in turn and yield bulbs for my grandchildren. With a little luck, the flower named Charles Kuralt will appear from the earth to bloom in the spring long years after the man of the same name is gone.

I guess that's not exactly immortality, but it's as close as I will ever get.

MAY

. . . . .

Grandfather Mountain, North Carolina

~

The temperature dropped 30 degrees as I drove up into the North Carolina mountains. It was a 94-degree afternoon down at Lenoir. Half an hour later, when I turned south onto the Blue Ridge Parkway at Blowing Rock, a storm was blowing up and the temperature gadget on the dashboard of the rental car told me it was 63 degrees outside. I turned off the air conditioner, opened the car window, and let a great rush of cool mountain air wash over me. I felt that I was home.

I've always felt at home in the mountains. I don't know why. I was born in Wilmington, on the flat coast, way at the other end of the state, and brought up in the rolling Piedmont near Charlotte, which passed at the time for a big city. I get no particular tingle in either place. I feel embraced by the mountains.

The Parkway, which follows the ridges, was fogbound that afternoon. I turned on my headlights and went slow. It would have been easy to make a wrong turn in the fog, and you don't want to make a wrong turn on the Blue Ridge Parkway. There are places where you could whistle two choruses of "Barb'ra Allen" in the air before you landed down in the valley.

I was headed for Hugh Morton's mountain. He's the only man I know who owns one, Grandfather Mountain above Linville, so named because if you look at it in the right way from the back side, it has the aspect of an old man staring up into the sky. The top of Grandfather is the highest point in the Blue Ridge, a little short of six thousand feet. On a clear day, you feel that you can see the whole world from up there. In fact, you *can* see a long way. Hugh Morton is a great and patient photographer, and one clear winter morning, after waiting patiently for the sun to rise, he made an astounding photograph of the dawn lighting the skyline of Charlotte, more than one hundred miles away, with many waves of dark blue mountain ranges in the foreground.

Long before Charlotte had a skyline, and before any road wider than an Indian footpath led to Grandfather, the great French naturalist, André Michaux, climbed to the top. This was in 1794, five years after the French Revolution, and Michaux, thinking he was standing on the highest peak in North America, sang the *Marseillaise* up there and shouted, "Long live the Republic of France!" and "Long live the United States of America!" Part of his excitement, no doubt, was that he had been finding botanical species he had never seen before, or imagined. He couldn't have known it then, but from the top of Grandfather Mountain, his eyes were falling upon a greater variety of trees and plant life than exists in all of Europe from the Scandinavian capes to the Mediterranean Sea. Grandfather Mountain is a special place in the world, designated by the United Nations as a Biosphere Reserve, the first privately owned one in the world.

I wasn't thinking about any of this on my drive toward Grandfather. I was squinting into the white mist and thinking about keeping the car on the road. A wild turkey appeared in the vapor ahead of me, glided across the Parkway, and disappeared on the downhill slope as I went by. A bushy critter, maybe a woodchuck, started across the road, thought better of it, and lumbered back into the bushes. I met no other cars. I felt alone in the cool white world with the creatures of the forest. A great happiness came over me.

Hugh Morton was letting me use a secluded one-room cabin he and his brother had built on an anvil-shaped ledge of the mountain. When I got there, the coffee pot was on the stove, the refrigerator was stocked with orange juice and milk, and somebody, his wife, dear Julia Morton, I imagine, had arranged two beautiful pink rhododendron blossoms in a vase on a windowside table. I carried my bags in just before the first raindrops spattered on the roof. I lighted a fire in the huge stone fireplace that occupied one end of the room and sat down before the fire to listen to the gathering storm. Only a bumblebee buzzing around my head was out of place. Or maybe he was *in* place, and I was out. He liked the rhododendron blossoms, too. It was raining and the night was coming on; I figured the bee and I could coexist until morning.

A big wind built in intensity all night. I woke up to the roar of it and felt the cabin shuddering. I was elated by the storm, don't ask me why. I rolled over and went contentedly back to sleep, feeling privileged to be there, safe and warm and dry. At first light, I could look down into the Linville Valley from my snug aerie and see the tops of small trees bending nearly to the ground in the gusts, and when I stepped out to drive down the mountain to buy the morning papers in Linville, the light rain, blowing horizontally, stung my cheeks. By the time I returned and had a big bowl of cereal and a cup or two of coffee, the wind was dying down and the wild sky was beginning to show patches of blue. An hour later, the sun was out and the world felt washed and fresh and new.

I went out to have a walk around. The cabin was anchored on the lip of a thousand-foot gorge—no walking that way. Deep woods extended along the cliffside almost to my front door. At the fringe of the forest, a patch of bluets grew, still moist from the rain; of all the wildflowers, I think bluets are my favorites. A baby rabbit hopped out of the woods. He settled himself amid the flowers as I walked around, in the naive belief of rabbits that they become invisible if they stay perfectly still. In fact, any passing hawk could have spotted him easily in his bed of bluets—but none did. When I left the cabin three weeks later, the rabbit was still nibbling the grass around the edge of the woods, and the flower patch was still his favorite resting place.

A wild pinkshell azalea was in bloom behind the cabin, a pastel, delicate, beautiful thing, native only to North Carolina, and rare, though it grows all over Grandfather Mountain.

And standing beside the stone steps that led up to the door was a single, doomed chestnut tree. All American chestnut trees are doomed. This one was about twelve feet tall, the size when they are afflicted by the chestnut blight, and this one was—covered with scale on the trunk and rotting at the junction of the branches. Chestnuts are the great arboreal tragedy of America. In the nineteenth century, they blanketed the land and amounted to about one-fourth of all the trees in the southern Appalachians. They grew a hundred feet tall and lived five hundred years or more. They provided a lively timber business, food for settlers and animals, and shade for many a dwelling. (Remember that it was "under the spreading chestnut tree" that the village smithy stood.) The blight struck in 1904, and in the next half century killed virtually every chestnut tree in the United States. Researchers have been at work for years in Maryland, Virginia, and elsewhere, trying to breed a blight-resistant chestnut. I hope they succeed someday. It would be wonderful to think of our grandchildren roaming through the woods as our grandparents did, coming home with a hatful of chestnuts.

I spent most of that day sitting on the cabin steps, gazing out over the valley to the mountains, inventing reasons not to go anywhere or do anything.

I got out my binoculars and tried to spot a woodpecker who was hammering on a tree part of the way down into the gorge. (How do woodpeckers manage always to stay on the *other* side of the tree?)

I watched a pair of ravens circling in an updraft, apparently just for the fun of it; I've heard that ravens are the most playful, as well as the smartest, of birds. These two found a thermal they liked and rose higher and higher overhead until they were two tiny dots against the sky.

In late afternoon, I listened to birds singing in the hills above me and in the valley below. I can't identify many birds by their calls, one of the gaps in my knowledge I want to correct someday. I'd rather know bird songs than know French.

The next day, I took a drive—from Grandfather to Blowing Rock on the road that Hugh Morton's granddaddy built, and which some old-timers still call the Yonahlossee Road, then the big counter-clockwise circle to Boone, Vilas, Valle Crucis, Banner Elk, Linville, and back to Grandfather Mountain. On the narrow and winding Valle Crucis–Banner Elk road, I saw great sprays of blackberry and sourwood blossoms, a benediction of the mountain spring. It was planting season in the valleys, of course, and I took notice of the things people had hung on wires above their garden plots to keep the birds away—old mirrors, hubcaps, strips of tinfoil, bandannas, highway reflectors, and more than one dead crow hanging upside down. If the crows don't get that message, they are impervious to messages.

I stopped at a crossroads store with a soda fountain, noted the price of a small Coke—seventy-nine cents—and handed the teenaged girl behind the counter a dollar. "That's twenty-seven cents with tax," she said. That was when I noticed the sign on the side wall: "Senior Citizens, small coffee or small soft drink twenty-five cents at all times." I thought the damned kid could at least have asked my age. I wasn't quite sixty years old. I had just experienced my first Senior Citizen's perk, saving fifty-two cents, and I was a little irritated!

This was the first direct human contact I'd had in a couple of days. It sort of snapped me back to reality. I hadn't come to the mountains just to gaze at the flowers and listen to the birds, as much as I was enjoying both. What I really wanted to do was meet a few people and hear a few stories. I spent all those years in television making a living by talking. I knew that in the North Carolina mountains, the pleasure is in listening.

"My mother didn't believe in music or dancing or drinking. My father was a fiddler and a dancer and a drinker."

So I spent the rest of May listening. This was Bertie Burleson telling me about her upbringing on Roaring Creek, in a house with no electricity or indoor plumbing. She remembered her mother doing the washing with a washboard down at the spring.

"My mother was a good woman, and worked hard all her life. But Daddy . . ."

She smiled to think about him.

"Daddy was a real man and free as any bird. He was an old-fashioned fiddler. He played with whatever clawhammer banjo player he could find. He was a sawmill worker. He always had sawdust on the brim of his felt hat . . . I sure did love my daddy."

Bertie never got to go to college, but she decided when she was young that she was a writer.

"I worked in the general store, and all the time I was filling gas tanks and making baloney sandwiches and sacking groceries, I told everybody I was a writer and someday I'd be paid for it."

I was making notes while Bertie and I had barbecue sandwiches at Dorman's Smokehouse and drank our sweet iced tea from Mason jars. Before we finished the meal, I checked back in the notes and said, "So you knew you were going to be a writer when you were still a little girl?"

"No," she said, correcting me. "I *was* a writer. I knew someday I was going to be paid for it."

She's the well-respected editor of the *Avery Journal* now, the weekly newspaper in Avery County, a tract of land so far back in the hills that it was the last North Carolina county to be named. It was named for Colonel Waightstill Avery, a Revolutionary patriot who was challenged to a duel by impetuous young Andrew Jackson. Colonel Avery let Jackson fire first, then holstered his own pistol, marched up to the future American hero, and rebuked him at length for being such a hothead. Andrew Jackson never got over his hotheadedness, but the old-time mountain duels, among many other things, gave Bertie Burleson stories to write about. She gets paid for it.

Nearly everybody in the Blue Ridge can tell you a story of growing up poor but happy. Some of the people who tell the stories are more or less successful now, like Bertie. Plenty are still poor but happy. Either way, North Carolina mountain people are the best storytellers in the world. The old Scots-Irish language and dialect survive in the mountain hollows, and the easy, brilliant seventeenth-century way of telling tales. They are almost always tales of old times.

I think back now to some of the stories I heard in my mountain month of May.

My friend, Dr. Ted Ledford, with whom I've gone trout-fishing in the mountain streams in springtimes gone by, was born and raised in that Shakespearean tradition of mountain storytelling. Now he *teaches* Shakespeare at Lees-McRae College. He told me this one:

"I knew a man who got into a quarrel with a friend in a timber camp. One night, his friend shot him in the face as he came into the mess hall. The bullet knocked out two of his front teeth and lodged in his head above his palate. He used to put chewing gum over the hole so he could drink without having his beer coming out his nose. Forty years later, sitting on his porch in Bakersville, he sneezed the bullet into his hand.

"People always said someday those two will meet again, and the quarrel will be settled one way or another.

"The years went by. Finally, it happened. They met on the street in Bakersville. The people around them all held their breath."

"What happened?" I asked.

"Well," Ted said, "the two of them just stood there. Neither one knew what to do."

He thought about it for a while, the way good storytellers do, to let me think about it.

"And then—well, they *hugged* each other!

"They talked a while and went on their way.

"It was over."

I thought it was a terrific story. Shakespeare isn't around to make a play out of it, so I guess Ted Ledford will write it himself someday.

Hal McClure is a mountain wood-carver with a great drooping moustache. I think it might be worth the trouble of growing a moustache if I could have one like that before I die. While Hal worked on an owl-head letter-opener, with wood shavings all over his chest, he told me stories:

"I come from a long line of carvers and coopers and cabinet makers. This is the truth: Instead of a pacifier, I cut my teeth on a pocket knife my mama gave me. Her mother was a good carver and she was a good carver.

"I had great-grandfathers who fought in the Revolution. A lot of them went west. I've been told the Platte River was named after my great-great-great uncle. My granddaddy met Davy Crockett. Said Davy was about five-foot-five or five-foot-six, red-headed and red-bearded and mean as a striped snake, that's exactly what he said. My granddaddy said Davy lay around drinking whiskey and fighting, that's all he done."

Bea Hensley is the best-known blacksmith in the mountains. He and his son, Mike, were working on a pair of 1800-pound gates at their shop in Spruce Pine, using 2 3/4-inch iron stock. That is hot, heavy work, and I felt bad about interrupting.

"No," Bea said, "I'm like a freight train. I couple and uncouple just when I'm ready. I've worked at this fifty-three years and I've loved every minute of it, but now I'll stop and talk if I want to."

We fell to talking about big trees.

"The largest poplar tree in the world growed at the head of Cane River," Bea said. "I saw it growing and I saw it cut down. Four squares of square dancers could have danced on the stump, with room for the band."

I said that sounded like a big tree, all right.

"And up here on Armstrong," Bea said, "they cut down the biggest chestnut ever growed in the United States. It took thirty-four head of horses to pull it out."

"We made J-bars and grab-hooks for logging," Mike said. "You ought to see a team of horses ball-hooting, going down hill, dragging tons of logs. At just the right moment, the teamster would cry 'Jay-ho!' as loud as he could. When they heard that, the horses knew to pull aside, and the logs would go on down the mountain. There was only two kinds of horses, live ones and dead ones, and the good ones stayed alive."

Mike showed me his hammer, with a handle of curly hickory. "That wood is as rare as an honest congressman," he said. He told me the old way of learning to use the hammer:

"The first four years, you stood across the anvil from the master, and you didn't say a word for four years. There was a reason for that. Some things you just have to know, like two plus two equals four. You don't ask why.

"The master's little hammer told the apprentice where to strike with the big hammer, what spot to strike, how hard, and most important, what angle. That was hard to see, but the apprentice had to learn to see it.

"The apprentice spent four years just learning this language of the hammer and cleaning the shop, starting the fire, and such as that. Then he'd spend six years on the master's side of the anvil, and he could talk, ask questions. Then he'd spend four years at his own anvil but subject to inspection by the master. He'd go from apprentice to journeyman to master in those fourteen years, and he had to complete it with the same master. He hoped the master wouldn't die, because if he did, he had to start all over again with somebody else. That was how you became a blacksmith. The old Germans in this country were the last to give up that rigid way of doing it."

Bea and Mike Hensley told me such stories for half the afternoon. Mike's son, Luke, stood there the whole time, listening to his father and grandfather, learning about blacksmithing, learning about storytelling. Someday, I thought,

Luke will be telling *his* grandchildren about the poplar stump big enough to accommodate sixteen square dancers and a band.

"We aren't inhibited in our talk," North Carolina's Roy Wilder, Jr., once wrote. "We turn the spigot and let it burble . . ."

There are many good reasons to spend the month of May in the Blue Ridge, and listening to the good talk is one of the best.

The southern Appalachian chain used to serve as a barrier to flatlanders from elsewhere, leaving the mountaineers isolated to talk their own language, brew their own whiskey, and live their own lives. They were fiercely independent lives. In colonial times, mountain people ignored the British laws, including the one that forbade settlement west of the mountain ridges; a historian wrote that the Scots-Irish settlers "were determined to keep the Sabbath and everything else they could lay their hands on," including the land of the much lied-to and mistreated Cherokees.

Later, during the Civil War, the mountaineers mostly shunned the Confederate cause. They had no quarrel with President Lincoln—were rather proud of him, in fact, his mother being a North Carolinian and all. They didn't like the Confederate conscription—the absence of a male from the mountain farms caused great distress—and they didn't like the Confederate taxes. Most of them stayed loyal to the Union, true to their independent way of thinking. The mountain generation that followed the war suffered for this when the former Confederates came back into political power after Reconstruction. Remembering the Union sympathies of the mountain counties, the Democrats of the populated East withheld tax money for mountain roads and schools, and this smoldering animosity still has echoes in the politics of the present day.

The mountains were isolated, but now things are changing, and not in a way that any mountain dweller likes.

The natural blue haze that gave the Blue Ridge Mountains their name is getting thicker and grayer. The winds from the west are no respecters of the geographical barrier. Chemicals from smokestacks in Michigan and Ohio fall on the mountains in acid rain, and once-beautiful stands of Fraser fir and red spruce now stand dead on the tops of the ridges; a scientist tested the soil atop Mount Mitchell, highest point east of the Rockies, and found its acidity to be halfway between that of lemon juice and battery acid.

An even more noticeable change is in the nature of the population. "The only way to get to Boone," it used to be said, "is to be born there." But the highway builders have been at work, and outsiders escaping the heat of Florida and South Carolina now flock to the North Carolina high country in the summer. They barricade themselves behind locked gates in their houses and condominiums. Most of them care a lot about their bridge hands and golf scores and nothing at all about the life and traditions of the mountain people.

The newcomers have money, of course, as hardly any of the old-time residents have, and this causes a strain. The *Watauga Democrat*'s local correspondent, "TLC," wrote from Sugar Grove, "We need to take pride in ourselves and our way of life. Ain't a soul the good Lord made that is any better than the rest." She said she and her husband saw five men in expensive outfits taking fly-fishing lessons in a meadow, casting their lines onto the grass. She said this scene caused her husband to remark, "The end of time is coming fast!"

"It was a strange sight to behold," she wrote. "Let's all remember, as the tourist season again falls upon us, to be as pleasant as possible, but keep your backbone straight and strong, for we and our mountains will be here after they are gone."

In the same paper, an old-time country store which used to deal in crosscut saws, chicken feed, and lamp oil advertised two new coffee bean flavors, Chocolate Cherry Kiss and Chocolate Streusel. The end of time is coming fast.

But for all the changes, the mountains are still beautiful—as beautiful as any place on earth, I think—and they still have a strong pull on those born in their folds. Ted Ledford told me, "Mountaineers have a sense of place, a sense of home. We say, 'Never move so far away that you can't see the smoke from your parents' chimney.' That's part of it. Then when we do go outside, we are always looked at as strange people from a strange land, so we can't feel at home anywhere else. There was a time when you had to leave if you wanted a job. I did. I went to Detroit to work in the automobile factory. After a month of that, I was back here. My brother went to upstate New York. The teacher sent his son home from school with a note saying the boy needed speech therapy. This from a *teacher*, who should have known better. We are four brothers, and we're all back—well, there's one who teaches at Auburn, but he's back every other weekend."

Ted Ledford is in the hills to stay. I think he renews his vows every year in the spring.

"I'm an outdoor man," he said, "and the winters are right hard on me. I watch that sun every day. I know right where it is going to be on December twenty-first, and I watch it start back up. By this time of year, whatever worries I had in the winter are all gone and forgotten. I'm a new man in May."

As a mountaineer with an education, Ted feels he has a responsibility to keep a record of the rich mountain customs. He showed me a film he made of Sadie Wiseman, wearing a long dress and a bonnet, stirring apple butter in a big black pot over a fire.

"Just bring the apples to a boil and add five pounds of sugar all at once," she says. "Some of them put in cinnamon, but that's not right. This is the real natural way."

And Jess Wiseman on how to make a banjo: "A gray squirrel makes the best drum. Go find your squirrel, shoot him in the head, soak him in lye and water for three days, take the hair off and stretch him on your banjo."

You have to be industrious to eke out a living in the mountains, but in the cold winters Ted dreads so much, sometimes there's only so much to do after you tend to the fire in the hearth. I think it was Ted who told me about a man who came down the hill to visit the clinic in Banner Elk one winter. The doctor asked, "Are you sleeping all right?" The man said, "Well, I'm sleeping all right at night, and I'm sleeping pretty well in the morning, but here lately, I've been having trouble getting to sleep in the afternoon."

Ora and Willard Watson

Bea Hensley and his grandson, Luke

That's the mountaineer stereotype, which mountaineers can laugh at, but the fact is, they can't afford to do much daytime sleeping; most of them have more than one job.

I went to see Luther Thomas on a back road near Micaville (turn left at the church and then back to the right across the creek). He lives in a house he built with his wife, Bea. "Really, I drew the plans," Bea said, "and did more work on the house than he did, until it came to working on the roof."

Luther and Bea grew up in the same mountain valley. She says they courted for three years and he never said thirty words to her until they were married. But she had no complaints about her husband as a worker. He's been a miner, mineral collector, carpenter, naturalist, self-taught archaeologist, carver of birch brooms and hickory flowers, and jack-of-all-trades for most of his eighty-two years. Since his early childhood, I would guess Mr. Thomas has worked at something every waking hour of his life.

"I went to work when I was thirteen years old," he said, "driving steel in the feldspar mine with an eight-pound sledge. I worked with three men driving, one turning."

(You wouldn't want to have been a turner; he's the man who held the steel chisel and reset it while the other three pounded it with their hammers. If you see an old man in the mountains with a permanently smashed and crippled hand, he was probably a turner.)

"I worked ten hours a day for ten cents an hour," Luther Thomas said. "I never got through the third grade. I loved all kinds of rocks. I didn't know the names of any of them. My cousin gave me a rock book, but I couldn't read it.

"My daddy was an old man when I was born. He took me with him when he went a-walking. We traipsed all over these mountains looking for mica. Mica had hundreds of uses, and my daddy always thought he'd find a big deposit. When we'd find some mica, we'd walk up the mountain looking to see where it came from, then dig it out. My daddy spent more money looking for mica than it ever made money for him.

Square dance caller Frank Mast

John Derych and Gerry

"I'd pick up pretty rocks and bring 'em home. They were pretty rocks, that's all I knew. I still have some of 'em."

He showed me a rock the size of a watermelon.

"This here's kyanite," he said. "See those big crystals? There's seven different colors in this one deposit. Charles, you could lay a thousand dollars on the table for this one rock and I wouldn't touch it."

He opened some wooden cases and rummaged around in them.

"Here are some rocks I found and my son Icket cut," he said. "These are quartz crystals here, these are rubies, citrines, emeralds from Crabtree Mountain—I think that may be the only emerald deposit in the United States. These are opals, rose quartz, Morganite beryl, golden beryl, tourmalines, blue topaz—see how them topazes shine? These are amethysts. They all come from right around here. I have heard there are three hundred and sixty minerals in these three counties, Yancey, Mitchell, and Avery."

I said he seemed to have made himself a real expert on gems.

"Well," he said, looking a little abashed, "I finally learned to read so I could read the rock books."

"He has some very technical books that he reads now," Bea said.

"I still don't have no education," Luther said, "but if you're around people and keep these things open [holding out his ears] and these things closed [pinching his lips], you can find out things."

"Do you still go gem-hunting?" I asked.

"Many a day," Luther Thomas said. "The rocks are maybe a little harder to find now, but there's plenty of them out there. This old earth ain't been scratched yet."

He unlatched the door to a cabinet and invited me to look inside. There were soapstone pots, stone axes, and spearheads on the shelves.

"Indian things," Luther said. "I found 'em under a big camp rock over here, a ledge sticking out about eighteen feet. Local people, white people, always camped under it. Icket and I got to digging there and found part of a clay pot, so we went on down through three layers of beautiful rock work, big flat rocks the Indians had to have carried in there. They fit together prettier than anybody could do it today. The Indians were better craftsmen than we are, considering what they had to work with. I offered to put all this stuff back where it come from if the archaeologists would fence it in and protect it, but they said they didn't have no funds for it."

We walked around the yard a while. Mr. Thomas wanted to show me his wildflowers.

"These are cardinal flowers. That's a lobelia, you know. They're all voluntary here by the creek. The hummingbirds will leave the feeder and come down here for these sweet red things . . .

"This is what we call golden seal. I've found only two little patches of it in all my treks through the mountains. This is one the Indians used for medicine, must have. . . ."

When it was time to go, I bought some of Mr. Thomas's beautiful carved daisies, dainty hickory flowers on eight-inch stems. He wouldn't let me pay more than three dollars each for them. "That's what I've always asked," he said. And he gave me a little pail he had made of poplar bark.

"My daddy showed me how," he said. "If we were out in the mountains and we got hungry of a morning, my daddy would make him a bark berry bucket and we'd pick blackberries or huckleberries and fill it up. When we got home, he'd throw the bucket into the fire. I make 'em now, but I'd give anything for one of his."

I thanked Mr. Thomas for letting me visit, and especially for showing me the treasures he had brought down from the hills, his gemstones and Indian artifacts.

"Well, they're not mine," he said.

He saw that I didn't understand at first.

"I found 'em, but I can't take 'em with me. They all belong to Him. He loaned every bit of this to me and let me have it for a little while."

In every mountain valley, there's a rushing stream, and in every stream there are quiet pools, and in some of the pools, there are trout. Toward evening one day, I strung up a fly rod and pulled on a pair of hip waders and tried to find the trout in a stretch of the Watauga River. Trout cannot live except in beautiful places, as a wise old fisherman once told me, so if you have bad luck trout fishing, you can always relax and enjoy the beautiful place. That's more or less what I did on the Watauga. I caught and released two small brook trout, the beautiful speckled native of these mountains, and had a larger fish spit out the fly after a few seconds on the line. I think I could have fished well into the evening without putting a serious strain on my fragile number-6 leader.

But big fish were not always scarce in these small streams. Hugh Morton told me about a twenty-two-inch brown trout he caught as a boy in a pool of the Linville River. With his heart beating fast, he took it to Hampton's store to be weighed. Mr. Hampton put the fish in the Coca-Cola cooler while Hugh ran home to tell his father. His father was a little skeptical about the reported size of the trout, but when he accompanied his son to the store, he had to acknowledge that this was a big brown, all right. The fish was swimming around in the ice water among the Coke bottles, and Mr. Hampton's customers were all lifting the lid of the cooler to have a look.

My friend Frank Mast told me that back in the Forties, he caught an eighteen-inch rainbow trout in Dutch Creek in Valle Crucis. On the way home, he showed the fish to everybody he ran into. But he didn't run into everybody he knew, so when he got home, he pinned a safety pin on his shirt sleeve up near the shoulder to show how long the fish was, measuring from his fingertips to the safety pin. He said he wore that safety pin on his shirt for a long time.

Frank Mast is better known today as a square dance caller than as a fisherman. He learned calling from an uncle who used to call at pie suppers and cakewalks, and he met his wife, Thelma, at a square dance forty-five years ago at the Mission School in Valle Crucis. When I expressed surprise that they allowed dancing at the Mission School, Frank said, "Oh, that's Episcopalian, you know. You can dance there. You can tip up a jug there, too!" Thelma said people in

Valle Crucis still serve two kinds of punch at their parties, Episcopalian punch and Baptist punch. She said Episcopalian punch is better.

I went to hear Frank call at Shadrack's, a big barn of a place in Boone on the Blowing Rock Road. Shadrack's offers food cafeteria-style—good ribs, barbecue, fried catfish, fried okra, fried shrimp, hush puppies, stewed apples, string beans and the like, and sells soft drinks and iced tea at the "drink bar." People in Boone freely predicted the place would never make it as a dance hall serving no alcohol, but I guess six hundred people were in there on a Friday night, having a wonderful time. A band played for every kind of country dancing—slow dancing, clogging, line dancing, two-step, and square dancing. Frank called a "Paul Jones," in which men circle one way and women the other. Every minute or so, when the caller blows a whistle, you grab the partner you're facing. This results in wonderful pairings—old men dancing with teenaged girls, for example, all entirely unselfconsciously—and was great fun to do, obviously, and great fun to watch.

"Circle right and *(whistle)* grab your partner and swing!" Frank would holler. Then, after a little while, "Turn 'em loose and circle . . . and *(whistle)* grab your partner and swing!" And finally, ". . . swing your lady HOME!" as the music ended.

A young man crossed the floor to where I was sitting to be an emissary: "That pretty dark-haired girl over there wants to know if you would slow dance with her." I protested that I couldn't dance, which is more or less true, and he went back to convey my rejection. I could tell by the reaction of Frank and Thelma that I had done the wrong thing. To fill the awkward silence, Frank said, "These mountain girls are real forward, Charles." Next time, when a pretty dark-haired girl asks me to dance, I'm going to dance.

Hugh and Julia Morton's daughter, Catherine, who lives near Grandfather Mountain and pays close attention to the subtleties of solstice and equinox, calculates that spring comes up the mountains at two hundred feet per day. So now, in the middle of May, I began to see some of the same blooms I saw in Charleston at the beginning of March. A dogwood behind my cabin transformed itself from pale yellow to brilliant white in the space of a week. I took the chill from the nights with crackling fires in my fireplace, and welcomed the refreshing mornings. As one who has always been willing to go to any latitude or altitude to escape hot weather, I could be secure in the knowledge that real summertime never quite makes it to the high country; the warmest temperature ever recorded on Grandfather Mountain was 82 degrees in a still-remembered long-ago heat wave.

With spring in bloom, visitors arrived at Grandfather in greater numbers. They pay a fee at the gate and spend the day in a place of great natural beauty, hiking, picnicking, daring one another to walk across Hugh Morton's "Mile High Swinging Bridge," and admiring the black bears and cougars in the spacious animal habitats on one of the mountain's slopes. I made the acquaintance of one of these visitors when Hugh took me into the bear enclosure to see some of the animals up close.

John Derych works for the Post Office in Commack, Long Island. One day in 1990 ("I was a typical postal worker, reading somebody else's mail!") he was thumbing through a copy of *Natural History* magazine and came across a story about bears. Something clicked in John's brain. He remembered the time when he was a kid and the animal trainer for the Clyde Beatty–Cole Brothers Circus let him stand outside a fence a couple of feet from the bears. The thrill of it came back to him. He resolved to spend the rest of his life as close as he could to bears.

John went to Minnesota in the dead of winter and talked the Forest Service's Dr. Lynn Rogers into letting him tag along on a trip into bear country. He went to Montana to travel the wilderness with another expert, Charles Jonkel of the Great Bear Foundation, on the trail of grizzlies. Now John saves all his vacations for bear trips. He comes to Grandfather Mountain three or four times a year to visit a hulking four-year-old female black bear named Gerry. He has special permission to enter the enclosure. He was walking around looking for Gerry, when Hugh and I came through the gate.

"Will Gerry remember you?" I asked John.

"I think she will, I feel she will," he said. "I always bring her shelled sunflower seeds. I think she remembers. I think she'll be glad to see me."

Gerry appeared from behind a boulder, looking enormous. I took a few steps back. John Derych walked right over to the massive animal.

"Hi, Gerry," he said.

The bear keeper was in the enclosure, a can of pepper spray in his hand for protection. "Don't try to pet that bear!" he commanded. "That bear cannot be petted, nohow!"

Gerry walked up and nuzzled John Derych.

"Careful, careful!" the keeper said.

John sat down on the ground. Gerry sat down too. John started rubbing her belly. Gerry rolled over on her back with what I thought was a kind of bear smile.

"All bears like marshmallows and apples and cookies," John said. "But Gerry is nuts about shelled sunflower seeds." He fed her sunflower seeds from a paper sack with one hand and kept rubbing her belly with the other.

I leaned on a rock and talked with John while he and Gerry had their reunion.

"Yeah, Gerry remembers me," he said. "She knows me."

The thrill of being remembered was written all over his face.

"I'll tell you," he said, "when I'm with Gerry, I just have a feeling about myself that I never had before I got interested in bears. It's the feeling that I've done something with my life, something almost nobody else has done."

He unlimbered his camera and made a few photographs of Gerry, whisker-length closeups.

He said, "I'm known at the Post Office as the bear man now. The kids in the neighborhood call me the bear man. At the place where I process my film, they have some of my pictures blown up on the wall, and when I walk in, the guy always says to whoever else is in there that I'm the bear man, the one who made the pictures."

I felt John's enthusiasm and found myself admiring him for his passion. He told me he has accumulated one hundred fifty books on bears. He saves up for his bear trips, waiting for the low air fares. He gets his job done at the Post Office, but bears have taken over all his spare time.

Most people never find a burning purpose in life. Maybe it wouldn't have happened to John Derych if he hadn't been "reading somebody else's mail" that day.

"I'll tell you," he said, "if I had known when I was a kid what I know now, I wouldn't be working at the Post Office."

Even the nervous bear keeper was beginning to relax a little by then. Hugh Morton and I left John and Gerry and walked up the hill for lunch.

Lunch in the mountains for me was almost always a barbecue sandwich. I have spent a good part of my life looking for the perfect barbecue. There is no point in looking in places like Texas, where they put some kind of ketchup on beef and call it barbecue. Barbecue is pork, which narrows the search to the South, and if it's really good pork barbecue you are looking for, to North Carolina.

There may be a law still on the books in North Carolina that if you don't cook it over hickory logs, you can't call it barbecue. Most barbecue places in eastern North Carolina can't find the hickory any more (or that's what everybody tells you in western North Carolina), and no doubt something has been lost in such famous barbecue outposts as Rocky Mount and Kinston, where they now do their cooking with a gas flame. But eastern North Carolina barbecue still can be very, very good. My sister Catherine so favored the barbecue served at a Texaco station between the two branches of the Intracoastal Waterway in Currituck County that she used to buy it there by the pound, freeze it, and take it all the way home to Seattle, where she lives. You might have thought her neighbors would have wondered at this, but they never knew. She kept it all for herself.

Barbecue is one of three highly subjective subjects in North Carolina, the other two being politics and religion. Some people prefer their barbecue chopped, some sliced, some shredded. Western North Carolina barbecue usually has tomato in the sauce. A little less tomato appears in the sauce in the Piedmont, around Lexington, and in the vinegar-based sauce of eastern North Carolina, there is no tomato at all. All North Carolina cooks are contemptuous of South Carolina barbecue sauce, which contains mustard. One of them told me, "If French's went out of business, there'd be no such thing as South Carolina barbecue."

Some barbecue makers, like Gene and Linda Medlin of Carolina Barbecue in Statesville, cook their barbecue over a hickory fire all night, at least twelve hours, which is right; and they baste it with a mild vinegar sauce they call "kitchen dip," which is right; but they cook only whole pork shoulders, which is wrong. It results in a barbecue which is too refined, without the necessary grease and gristle. I believe in serving up everything but the skin and the bone, "going whole hog." That's where the expression came from, from some epicure who knew how to make barbecue right.

Catherine Morton and I drove all the way to Pineola just because she likes the sliced barbecue at the Mountain Top Restaurant. I tried the barbecue at Hampton's Country Store in Linville, and the Smokehouse outside of Newland, where Bertie Burleson told me about becoming a writer, and the Woodlands in Blowing Rock, and a number of other places. I liked the odd savory cubes of barbecue they serve between two slices of white toast at Pappy's on the Linville-Boone road. But if you ever buy a barbecue sandwich from Pappy's, don't try to eat it while driving. You'll end up with sloppy brown cubes all over your lap. And Pappy's barbecue sauce is abiding; it doesn't all come out in the wash.

I hate to admit it, but the best barbecue I had in the mountains was at the little cafeteria at the Nature Museum on Grandfather Mountain, which buys it from somebody else, perhaps that Texaco station down in Currituck. It was the genuine shredded item of the whole hog variety, served in a soft hamburger roll with the usual barbecue accompaniments—sweet iced tea, Brunswick stew, cornbread, and coleslaw. I like a few drops of Texas Pete hot sauce on my barbecue to heat it up, and then I like to put the coleslaw right in the sandwich to cool it down. Not everybody agrees. I have a friend who says Senator Jesse Helms is God's retribution to North Carolinians for eating coleslaw on their barbecue.

Every little store in the mountains sells many common items of country food I can't find in New York. So I stocked my cabin with down-home delicacies: eggs fresh from the farm, trout fresh from the pond, good hard salt-cured country ham, and stone-ground grits and cornmeal.

Northerners who don't like grits never tasted the real thing. At Hampton's Store, a waterwheel operates a gristmill, and Jeff McManus, the proprietor, took me out back to show me the 1934-model mill which turns out stone-ground grits, the real thing. Corn, shelled from the cob, goes in the top of the mill. Corn meal comes out one side; grits, being heavier, come out the other side, and the husks of the kernels come pouring out the front. All three commodities are sacked and sold, the husks for use as chicken scratch or for aerating gardens. That 1934 mill must be the most efficient machine ever invented for separating a bushel of corn into the elements God intended.

I bought a sack each of stone-ground grits and cornmeal to take home. I soaked a cup of grits in a pot overnight, brought the water level up to the top of the grits in the morning, added salt, and boiled the grits for about twenty minutes. Then I had my reward for breakfast: fresh eggs, country ham and grits with red-eye gravy. If I were a condemned man, I would ask for this breakfast as my last meal. But only if the grits were stone-ground. If the grits came out of one of those round cardboard boxes, I would tell them I could wait.

Cornbread made of stone-ground meal is also the only kind worth eating, by the way. It has the right taste and the gritty texture. Some people use cornmeal from the supermarket, which is bad enough, and then put flour in their cornbread, which is worse. Some put *sugar* in! I feel sorry for them. They know not what they do.

All the country stores are satisfying to visit, but one of them, the Mast Store, is a destination. It has stood beside the road in Valle Crucis for more than a hundred years. Valle Crucis was not a very big community when the store first opened for business, and it's not a very big community now. Put it this way: When you get to the Mast Store, you have pretty much arrived in Valle Crucis, and when you leave the store, you have pretty much left.

In years past, I have spent hours just wandering the aisles of the old store, looking at the merchandise. It's one of those places that can say if they don't have it, you don't need it. I was happy to find it hasn't changed much. There was the Post Office to the left as I walked in, with three or four old-timers who'd come for their mail maybe an hour before still standing around the letter boxes passing the time of day. There were the signs beside the door, one advertising "Sheep for Sale, Ewes and Lambs," one calling attention to a revival at the Foscoe Christian Church. There was a notice of a mule-pull and log-skidding contest on the Tweetsie Railroad grounds, and of a square dance coming up at the Apple Barn. And beyond, there were the familiar counters and hooks and shelves and barrels holding penny candy and chewing tobacco, work gloves and straw hats, mixing bowls and picture frames, clothespins and roofing nails, haying scythes and pitchforks. It's hard to get out of the Mast Store without buying something, and I didn't. I bought a box of hand-tied fishing flies and a denim shirt, neither of which I really needed.

There's a trap door in the floor behind the cashier's counter. Frank Mast, whose granddaddy, W. W. Mast, founded the store in 1883, told me that used to be the chicken door. When Frank worked there as a boy, the store did a considerable barter business. Customers would bring in chickens to swap for goods, and one of Frank's jobs, he said, was to weigh the chickens on the scale and then toss them down through the trap door into the chicken roost under the store. Once a week or so, the chicken buyer would come by and pay so much for roosters and so much for hens. The store also accepted garden vegetables and wild roots and herbs, pretty nearly anything any of its customers brought in from the countryside to trade.

Out of habit or out of necessity, a few mountain people still roam the woods collecting plants and digging roots for sale. Some of them are old enough to remember a time when there were no doctors, so families doctored themselves with the medicinal plants they found growing wild. This lore lives on in many a mountain cabin.

The "wildcrafters," as they're called, bring whatever they have cut or dug to Wilcox Natural Products in Boone ("Botanicals Since 1900. Your Best Dependable Market for Roots and Herbs. Contact Us Before You Sell!"). Wilcox resells the products of the hills all over the world. The day I visited, witch hazel leaves (good for sore throats, hemorrhoids, and eye ailments) and wild indigo (a cure for toothaches, cuts and sprains, and stomach cramps) were being loaded into a tractor-trailer to be driven to Charleston for shipment to Germany. There, pharmaceutical companies turn the practical knowledge of the North Carolina mountains into over-the-counter products, some of which eventually show up in the North Carolina mountain drugstores.

I asked Ray Bowkley, the purchasing agent, if you could make a living as a wildcrafter.

"Well, maybe," he said, "if you don't care very much how you live. It's always been a subsistence living. Herb and root gathering kind of goes with scrap metal dealing. The same kind of people do both and make a living any way they can. Some of them are very good people, but not educated people. You know what I mean."

Ray said the Wilcox Company had survived nearly a hundred years by honest dealing.

"There are a lot of crooks in the root and herb-buying business," he said. "They won't give fair weight and won't pay what they owe.

"Charlie Wilcox was different. He made a point of keeping this business going year round. He didn't particularly want to do a fur trade, but he said we had to, so our people could make a living in the winter.

"There are probably people who resent the Wilcoxes. They've made a lot of money with this business. But another way of looking at it is that we provide an income to people who don't have any other income, and we're fair to everybody and consistent, and we're always here to buy even if we don't always need what's being sold."

I looked over the "Root List" and asked Ray about some of the items on it— pink root, for example, which Wilcox was offering to buy for a good price, ten dollars a pound.

"Pink root is good for getting worms out of the belly," he said. "But it's scarcing up. We don't see five pounds of pink root in a year.

"Most of the items on that list are not worth fooling with. You'll see that this year we don't even list a price for Mayapple. It was known as a wart remover. There's no more demand for it. But now there's a doctor in Chapel Hill who's using Mayapple in an experiment to see if it might be a high-tech cancer medicine, so you never know.

"Bloodroot, same thing. It's a real powerful root. The Indians made a love potion out of it. If you chew it raw, it'll about make you go blind. Now they say it may turn out to be a cancer cure.

"Snakeroot, that's a cure for snake bites. They're experimenting with it as a stimulant to the immune system.

"Everybody thought modern times would put wildcrafting out of business, but if these roots and herbs do some of the things the doctors think they might, it could become a bigger business than ever."

Ray went down the items on the list.

"The ones in bold type," he said, "those are the ones in good demand— blackberry root, golden seal root (the plant I'd seen growing in Luther Thomas's yard), snakeroot, slippery elm bark, sassafras leaf, star grass root and star grub root, white willow bark, wild ginger root, witchhazel leaves . . .

"And ginseng. That's an entirely different thing. The price has been up in the hundreds of dollars a pound because it definitely is a tonic and a sex stimulant. Almost all of it is sold to China, and there's a lot more demand than there is ginseng. There are greedy 'sangers' who dig it in the spring, which kills the plant. We won't touch ginseng until the fall."

The Wilcox Root List cautions: "The law and our conscience prevents us from buying ginseng before the legal season opens. We urge you not to dig before the berries ripen and fall . . . Leave the ripe berries under a few leaves. This will assure ginseng for years to come."

I bought a couple of books on medicinal plants and herbal healing and read them in the evenings beside the fire back at the cabin. It's obvious that the Cherokees and the early settlers shared some secrets about plants which modern medicine is only beginning to catch on to.

"If you need to cure hives on a baby, find you some blue blossoms of the ground ivy and make the baby some tea. That really works."

Ora Watson shared some of her healing knowledge with me a few days later.

"If you're sick to the stomach, go to a swamp and find some boneset blossoms. Dry them good and make a tea. It's bitter as quinine, but it cures the stomach flu and the gout and I think some other things."

Ora's husband Willard remembered some cures, too, but Willard never tells you anything without adding a story.

He said, "Henry Parsons's wife used to use red-stemmed ivy to make ooze."

"Ooze?" I asked.

"That's what she called it," Willard said. "It was a poultice for Henry's arthritis, but he couldn't stand the burning. I was there when his wife asked him, 'Can I do anything for you, Henry?' He said, 'Next time I pass by you, just throw a bucket of cold water on me.' "

Willard and Ora have lived in the same spot on Wildcat Road in Deep Gap since they were married sixty-eight years ago, and Willard twenty years longer than that, since he was born. Except that there was no Wildcat Road back then, only a footpath. Willard had to walk in and out of the hollow to school, to the store, and when he started work, to work.

"For years," he said, "I walked six mile to the sawmill and six mile back, for two dollars a day."

"I remember seeing you come over that hill from the mill carrying a hundred-pound bag of chop, food for the hogs," Ora said. "You hauled it on your shoulder all the way."

As an old moonshiner, Willard is partial to cures flavored with corn whiskey—dry pokeberries in corn whiskey with sulfur for arthritis, camphor with corn whiskey for pneumonia. "That cured Sally," he said, "and she's still living."

"For yellow jaundice," Ora said, "you need to parch rye and grind it up to make tea. That cured Helen."

Helen, their daughter, who was sitting with us, said, "Yes, and I ain't been fond of tea to this day."

Willard said, "Blackberry wine builds up the blood. Doctors don't know all this yet."

Whatever you wanted, in Willard and Ora Watson's day, you made for yourself—your medicine, your food, your house, your clothing, your furniture, your bedspreads and rugs. If you wanted a toy, you made your own corn shuck doll. If you wanted music, you carved your own dulcimer.

"I remember the year I got an orange for Christmas," Helen said. "I think that's all I got, but I was thrilled. Everything I'd ever had to eat was homemade, except that."

Ora Watson is one of the great quilters of the mountains, and Willard—first cousin to the famous musician Doc Watson, who lives down the road—is one of the best flat-foot dancers and banjo players. He's even better known as a wood-carver. He admitted to me, "Well, I've never seen a piece of wood that could beat me."

For many years, since I first met the Watsons, I've enjoyed owning a pair of Willard's carved roosters, which he can turn out in a minute or two with his pocket knife, and I've long slept under one or another of Ora's log cabin quilts, which she still pieces out of bright fabric. I've been back to see them a number of times, and I've always left knowing things I didn't know before. Never cut shingles in the light of the moon or they'll warp; never kill hogs in the dark of the moon or the meat will spoil; if a rooster crows at night, there will be snow before morning. The Watsons always dispensed this knowledge freely and cheerfully.

But on this visit, Willard seemed depressed. Out of the blue, he said, "Charles, with a certainty, inside of ten years, they'll throw the Book away." He still remembered with pleasure his world as it was, but didn't think much of what it was becoming.

He said, "If you were sick in the old days, your neighbors would come to you. If it was winter, the first thing they'd see about was your woodpile. If it was crop season, the first thing they'd see about was your crop."

He shook his head. I think he was in need of visitors, and I was glad I had come visiting. When I left, Willard walked with me to the porch, took my hand, and said, "I'd rather have your friendship than your money."

Of course, hardly anybody in the mountains today lives the purposefully plain life Ora and Willard Watson have had together. But I went to see one family that is making a pretty good attempt at it. They are my own distant relatives, Cecil and Julie Gurganus.

Cecil's father, Ransom, was my mother's favorite first cousin when they were growing up together in Onslow County, the adventurous one, my mother used to tell me, who was always leading the other children into and out of mischief. By the time I came along, Ransom had lived in New York City, known Thomas Wolfe and other literary figures, and led a spare-time writing life of his own. He was a romantic figure to me, and remains so in my memory. When I was only eight or nine years old, he treated me as an adult. It was Ransom who encouraged me to plan a career in journalism and to prepare for it by studying history and English in school. If this advice had come from anybody else, I might have shrugged it off. Because it came from Ransom, I followed it.

I knew his son, Cecil, lived in the mountains, and one day I drove over into the New River valley to find him. The drive from Boone took me past neat farmsteads on the Big Hill Road and through miles of unspoiled countryside. I saw only one sign the whole distance, a hand-painted sign on a barn that read "Fresh Mountain Apples."

Cecil and Julie Gurganus, their son, John Brinn, and their daughter, Sallie, live in a house in the woods with flowers blooming around it. The house looks old and traditional, but Cecil, a handsome man with a great black beard, told me he built it himself of white oak trees he cleared on the place and sawed into lumber. After graduating from college, he built houses and hired out as a carpenter. Now he's his own man, having remodeled an old cattle barn nearby into a cabinet shop. He also makes musical instruments and plays fiddle and banjo in a traditional group called the Laurel Creek String Band. Julie plays guitar with the band when she's not too busy with the children. They grow their own vegetables and split their own firewood and devise their own family entertainment.

Julie served a wonderful meal of Cornish hen and brown rice and vegetables—an obvious "company's coming" dinner for me—and Cecil found a bottle of wine that had been around the house for years, "since before Mama died, I'm afraid." The children, who are learning music and doing well in school, entered into the talk at the table. They listened with interest when their father explained to me the difference between "Bluegrass" and "traditional" music.

"In the first place," Cecil said, "not everything called Bluegrass is Bluegrass. That started with Flatt and Scruggs and Earl Monroe, playing the banjo with three fingers and picks, and with breaks—solos—for the musicians, which we don't do. Somebody put the real difference in one short sentence: 'Bluegrass is played at a frantic pace.' The old-time bands like ours have more rhythm. We're better for dancing. The flat-footers would rather have our music for dancing to, I think. And there's just a tremendous repertoire for traditional bands, the old Civil War songs, for example."

As we talked, it was clear to me that Cecil and Julie have intentionally chosen a simple life, close to nature, rich in music and reading and conversation with friends. I was impressed by their children, who are growing up to appreciate this way of living.

If two college-educated Americans can start a family and reach a very nearly perfect harmony in the United States, it occurred to me, Cecil and Julie probably have done it. They have methodically turned their backs on everything that is facile and shallow and mass-produced and harmfully addictive about American life—smoking, drinking, drugs, television, the urban rush, the acquisitive instinct.

I drove back along the lonely North Carolina mountain roads with the dark coming on, reflecting on this. The hunger for worldly success is what sends people into the commotion and flurry of the big city suburbs and puts them in neckties and cocktail dresses, and keeps them in their offices and commuter trains and country clubs for the rest of their lives. I tried to think of something Cecil and Julie and their children are missing by deliberately living so far off the beaten path.

But I couldn't think of anything.

Ketchikan, Alaska

~

It was raining in Ketchikan.

This is like saying it was hilly in San Francisco or it was crowded in Tokyo or it was romantic in Paris.

It is always raining in Ketchikan. Seattle, which has a reputation as a rainy city, gets thirty-eight inches of rain a year. Ketchikan gets fifteen *feet*. June is the dryest month in Ketchikan. It rained the whole time I was there.

I didn't care. It wasn't the kind of downpour that drives you indoors to stare glumly out the window. Ketchikan's rain is what you'd call a soft drizzle or a hard mist. It's steady, but it's gentle. I wore an old, oiled green jacket and a Norwegian fisherman's cap every day and hung them both in the hotel bathroom every night. By morning, they were almost, but not quite, dried out.

The rain reminded me of everything I love about southeastern Alaska: the rain forest, the mountain lakes, the waterfalls, the fjords, and the glaciers. (When

more rain and snow comes down on a mountain in the winter than melts away in the summer, eventually you have yourself a glacier. Alaska has tens of thousands of them.)

When I was planning my perfect year in America, I knew I had to spend a month of it in Alaska. But Alaska is way too big a place in which to contemplate spending a mere month—2,500 miles across. There used to be four time zones, Pacific, Yukon, Alaskan, and Aleutian, before the bureaucrats, playing God with the sun, reduced the four time zones to a mere two sometime in the Eighties.

If I wanted to explore only along the coast—well, the tidal coastline measures 47,000 miles!

So I thought, well, I'll just poke around in Southeastern, as Alaskans call the panhandle which stretches down toward the Lower 48 states, and see how far north I get. I got only as far north as Glacier Bay, revisiting a few favorite places along the way. But the beauty of this trip along the Inside Passage took my breath away, the effect it always has had on me, the effect it has on every visitor. I said to a Tlingit Indian woman one time that I thought she lived in the most dazzling place in America.

"It's God's thumbprint," she said.

And it is.

I started in Ketchikan, which is only an hour and a half on Alaska Airlines from Seattle, but a world away. There's no place for a jet to land at Ketchikan. There's barely room enough for a town between the mountains and the sea, and no room at all for a runway. In the old days, the jets landed on Annette Island and you caught a Grumman Goose amphibian to Ketchikan. The Goose would set itself splashily down in the harbor, reverse its engines with a mighty roar, and taxi over to the Front Street boardwalk. You'd climb out, pick up your suitcase, walk across the street to the Gilmore Hotel, or the Ingersoll, and you were there.

Today, they've taken some of the romance away, possibly because of Goose obsolescence. The jets land at a new airport on an island just across the Tongass Narrows and you get to town by short-haul ferry.

It's still a wonderful town to get to. Right into the second half of this century, Ketchikan was a wild little burg given to temporary employment in the canneries and shingle mills on the harbor, and temporary pleasures for the gill-netters, loggers, and miners in the bars, bordellos, and dance halls on Creek Street. Part of the town's charm is that it doesn't seem quite respectable yet.

Creek Street is no street at all, merely old houses on pilings connected by a boardwalk along Ketchikan Creek. At the foot of the street, the mouth of the creek, I could see hundreds of salmon feeding, some of them leaping clear of the deep, cold, dark water, preparing for their annual journey upstream. The salmon were what attracted the Tlingit Indians to the spot hundreds of Junes ago, and when a prosperous Tlingit known as Paper Nose Charlie sold Ketchikan to Mike Martin, an Irishman from County Cork, it was the salmon Martin meant to be buying. Almost immediately, the rough-hewn pleasure palaces sprang up. Creek Street became known as the place where "both the fish and the fishermen go up the creek to spawn."

The old bawdy houses are jewelry stores, souvenir shops, and cafes now. All you get for your $2.50 at Dolly Arthur's famous establishment on Creek Street is a bordello museum tour. But it's easy to imagine the days of the "Alaska Bone Dry Law," two years before national Prohibition, when bootlegger skiffs slipped into the creek at high tide and unloaded their cargo through trap doors right into the parlors of the fancy houses. The Alaskan word for the cargo entered the American language. It was "hootch."

Logging and fishing are still the mainstays of Ketchikan's economy. When the local government needs money, it sometimes just goes out and cuts down some trees. The week I visited, the Borough Assembly voted unanimously to log five hundred forty acres it owns near Whipple Creek and use part of the expected receipts, seven million dollars, to build an indoor recreation center. Financially strapped places like New York City can wish they also had a few stands of Douglas fir to tide them over.

Hootch is still available, but these days most of it is consumed in the form

of Bloody Marys by the tourists who gush from the newly arrived cruise ships by the thousands every morning at breakfast time and wander around looking for a warm place to get in out of the rain. Creek Street is ready for them. The bars open early, with vodka bottles at the ready and the ice already in the glasses. The shopkeepers stand by. The cruise passengers have their brunches and buy all the T-shirts, postcards, gold nuggets, Haida carvings, and oosiks they can carry. (An oosik is a popular Alaskan souvenir, a long, white bone, the awe-inspiring organ of a male walrus; it awakens a sincere compassion for female walruses.) Then the ships sound their loud, mournful horns, signaling that they are preparing to get underway, and the passengers stream back to the dock. Creek Street empties out by midafternoon, and solitary strollers have the place to themselves. This was the time of day I liked best, when the ghosts of Mike Martin and Paper Nose Charlie and Dolly Arthur were back on the boardwalk, and of the other old-timers, Whiskey Pete and Gold-stick Johnny and the rest, whose reputations live on from the frontier Ketchikan of not so long ago.

One afternoon, I walked down to the waterfront and watched a couple of Indian kids casting copper spinning lures into the teeming schools of salmon at the mouth of Ketchikan Creek as the tide came in. I don't know what attracts king salmon when they're about to spawn, but apparently not copper spinners. I saw several gigantic fish turn to watch the lures go by, but not one was tempted to strike. The fishing wasn't much.

The tide, however, was fabulous to see. At Key West, where I spent my February, the tide rises and falls eight inches or so every twenty-four hours. Nobody even notices. Ketchikan has two high tides a day with a height of twenty-two feet, and you'd better notice. If you anchor your sailboat on too short a line, the tide will pick your anchor right off the bottom and float you away. You can actually see the water rising by the minute, lifting the boats in the harbor. There used to be a sandlot baseball field on the beach. It was abandoned after a few years when the players got tired of their games forever being cancelled by high tide.

The normal twenty-two-foot tide is impressive enough, but occasionally, in storms, Ketchikan catches a thirty- or forty-footer. An old gent in the Alaska Bar on Front Street ("Celebrating the Repeal of Prohibition Every Day!") said he used to do his drinking in the Arctic Bar until one day a flood picked the building up, washed it down Ketchikan Creek, over the highway bridge, into the harbor, and out to sea. He said the Arctic Bar ended up aground ten miles north of town. Luckily, he said, all the customers had gone home to bed before it happened.

On one of my waterfront walks, I met a man wearing shorts, a mismatched suit coat, a bandanna, a floppy white hat, black socks, and tennis shoes, an outfit guaranteed to turn the head. This was the idea. Dave Button is a tour guide whom the city of Ketchikan officially banned from the cruise ship docks for soliciting customers, which tour guides are not supposed to do. So he donned his bizarre outfit to call attention to himself wherever in town he happened to be. It worked with me. I struck up a conversation with him one minute, and the next minute I found myself climbing aboard his rattling, green, flag-bedecked school bus for a "complimentary" nature tour. He entertains his passengers so well that they feel obliged to give him generous tips, which he accepts as his due and as a victory over the town fathers.

The "highway" out of Ketchikan goes only a few miles along the coast before reaching dead ends in both directions. To the south, it leads to a boat-launching ramp, where you can walk a few feet through the woods to the shore and watch eagles soaring. This is the "nature" part of Dave Button's tour. The day I went for a ride with him, an eagle obligingly plucked a fish out of the water and flew with it back to his nest at the top of a tall tree.

Meantime, Dave talked. He talked all the way out of town, he talked at the boat landing, and he talked all the way back. What do you want to know? You name it, Dave will talk about it.

He praised the modern Tsimshian Indians of nearby Metlakatla for achieving prosperity by logging, fishing, and canning while disdaining to open a gambling casino.

He praised the ancient Tlingit Indians for paddling their canoes as far south as Baja California and as far west as the Aleutians. (I don't know whether the Tlingits actually did this; I am just saying Dave praised them for it.)

He said it costs $850 a month to rent a decent house in Ketchikan, but you can live on your boat for $400 a year in moorage fees.

As we passed the fish cannery, he said the cannery workers make five or six dollars an hour. They make up for the low pay with hard work, he said. They work fourteen hours a day, some of them, seven days a week. He said college students were now arriving from everywhere in the country to work like that all summer, hoping to make enough money to go back to school in the fall.

He said the cannery was owned by the Japanese. He said the pulpwood production was owned by the Japanese. He said Ketchikan's moderate climate is due to the Japanese Current. "The Japanese even own the Current!" he said.

Dave was a memorable character. I think he lives somewhere in the Lower 48 during the winter. But every summer he returns to Ketchikan, puts on his ridiculous outfit, gasses up his school bus, and goes back to war with the city.

Not that you ever see the sun in rainy Ketchikan, but in June, it doesn't set until 10:30 P.M. or so. It doesn't get really dark until nearly midnight. You have to remind yourself when to have your supper. Most nights, I had mine in the solarium dining room of my hotel, the Cape Fox Lodge, on the hill above town. A solarium sounds like a nonsequitur in a place with no sun, I know, but the room was beautiful and the food was good, and I liked the sound of the rain on the roof.

Many people in Ketchikan go home by climbing endless outdoor flights of rickety wooden stairs up to their houses in the hills. The Cape Fox makes it easy for its guests by giving them a scenic tramway ride from Creek Street right up into the lobby. The Cape Fox is the newest hotel in Ketchikan, and I suppose the nicest anywhere in southeastern Alaska. It took a day or two to get used to the luxury, but I managed it. On previous trips to Alaska, I've slept in one-room Forest Service cabins in the wilderness, in the kitchen of an Eskimo woman's house on an island in the Bering Strait, and often in a sleeping bag beside a campfire, and all these accommodations suited me just fine. This time, I confess that I enjoyed coming home to a warm, dry room with an easy chair and a reading lamp.

The hotel is owned by a native corporation, a monument in polished cedar to the prosperity of the local tribes. The public rooms are adorned with massive native carvings. The restrooms are marked Haa and Shaa, which didn't take too much figuring out once I thought about it. A semicircle of five fine totems by a famous young carver named Lee Wallace stands outside the hotel's front door. There is space for a sixth, and I went down to Saxman, the native village a few miles south, to watch Lee Wallace working on it.

Lee comes naturally by his ability with chisel and adze. His father, Bill, was a carver, and one of the last fifty pure-blood Haida elders. Bill's father was John, known as S'duuts, chief carver of the Haida village of Hydaburg on Prince of Wales Island. (Lee said that when he is really hard at work on a totem pole, he can finish one foot a week; he said his grandfather John could carve one foot a day.) John's father, Dwight, was a carver. And Dwight's father was a carver, too. So totem-carving goes back five generations in the family. Lee said his young son, Xuuts ("Brown Bear"), is already playing with the carving tools.

I looked on for a while in silence as Lee Wallace worked. I knew better than to ask him the meaning of the totem he was carving. To know the meanings of totem poles, you have to know that Raven created the earth out of rocks and mud, and stole the sun, the moon, and the stars from his grandfather to give to human beings. You have to know this and hundreds of other stories about Eagle, Wolf, Bear and Frog, Fog Woman, Tide Woman and Thunderbird. Most Tlingits, Haidas, and Tsimshians don't fully understand the totem poles their grandfathers created; you had to be there at the time, to hear the stories told at the big parties, or potlatches, that were held when the poles were erected.

Some of the old totems told the stories of families, and used figures that could never appear on another family's pole. Some totems served as a record of wealth, with potlatch rings counting the number of great feasts the family had given, with gifts for all the guests. (When your family gave another potlatch, you didn't add another ring. You carved another pole with one more ring on it.) Others served as mortuary poles; the ashes of a dead chief were placed inside in elaborately carved boxes. Still others were heraldic, serving the same purpose for a family that a coat of arms did in old Europe. You can see more totem poles around Ketchikan than anywhere else in the fabulous world of the northwest Indians, and some of them are art of the very highest order.

Lee Wallace's wife, Winona, however, can't quite get over the thought that the totem poles were a way of bragging. She's a Navajo from Arizona. Navajos never brag. In the non-materialistic Navajo way of thinking, fine clothing and big houses and great wealth are not much valued. The goal is harmony within.

"I've had a little trouble with the Tlingit-Haida culture," Winona said with a smile, "this whole caste system based on money and possessions. Potlatch rings on the totem poles were a way of saying, 'Look, I have so much money that I can give it away!' Well, that goes against everything I was taught."

I was charmed by Winona Wallace. She is exceedingly proud of her totem-carving husband, but she said she was thinking about organizing a Southeast-Southwest cultural exchange. I got the impression she'd like to put a little Navajo humility into these proud Haidas and Tlingits.

I huffed and puffed up the steep hill beside the falls of Ketchikan Creek until I reached the Totem Heritage Center, a handsome building where some very old, unrestored totems are protected from the elements. I had a little shock when I walked inside: the first thing I heard was the sound of my own voice!

Twenty-five years ago, I visited some of the empty native villages and filmed an "On the Road" story about abandoned totem poles. They were playing this very story in an anteroom of the Totem Heritage Center to show visitors where the Center's totems had come from. I sat down and watched it myself.

The slender thirty-five-year-old Charles Kuralt stood in a clearing and explained to the fifty-nine-year-old Charles Kuralt things about totem poles that he had forgotten. Very interesting. Some of the old poles were obviously the work of master carvers. Even neglected out there on the island, tilted and fallen and forgotten, victims of fungus and carpenter ants, the poles were magnificent, and one of them in particular.

I walked into the main museum and there it was, facing me head on—the same majestic totem I had just seen on screen, the one I had filmed covered with moss in the overgrown village of Old Kasaan in 1970!

When the people abandoned their island villages decades ago to find work in the canneries of the growing cities, the ancient totem poles stayed where they had been erected, staring out to sea. The people didn't realize they were leaving behind part of their identity. Now, they can walk up a hill in Ketchikan to the Totem Heritage Center and find it again.

I remembered hearing Dennis Demmert, then head of the Ketchikan Lodge of the Alaskan Native Brotherhood, and Jane Wallen, then the twenty-seven-year-old director of the Alaska State Museum, talking about how wonderful it would be to have a fine indoor repository for the old totems. My first thought on seeing the Old Kasaan masterpiece again was: good for Dennis and Jane! They did it! Ketchikan, I found, supplied the museum. Dennis and Jane supplied the totems, thirty-three of them, which they salvaged from the islands, towed to Ketchikan behind a tugboat, and stored in a cannery until the museum was finished. Some things really do work out in life, I thought.

Later I found that for Dennis and Jane, things had worked out better than I knew. They were married to each other soon after I met them; they're living up in Juneau now and still doing good works for Alaskan natives. Happy ending all around.

I thought I would meander north from Ketchikan by sea along the Inside Passage. I thought I'd stop in the picture-postcard fishing port of Petersburg for a supper of plump, sweet Petersburg shrimp—a meal I had there years ago and have never forgotten. I thought I'd revisit Sitka, once the capital of Russian Alaska, which was an elegant city with a cathedral, scientific institutes, mills, foundries, and fancy shops when San Francisco was still a muddy village. I

Carver Lee Wallace and a
Wallace totem

Creek Street, Ketchikan

Butch Laughlin and his plane

Dave Button

thought I might make it all the way up to Skagway, where the Klondike gold rush started.

That's what I thought. But when I stopped by the Alaska Marine Highway ferry terminal to reserve a cabin, the guy practically laughed at me. He said the cabins on all the northbound ships were fully booked through September. He said he could sell me deck passage but warned me that the covered decks were crowded and the open decks were wet. I was forced to do a little rethinking. The only ways to go anywhere in southeastern Alaska are by sea or by air. I packed my bags and went out to the airport.

I flew to Juneau (imagine, a state capital with no roads leading to it!) and spent the night at a hotel on the waterfront, after arranging a trip for the next morning to Glacier Bay. I remembered Glacier Bay as one of the most spectacular places on earth, and I wanted to go back there, no matter what.

I am a fan of state flags. I like Maryland's gaudy flag, and Ohio's, and Arizona's, but Alaska's is my favorite. It's Ursa Major, the Big Dipper, in gold on a field of blue, with the lip of the dipper pointing, as it does in the sky, to Polaris, the North Star. The flag is brilliant in its simplicity, and unmistakable in its symbolism, and it's pretty. And it wasn't the idea of some professional designer. It was the idea of Benny Benson, who was a thirteen-year-old from Chignik, Alaska, when the Territorial Legislature adopted his design in 1927.

The flag was waving gently from its pole in front of my hotel at five o'clock in the morning. It wasn't raining. The sun was coming up. It was going to be what they call a "blue day," perfect for my 7:45 A.M. flight to Glacier Bay. I was standing at the window, trying to wake up and admiring the flag and wondering whether it might be worth it to find Benny Benson, if he was still alive, and talk to him.

That was when the lights went out.

At first, I thought maybe a fuse had blown in the hotel. But then I noticed the street lights were out, too. I rummaged around for my battery-powered radio and turned it on. Nothing but static. If the radio stations were off the air, that meant the power was out all over Juneau.

I pulled on my clothes in the half-light of the room and walked down seven flights of stairs to the lobby. The breakfast room was unlighted but still had some hot coffee in carafes. "It's been happening all year," the waitress said as she poured me a cup in the dark. "They think it's the eagles."

They think it's the eagles! They really do. Juneau's electricity comes in from the south on lines supported by tall steel towers. This time of year, the eagles nest in the towers and cause massive short circuits. The power company, I discovered later, was commissioning a study of what kind of bird-discouragers they might install on the towers, to keep bald eagles from periodically plunging the capital city of the state into darkness. This is a very Alaskan thing to have to worry about. So far as I know, no other power company in the world has an eagle problem.

The lights came on again after a while, and I made it to the airport in time.

I have a cigar box full of old baggage tags at home. Some directed my luggage to places that no longer exist, IDL for Idlewild (now John F. Kennedy Airport, New York), CTJ for Ciudad Trujillo (now Santo Domingo), LPV for Leopoldville, the Congo (now Kinshasa, Zaire). Some are souvenirs of long trips to small places, YDS for Desolation Sound, TVF for Thief River Falls, MSA for Muskrat Dam.

I picked up a new one that morning in Alaska—GST for Gustavus.

You get to GST on LAB. The airline is named for its owner, Layton A. Bennett, who has several single-engine and twin-engine Pipers lined up in a row at Juneau. At the counter, you tell them your weight and they assign you to a pilot— "You'll fly with Steve, you'll fly with Travis . . ." My weight was enough to get me Steve, a competent-looking lad in his twenties, and a twin-engine Piper Chieftain.

Steve took us over the Stephens Passage, over the Lynn Canal, through a narrow gap in the Chilkat Range with mountain walls rearing up on either side of the wing tips, and down to a World War Two landing strip at Gustavus. The LAB terminal is a little one-room plastic igloo set in a patch of fireweed. Broken-down old trucks were rusting in the grass nearby. "That's our long-term parking lot," they said.

I could live in Gustavus. If I did, though, it would be a little hard to explain to people where I lived. Gustavus is a stretch of woods and open fields along Icy Strait near the entrance to Glacier Bay, home to about four hundred loners and rebels and seekers of peace and quiet. They live in widely spaced cabins in the woods. There's no town, because a town would mean elections and laws and taxes, and nobody wants the hassle. If Gustavus had a government, paved roads and streetlights would probably be next. Gustavus has no police, no bank, no hospital. It does have a gas station with ancient Flying Red Horse pumps, but the gas station is open only two hours, and only on Tuesdays, Thursdays, and Saturdays. If you have a car full of gas, you have a choice of three destinations— the airport, the dock, and the Glacier Park Lodge.

So there's no town, but there is a community. There is a community school, with five rising seniors. There are community celebrations; they were planning for the Fourth of July when I was there. On the Fourth of July in Gustavus, they have to wait until midnight for it to be dark enough for the fireworks, and then they have to shoot the fireworks off fast before the sun comes up again.

Only one hundred fifty years ago, Gustavus was under millions of tons of ice, but the glacier receded (glaciers are always coming and going), and they have figured out that the altitude of Gustavus is increasing an inch and a half a year as the land rises in relief of being rid of all that weight. The glacier left behind a rich flat field along the water, known as Strawberry Point. Anybody can walk out there and pick a hatful of sweet wild strawberries. I did, and it was the best lunch I had in Alaska.

There are at least a couple of hostelries in Gustavus, one of them an attractive old house in a former pasture with a big garden. The house was the headquarters of a pioneer cattle ranch run by the Lesh family. But the cattle kept getting eaten by the bears, so now the house is the Gustavus Inn, run by David Lesh and his wife, Jo Ann, with meals served family style—fish from the nearby waters and vegetables from the garden. The Leshes had a full house; I hitchhiked ten miles down the road to the Glacier Park Lodge.

I've stayed in a lot of National Park Service hotels in my life, and the Lodge was the best of them, with a reception area, dining room and bar downstairs, and upstairs a marvelous diorama explaining the geology of Glacier Bay and its plant and animal life. Boardwalks lead from the main building to little clusters of modern guest rooms in the woods. A raven perched on the porch railing outside my room, and under the boardwalk, a blue grouse was walking around in a berry patch clucking to her brood of five chicks. She was obviously raising them right there, safe from the bears, with plenty of food for foraging.

The waiters and maids at the Lodge were all college kids, bright and energetic and aware of their good fortune to be spending the summer in such a place. They were mostly veterans of other lodges in other parks. They talked knowledgeably of Grand Teton and Great Smoky Mountains and Yosemite. One of them, Rebecca Bodrero of Kirksville, Missouri, assured me, "When I have children, I'm going to be sure they all work in the National Parks in the summertime."

The weather was holding, and everybody having drinks on the porch before dinner was talking about the glorious sunny spell. To me, it seemed a little strange. This was my third trip to Glacier Bay, a place I'd thought of as misty and moody. For the first time, it sparkled. I could see the snow-covered Fairweather Range of mountains on the horizon fifty miles away. (The Fairweathers were named by Captain Cook while searching for the mythic Northwest Passage. They are spectacularly mislabelled. Cook must also have been dazzled by an unexpected sunny day.)

Before breakfast the next morning, I went for a walk on a trail through the spruce and hemlock-scented rain forest. Alaska's forests are the most welcoming I know. There are no ticks, no snakes, no poison ivy in Alaska. Moss, which was everywhere underfoot, is spongier in Alaska, and ferns are greener, and grasses are lusher, and trees are larger. Fallen hemlock giants beside the trail were covered with lichen and forest mushrooms. The woods looked moist even on a dry morning. Patches of sun in the deep, cool woods illuminated great expanses of delicate ferns.

I picked blueberries along the trail and ate them, ignoring the intelligence I had picked up from one of the kids that most of them were supposed to be full of worm larvae. Strawberries and salmonberries also grew, and bush cranberries (which are not cranberries) and nagoon berries, all ripening, and all except the blueberries in bright shades of red or orange. Most other plants seek to preserve themselves, but the berries cry out to birds and animals, "See me! Pick me! Eat me!" And then, they might add, "Excrete me!" so as to spread their seeds far and wide.

Little squirrels scampered away as I walked. Birds flitted through the shadows. On a stretch of the trail that ran along the edge of the woods above the ocean beach, a thrush kept me company, hopping along in front of me, pausing for me to catch up, then hopping ahead again. Once, when I stopped to pick blueberries, the bird looked back as if to say, "Well, are you coming?"

After a breakfast of blueberry pancakes, which I figured my long walk had earned me, I was looking through the books in the Lodge gift shop when a man came up to me and said, "You want to see the glaciers from up top?" He said he recognized me from television. This was Steve Pierce, who had flown his float plane over from Juneau for the day with his wife, Neala. The two of them, it turned out, were owners of the Waterfront Gallery, one of the best of the many art galleries in downtown Juneau. Steve is one of those Alaskans who has been everything at one stage or another—firefighter, paramedic, halibut fisherman, and bush pilot. I accepted his invitation to take a ride.

Neala stayed behind, sunbathing on the dock. I helped Steve push his Cessna 172 off its mooring, and a few minutes later we were climbing away from Bartlett Cove above the Brady Icefield, which spawns many of the glaciers that plunge down into the west side of Glacier Bay. The view in the bright sun was resplendent, a fantastic jumble of ice-capped granite mountains close at hand towering above us to the north, the brilliant, broad icefield stretching to the horizon below, and farther below, the rippled surface of Glacier Bay reflecting bursts of sunlight back into our eyes like a thousand flashbulbs going off at once. My mistake was in leaving my sunglasses in my room. I had to squint to keep from being blinded up there.

Steve looked at me and grinned. He said, "Just another day in southeastern Alaska, eh, Charles?"

If I lived in Alaska, I would certainly learn to fly a float plane. Wings are great for city people like Steve and Neala just looking for a change of scenery on a sunny day; I don't think they could ever get used to the indescribable vistas of white snow, green forests, and blue waters. For those who live on the distant islands and along the rivers in the bush, an airplane is nearly a necessity. The alternative, an Alaska homesteader once told me, is to stay put in your cabin watching the porcupines gnaw on your ax handle and the moss grow on your roof. Without a means of transportation, it would be easy to develop cabin fever, the often-described thirty-foot stare in a twenty-foot room. All over Alaska, small planes are the preferred means of going grocery shopping, running errands, picking up the mail, and just getting out of the house for a while.

The other choice, of course, would be a boat—a slower option for covering Alaska's immense watery distances, but an even better platform for seeing the natural world close-up. One day, I boarded the *Captain Connor,* an elegant old twin-screw launch operated by the Park Service, for a whale-watching trip into Icy Strait.

We weren't underway five minutes before we had to steer around a sea otter lying on her back in a bed of kelp. All the sea otters I've ever seen in my life were lying on their backs, sometimes patiently dismantling a crab or abalone and using their bellies as breakfast trays. They seem to live their lives on their backs, feeding, nursing their young, watching the world go by. Now that human beings have left off murdering them for their fur, otters are all over the place, lying on their backs, living sweet lives.

Salmon jumped around us and splashed back into the sea. They say the jumpers are all females, loosening their eggs before going up the streams to spawn.

For nearly an hour, I watched a bald eagle circling, diving, obviously spotting plenty of salmon but failing to snag one. Eagles are powerful birds, but they're not always smart enough to pick on somebody their own size. Occasionally, they sink their talons into too big a fish, find they can't let go, and are pulled underwater and drowned; I've heard trawler crews tell about hauling big salmon with eagle corpses attached.

Our skipper was Jay Florey, Port Captain of Glacier Bay, a former Coast Guardsman from the Lower 48 who was assigned to Alaska and found a way to stay. His is usually an important but slightly tedious job ashore, keeping the Park Service boats fueled and working. So he was on a busman's holiday on the *Captain Connor,* wearing a big gap-toothed grin because he was out of the office for the day. He said, "This wheelhouse is the best office in the world."

Captain Florey found us some humpback whales traveling north off Point Adolphus, and fell in beside them, idling along at a respectful distance so as not to disturb them. I was trying to make photographs with a 500-millimeter lens and Jay gave me a handy tip. Humpbacks almost invariably "blow" four times—you can count the spouts: one, two, three, *four!* Then they roll their big backs out of the water. Then, on cue, they sound, with their great tails pausing in the air a few seconds for the benefit of photographers. I got the hang of it and made some good pictures of whale tails.

This nowhere near made up for my single great failure as a whale photographer. Years ago, I went out into the Bering Strait in a skin boat with some Eskimo walrus hunters. They spotted a group of walruses in the middle of a huge ice floe. While they crept toward the animals half a mile or more away, I was assigned the job of standing at the edge of the floe and holding on to the boat. It was made clear to me that if the boat floated away, there was a good chance that nobody in the world would ever see or hear of us again, so I held on tight.

As I stood there, the sea parted not fifty feet away and a giant dark form rose from the depths. It was a stupendous thing, a barnacle-covered whale's back moving through the water and arching high into the air. It seemed to travel on and on and on for minutes, so close to me that I felt I could almost touch it. At last, the gigantic flukes appeared, towered against the sky for an eternity, and fell slowly back into the sea. A great wake washed toward me, and I ran from it, towing the boat higher up on the ice to keep the wave from wrenching the mooring line out of my grasp.

Then I looked down at the camera hanging around my neck.

I had just seen a blue whale, the largest creature that has ever lived, and one of the rarest sights in all of nature.

And I had stood there paralyzed. It never occurred to me to point the camera and click the shutter.

Having that whale in my memory is enough for me. But I know a lot of photographers for *Life* and Magnum and Black Star who would have given years of their lives to have been standing on that ice floe with a camera. I never tell them this story.

I left Glacier Bay after a few days and went back to Juneau. The barometer stayed locked on high and the weather, incredibly, stayed clear. I walked along the waterfront, watching the cruise ships and tugboats and fishing trawlers come and go. I admired the tall blue iris in the beds on Egan Drive and the baskets of petunias hanging from all the light-poles in town. I went up to Evergreen Cemetery to find the graves of Richard Harris and Joe Juneau, the two down-and-out prospectors who came looking for gold in 1880. They found no more than a few flecks, until an Auk chief named Kowee got exasperated with their efforts and patiently walked them up Gold Creek right to the mother lode. The town was called Harrisburg at first, then Juneau City. It should have been called Kowee.

I stopped in at the Forest Service office to check on the wilderness cabins that can be rented in the Tongass and Chugach forests. There are 227 of them, nearly all accessible only by float plane, the Southeastern version of the rental car. They go for twenty-five dollars a day, up from five dollars when I last visited a few years ago, and, in the view of many locals, a scandalously high price for a wood stove, table and chairs, sleeping platform and roof overhead, with a bear probably nosing around outside. But I thought I might take a hatchet and a bedroll and try roughing it in some beautiful place for a few days. These cabins, however, proved to be as popular as the cabins on the State Ferry; they were all spoken for. Cherie Andrews, the friendly Ranger in a green uniform who broke the news to me, seemed genuinely sorry. "They're a great getaway," she said, emphasizing *away*. She told me about a couple from California who rented a cabin for a week. The man asked, "Where's the nearest place for my wife to go shopping while I'm fishing?" "Well," Cherie said, "about one hundred seventy miles north or two hundred eighty miles south."

If I couldn't live on pork and beans in the woods, I thought I might as well try poached salmon with a honey-mustard sauce in town. This was an elegant meal I remembered from the best restaurant in Juneau, the Summit, at the Inn on the Waterfront across from the cruise ship dock. The Inn, built in the 1890s, is identified on an old map of Juneau as a "cigar store." There are "cigar stores" all along the waterfront on that map. It's a euphemism, of course, for the same kind of establishment that made Creek Street famous in Ketchikan. A Juneau old-timer told me that when he was a kid, his mother wouldn't even let him deliver newspapers to the "cigar stores." Now, perfectly respectable tourists sleep in rooms that used to belong to Juneau's Jezebels.

When I walked in, I was greeted like a long-lost brother by Ann House and her husband, Bill, the proprietors—the kind of greeting that keeps their customers coming back, even after an absence of years. The food and drink were as marvelous as ever, but what I remember about that night were the patrons. Around the polished copper bar were three locals in an animated discussion of whether or not the Tongass National Forest should all be cut down, turned into pulpwood and shipped to Japan; a grumpy Swiss businessman from Zurich; the German wine steward from the cruise ship *Sagafjord,* which was parked outside and not leaving until midnight; two young traveling saleswomen, one of whom said she was a Basque from Idaho; and a free spirit named Terry Aitchison, identified by Ann House as "our accountant." It turned out that from time to time, when he needs money, Terry "accounts" for the restaurant dishes by washing them.

Terry told me his life story. After hitchhiking all over America, he got an undergraduate degree in English from Minnesota and a graduate degree in business from Tulane, got married, got divorced, taught school for a while in Mountain Village, sixty miles from the mouth of the Yukon, while coaching the Eskimo girls' volleyball team, and worked in Juneau as a carpenter and accountant while living in a tent. He said, "I prefer to keep my options open."

To make the evening complete, Terry introduced me to a friend of his who walked in—Richard Harris, great-grandson of the prospector who helped stake out the town. Richard turned out to be a nice young guy, part Tlingit, who's proud of both his white and Indian heritage. But times have changed in Juneau. Richard is no prospector like his ancestor, wandering in the wilderness. He works in the K-Mart.

All these characters were being waited on by the bartender, Afshin, who is a Persian, he said, from Azerbaijan. Ann and Bill's little provincial inn seemed the center of the world that night. I was going to say something like that to Ann, but I had to wait until she showed Afshin how to make a pitcher of sangría, which somebody in the dining room had ordered. It must not have been very good; the customer sent it back.

Everything else about that evening, though, was terrific. In thinking about it now, that particular collection of human beings coming together on the same night in the same room seems about as likely as an Azerbaijan Persian stirring up a pitcher of Alaskan sangría.

From any street corner in Juneau, you can look up into the wild mountains.

My month was running out, and I yearned to soak up some more wildness before I had to leave. I called Butch Laughlin, who makes a living by flying yearning souls to beautiful places. It's not necessarily much of a living, Butch said, barely enough to make the payments on his new blue and white $120,000 Cessna. He said he and his wife would starve if it weren't for the body shop he runs in the winter. But it's flying that Butch loves, and in the summertime, he flies.

I met him early in the morning at "the Pond," the float plane canal that parallels the airport runway. "Where do you want to go?" he asked. I said, "Some place lonely."

We took off from the Pond, flew south over the Gastineau Channel, and then turned west into the mountains. After a while, I could see a couple of mountain lakes down there, a small high one connected to a larger lower one by a ribbon of waterfall. Butch put the plane over on its wing and aimed us for the large one. "Lower Sweetheart Lake," he said. "I've never seen anybody here. I've never talked to anybody who's ever been here. I bet not five people a year ever come here."

We landed, taxied over to the outlet of the stream that was created by the waterfall, and tied the plane to a streamside tree. I stepped down on the pontoon and onto the shore and stood there looking down the length of the lake. After the racket of the flight in, the silence of the place was overpowering. The surface of the lake was utterly still and utterly magnificent, a deep blue jewel in a setting of steep green woods. From where I stood, everything I could see was as serene and virginal as on the day of Creation.

It's in the nature of human beings to *do* something, even in a place like that. So Butch produced fly rods and we busied ourselves casting into the current where the stream flowed into the lake. But my heart wasn't in it. I kept forgetting to fish. I just stared at the scene. Butch landed a small landlocked Chinook salmon and let him go, but I don't think his heart was in the fishing, either.

After a while, we climbed back into the plane and took off. I looked back to see the lake receding in the distance. I still put myself to sleep at night thinking of Lower Sweetheart Lake.

We flew up over the Juneau Ice Field, which is incredible, indescribable. It has snowed up there about one hundred feet per winter for thousands of winters, and the resulting glaciers plunge down from the mountains for ninety miles around. The glaciers flow into the Pacific to the west, into Canada to the east, and into one another, some advancing, some retreating, in an immeasurable chaos of ice.

The stunning thing was to be lost for an hour in that surreal white world, then, abruptly, to fly down over the Mendenhall Glacier, land on the Pond at Juneau Airport, and drive to the terminal—ten minutes from the trackless, frozen wilderness to pavement and taxicabs. It was a profound shock to the senses.

I made one other trip with Butch. His wife, Sarah Dunlap, came along. We flew down to Taku Harbor, a remote dent in the coast where I once spent a day with Tiger Olson, a prospector who lived alone on an ancient mining claim. At ninety, Tiger Olson was still hunting, fishing, and, as he had done every morning since 1918, splitting logs for firewood to make his morning coffee. That was twenty-five years ago. Tiger was indomitable, but, of course, not immortal. Butch and Sarah and I walked up the overgrown path to his cabin and found it empty and desolate. I don't know what else I expected to find. Tiger's ax and chopping block were just where they had been. His old skiff was upside down on sawhorses. His crab pots and buoys were stacked beside the house. Only Tiger wasn't there. It is pointless to mourn the death of a man who lived well into his nineties, but there at Tiger's cabin, remembering how much life was in him, I couldn't help it.

Sarah had brought along fish sandwiches and iced tea, and we found some rocks above Tiger Olson's beach on which to sit and have lunch. We talked about flying and fishing, but I suppose we were all thinking about Tiger and mortality.

Sarah drove me back to town from the Juneau airport. She is a lovely woman with poetry in her speech, and eyes that seem to be looking at something far away.

She said she loves the dynamism of Juneau, the constant change—by which she didn't mean the new K-Mart. She spoke of the glaciers receding, the land rebounding from the glaciers' weight, the cycle of freeze and thaw in winter and spring and the short, intense summer.

The fireweed was in full bloom in the fields and ditches along the road to town. "It will bloom another six weeks," Sarah said. "When it stops blooming, you have to start thinking about winter again."

She said, "I like living in a place where you measure your life by the wildflowers."

I didn't want to leave southeastern Alaska. It's God's thumbprint. Alaskans refer to everywhere else as "Outside." The day came when I had to go back Outside where I had come from.

On the plane to Seattle, I sat next to a Tlingit lawyer, Leroy Wilder, who had been out in the islands working on some land case. He talked about his youth and upbringing in Southeastern, and I talked about my month in his native country.

He was wearing a tie with a subtle totem design. When I noticed it and told him I admired it, he took it off and gave it to me.

"To remember us by," he said.

I still have your tie, Mr. Wilder.

I remember.

Ely, Minnesota

A birch tree grows on the shore of Moose Lake. A canoe lies on the bank beside it.

From that birch tree, you could paddle the canoe up to the end of Moose Lake and camp overnight and put the canoe in another lake the next morning. You could cross that lake, and camp for the night, and paddle across another lake on the third day. You could keep this up, visiting a different lake every day, for a *hundred years,* and you still wouldn't get to all the lakes.

Henry David Thoreau wrote, "A lake is the landscape's most beautiful and expressive feature. It is earth's eye."

I sat on a rock beside the birch tree, looking into the eye of the earth. I was watching the sun go down on Moose Lake and thinking about the universe of green forest and blue water I had come to in a day's drive north from Minneapolis–St. Paul. Loons called to each other out on the lake. Thunder rumbled away to the north in Canada. I stayed there until the night came on.

This was not the Moose Lake down there south of Kettle River, and not the Moose Lake west of Nashwauk, and not the Moose Lake that the Bigfork River flows out of. God knows how many Moose Lakes there are in Minnesota. This was that other Moose Lake, the one east of Ely where the roads run out and the Boundary Waters begin.

The Boundary Waters Canoe Area is a million acres of wilderness with no roads, no buildings, no sign that human beings have ever been there, except for Indian pictographs on some of the rocks and footprints on some of the portages and signs of old campfires on some of the islands. Motors are barred; no outboard motors, no airplanes, no generators compete with nature's sounds. No cans or bottles are permitted. It is unlawful to cut down a tree, or even to cut off a bough or chip away bark. Groups of more than nine canoeists must split up and go in different directions.

If it is absolute solitude you want, you have only to paddle far enough. If the vast and glaciated U.S. wilderness isn't big enough for you, a Canadian wilderness of equal size awaits across the border. Without a topographic map and a compass, there's no way to tell which country you're in, anyway. In two or three days of paddling and portaging, you can be reasonably assured of reaching the beautiful lake of your fondest dreams, where you can set up camp for a week or two without hearing another human voice.

I had not come to Moose Lake to embark on an arduous wilderness trip, not this time. I've done it in years gone by, and I remember how long those uphill portages can be with a canoe and a backpack to carry. I thought it would be enough to wait until July when the black fly season is over, go as far north in Minnesota as I could, find a cabin on the last point of land where cabins are permitted, and just look at the wilderness and think about it.

The cabin came close to qualifying as a log mansion. I was planning to stay in a sparse outfitter's camp, but Linda Fryer, the energetic woman who runs the

Ely Chamber of Commerce, called Chet and Nancy Niesel, friends she'd heard were planning to be away, and next thing I knew, I was ensconced in the Niesels' house. Or rather, in part of it. I occupied the spacious kitchen, a bedroom facing the lake, and the more extravagant of the bathrooms, without needing to venture into the rest of the dwelling, which was filled with the furniture and collections of an obviously well-lived life. I never met the Niesels, but I feel I know them. Sleeping in somebody's bed will do that to you.

The birch tree and the canoe belonged to the Niesels, and the shoreline where I sat to watch the sunset that first night and most of the nights that followed. How I envy them! Any time they want, they can drive twenty miles out of Ely nearly to the end of the Fernberg Trail, turn left on the road toward Moose Lake, pass through groves of pine and stands of aspen, ash, and maple for a mile or two, bump along a few hundred yards of fire trail, and pull into the dirt driveway of their own utopia. It was my good fortune that the owners were away. If it were my house, I think I'd never leave.

My trip up from the Twin Cities took me north past Duluth, past the piles of tailings from the great days of the Mesabi Range iron mines, some of the heaps of red earth sprouting scrubby pines now. Around Eveleth, the music on the radio turned heavily to polkas, the favored music of the miners who came from the Old Country to the Minnesota north. I crossed the Laurentian Divide, beyond which all waters flow north to the Arctic. I was getting close. Between Tower and Ely, I counted seventy-one cars with canoes tied to their roofs. The guidebooks list twenty canoe outfitters for this general region, and the guidebooks don't list them all.

Ely's main street has the shops and cafes and gas stations you'd expect at the place where the road runs out, but it would be a lonesome street without the outfitters. Their front windows in every block, full of fishing gear and lifejackets and ice chests and freeze-dried food, remind you where you are. You can arrive in Ely in a coat and tie with no baggage and push off in a canoe an hour later, properly dressed and fully equipped for two weeks in the wilderness.

Ely is a town full of good people. I know all towns are, but Ely has always seemed to me especially rich in neighborliness and good nature and the salt-of-the-earth virtues. It's hard to be a stranger there. If your name is Charles, everybody in Ely calls you Chuck.

Minnesotans are different from the rest of us to begin with, as I was reminded on the trip in. Minnesotans don't smoke; the Minneapolis airport was the first in the nation to ban smoking, even in bars. Minnesotans recycle; there are separate containers at the highway rest stops for cans, bottles, and plastic. Minnesotans return the grocery cart to the store. Minnesotans do not consume butterfat; at the supermarket in Virginia, Minnesota, where I stopped for groceries, they had abundant gallons of skim milk, one percent milk, two percent milk, and some kind of healthy milk substitute. I had to look a long time to find real milk, on a side shelf. Minnesotans bike with their helmets on. Minnesotans fasten their seat belts. Minnesotans hold the door for you. Minnesota men don't leave the toilet seat up. Minnesotans do not blow their horns behind you when the light turns green; they wait for you to notice. Minnesotans are nicer than other people. The farther away from the big cities you go, the nicer they are. Ely is about as far away as you can get.

I don't mean that there is anything bland or insipid about Ely. The town wasn't founded by canoe paddlers who came for the beauty. It was founded by miners who came for the iron. They were tough Swedes and Finns and Norwegians, durable Irishmen and muscular Slavs. The rough mining camp they staked out late in the last century was an ugly little place on the edge of a scenic paradise. The streets were so muddy in spring, somebody wrote, that they were "not passable, not even Jackassable." When Billy Sunday, the evangelist, passed part of a summer vacation nearby, he said the two worst places he'd ever heard of were Ely and hell, the difference being that there was a railroad out of Ely.

"Ely was hard on everybody," Bob Cary told me. He's a square-jawed outdoorsman of the old school in a flannel shirt and felt hat, "Jackpine Bob" to the readers of his stories in the Ely *Echo*.

"It was especially hard on the women, what with the mud streets and the brawling menfolks. There was all this beauty at the edge of town, but no beauty in their lives.

"Some of them tried to homestead, poor souls. They had always dreamed of a little farm, and the land was cheap. If you could prove it up in five years, it was yours. So some of them tried to grow something in these rocks. It was just impossible, of course."

This reminded me of Garrison Keillor's explanation for why so many Scandinavians located in northern Minnesota. They'd been brought up in a hard, rocky land with a short growing season, their lakes frozen solid most of the year, and they'd heard about the rich farming country of America. So they crossed the Atlantic and headed west. When they reached Minnesota—a hard, rocky land with a short growing season and the lakes frozen solid most of the year—it made them so nostalgic that they settled down, forgetting why they had left home in the first place.

The hard land bred strong characters. I was lucky enough to know some of them in years gone by, and now, in the evenings, sitting beside my birch tree and looking out at the lake, I thought about them.

There was Bill Magie, who lived in a shack just around the bend on Moose Lake with his springer spaniel, Murphy. As a young man, Bill spent years mapping the country. "I'm the only man alive," he said to me, "who's walked from Lake Superior to Lake of the Woods on the ice and carried a transit on his shoulder all the way. You could tie me up right now, blindfold me, fly me into some lake and drop me off, and I'd know right where I was and find my way back, damn right, and without any help, either." Bill took Knute Rockne and Grantland Rice on a long canoe trip back in the Twenties, and guided Margaret Mead into the wilderness, and drank his bourbon straight, and told great stories, like the one about the night he crawled inside a moose he had shot to keep from freezing. People told Bill he'd become too old to be a canoe guide. He said, "The canoe country is where I want to die. If the old Reaper is going to catch me, let him

catch me on a portage. Let it be the long portage to the happy hunting ground!"
He laughed. When the Reaper caught him, that's about the way it happened.

There was Bill Hafeman, who was eighty-three when I met him. He had lived over on the Bigfork River since 1921, when he and his wife, Violet, moved into the woods. He said, "I wanted to live in a wild country like the Indians did. I thought, now that would be a free life. I could work as I wanted to, and nothing holding me back. I didn't want to live in a city where you go to work by a whistle, come home by a whistle. I didn't like all that stuff. So I told Violet we'll go live in the woods. And we done it. We learned how to live. We picked berries, we had wild rice for our grain, we had venison, fish, fruit. This is a Garden of Eden. Everything grows here." Bill made his first birchbark canoe with nothing but a knife and an ax so he and Violet would have some way of getting to Bigfork, the nearest settlement, fifteen miles down the river. Every canoe he built after that was a little better than the one before. I watched him build one of his last, with "all its mystery and its magic, all the lightness of the birch tree, all the toughness of the cedar, all the larch's supple sinews," to quote from the *Song of Hiawatha,* and when the buyer he expected never showed up, I bought that beautiful canoe from Bill Hafeman myself. Bill is gone. I try to take good care of one of his last masterpieces.

There was Dorothy Molter, who lived on an island in Knife Lake for more than fifty years, harvesting ice in the winter to see her through the summer, making friends with the mallards and chipmunks and chickadees, if never quite the troublesome bears, and selling her homemade root beer to thirsty paddlers who came calling. I portaged and paddled the long trail into Knife Lake one long-ago summer and spent an afternoon with Dorothy on her island. She told me her life story while I helped her wash out her root beer jars. Bob Cary, who wrote a book about her, helped win Dorothy special permission to go on living in the Wilderness Area until she died. A few years ago, in the winter, alone on her island, she did. They hauled her cabin all the way back to Ely by dogsled and set it up as a Dorothy Molter memorial and museum.

Those three I met, and others I heard about:

Chief Black Stone, the Ojibwa from Kawa Bay, who snowshoed a hundred miles through unbroken snow to seek help for his people during a flu epidemic. He made it to Ely, but never made it home. He died on Agnes Lake and was buried there in a rabbit skin blanket with his beads and his calumet, a great hero whose name is still honored.

There was Uncle Judd Cleveland, who had a little mining claim near Moose Lake, an old prospector who spent his life looking for the mother lode, sure he was going to find it any day. He left nothing behind when he died, except his name on Uncle Judd's Creek, which I crossed whenever I went back and forth from Moose Lake to Ely.

And Mike Kelly, who lived on boiled potatoes, salt pork, and bannock in a little shack on Birch Lake. He had a crooked arm from the time he was chased up a white pine by a bear, and fell and broke his arm on the way down. He set it himself and tied it to his body, and it set crooked. He never complained.

The old-timers were tough.

Plenty of their descendants, who have a memory of the rough and ready past, resent the prissy wilderness that has arrived, complete with regulations and a federal bureaucracy, in what they used to consider as their own hunting and fishing grounds. I'm on the other side of the wilderness argument myself, but you can't meet the old pioneers, especially the miners, or hear about their time on earth, without according their opinions great respect. In their lives, they worked harder than you did, whoever you are, and they can be forgiven if they never got around to becoming environmentalists along the way.

I went to see Mike Hillman, the forty-two-year-old son and grandson and great-grandson of miners, in his house beside the old Pioneer Mine on the north edge of town. Mike wrote a good short book, a history of the Vermillion Range. Mike's wife, Julie, gave us coffee and blueberry pie made with berries they'd picked the afternoon before in "a nice berry patch only three portages from the house," and Iron Mike and I talked the afternoon away. Laconic phrases came out of Mike Hillman in a natural North Country poetry.

"I'm the keeper of this ghost mine right here on Miner's Lake," he said, "This was the richest square mile of iron in the world. They took 82 million tons of ore from the Pioneer and the other mines in Ely. Between 1889 and 1967, one hundred and fifty two miners died in mudslides and cave-ins in those mines. When there was a cave-in, the whistle blew for ten minutes. They called it the Screamer. I remember that whistle blowing, wondering who was in the cave-in, wondering if it was my dad."

(It never was. I met Mike's father later—they call him Checker, because that was his job in the mine—making his Ely rounds with a Santa Claus beard that caused little children to stop and stare. Checker's peers, the other old men, always greeted him with solemn deference.)

Mike said, "My grandfather hugged and kissed his children every day before he went to work, and I realize it was because he didn't know for sure whether he'd come home. More than a hundred and fifty of them didn't come home, and when I got to looking into it, I found that for every death by cave-in, there were five deaths by suicide! I asked my dad about it. He said you have to realize they came across an ocean with big dreams and ended up in a raw town in the north woods with no prospects, except to be given five candles every morning to wear in their hats and then to go down into that black hole day after day. The disappointment was too great for some of them.

"When World War Two came along, sixteen hundred miners volunteered for service. They didn't have to volunteer. They were working in an essential industry. Uncle Sam needed the iron. But they felt it would be safer to go to war, and really, the statistics show that it was. These guys were the elite of mining, and they were the elite of soldiering, too.

"People who look for the history of immigration at Ellis Island are looking at the wrong end of the funnel. They should look at Ely, one of the places where the immigrants funneled down to. They were great people, and their children and grandchildren are great people. I think people who live in Ely now have a genetic memory of how important it was to be an American."

I said I thought I had inherited some of that same fervor from my Massachusetts grandfather, Leo Kuralt, the son of an immigrant from Slovenia. Mike whooped, "You'll be a hero in Ely! Eighty percent of this town is Slovenian."

Mike then digressed—all good storytellers digress—to tell me, offhand and by the way, one of the most affecting small-town stories I've ever heard. It is a tale of patriotism:

The most popular man in Ely was Leonard Zupancich, the Slovenian owner of Zup's food store. Zup was a regular in the poker game in the basement at Vertine's, a leading citizen, a friend to all, and a benefactor of the community. He was also an old-fashioned patriot who loved Ely's Fourth of July celebration. If the collection for the fireworks fell a little short, the town could always count on Zup to kick in two or three thousand dollars to guarantee a great fireworks show. Nobody enjoyed the fireworks as much as Leonard Zupancich himself.

Last year, with the Fourth of July approaching, Zup failed to show up for the poker game. His friends knew something was terribly wrong. They went around to his house and found him dead.

Zup's death was a blow to Ely. Everybody wanted to give him a suitable memorial. The people in charge of the fireworks thought of one. On the night of the Fourth of July, without letting it be known, they loaded Zup's ashes into a skyrocket. After all the other fireworks—the pinwheels and serpents and candlebombs—had been discharged, there was a respectful pause. Then one last skyrocket rose into the dark sky, higher than all the others. Up it went, higher and higher, until it exploded with a great flash, the moment Zup always loved so much.

Everybody cheered, and there in the darkness, floating down on his town, came Zup.

I told Mike my patriot grandfather would have loved to have gone that way himself, if anybody had thought of it.

Mike's own great-grandfather, Bill LaBeau, came to Ely before the Zupan-ciches, or anybody else—by canoe in 1885. He was one of a party of eight, six French-Canadian paddlers escorting two professional mining men. "Those canoes held every skill that was needed then," Mike said. "They could paddle and they could drill."

Those eight men found the richest iron in the world. The first women came the next year.

"My great-grandmother, Mary Ellen LaBeau, walked in from Lake Superior, three days and two nights on the winter road, and she was six months pregnant. She delivered William LaBeau, my great-uncle, June 8, 1884. That was the first recorded birth of a white child north of Duluth."

The iron mining lasted eighty years. It enriched Rockefellers and Carnegies, but no miners. Then it ended.

"This little mining town dies a little more every year," Iron Mike said. "Really, what's left is only the memory of the rough town with forty-six saloons. Ely is gentrified now in a way nobody ever dreamed of.

"When the mines closed, it was a real shock. The miners resented change. Some of them became trappers and fishermen. Then the Wilderness Area came in, and most of the trapping and fishing ended, too. I'm all for the Wilderness Area, because I can see what it would have become—logged over and overfished and hunted out. But if I could turn the clock back to 1957, 1958, why sure, I would. We were really free. There were no restrictions. This was our own paradise. After the mines closed, my dad never wanted anything more than to fish and camp and hunt, and most of the guys I knew when I was growing up stayed here for the same reason."

I asked Mike what kept him in Ely.

"It's my place," he said. "Minneapolis is the biggest city I've ever been to, and when I was there, I wanted to be back here."

But how can you make a living in Ely today?

"Well," he said, "I'm a red-card firefighter. I've carried boxes for United Parcel at Christmas. I've run a canoe base camp and guided canoe trips. I've tutored English classes at the community college and taught at the Elderhostel. I've been an actor and radio announcer. I've guided tourists through the Soudan iron mine—it's a state park now.

"I was supposed to run a resort, but I found out there was a little hitch. When they drew the wilderness line, the resort cabins were on the wrong side. If I wanted to manage the place, I had to move it over to the other side of the line. And I was an English Lit major.

"But there's good men around here, as I've been telling you. And I went to them and brain-picked, and these guys were really wonderful to me. I said I've got a resort that I've got to move from one side of the line to the other, and I've got to go over the ice. See, as soon as you say 'over the ice' to them, that makes them responsible. And these guys, boy, they babied me. They sat there over coffee for hours and hours explaining here's what you do, and here's why you do it.

"In the old days in the mine, a young guy might say, 'I think we ought to do it this way.' And the old Slovenians would say, 'Hey, podner, I no pay you to think. I pay you to *do*. I do the think, you do the do!' And if the young guy was smart, he would shut up, and that's the way he learned to be a miner.

"These old men who did it, there was a reason for everything they did. Do what they tell you to do. And after you do it enough, you'll figure out why they did it that way. I did what they told me, and I got those buildings moved over the ice."

In Mike Hillman, I figured I'd stumbled upon the soul of Ely, Minnesota. He is a tenacious and able man of the north. In the spirit of his forebears, he can do anything he sets his mind to do—even if it's something he's never done before.

He said, "For a while there, I was the Head Howler at the Wolf Center."

Ely has wolves in the neighborhood, dozens of roving packs of them, at least ten times as many wolves as the rest of the Lower 48 states combined. In the middle of my first night on Moose Lake, I heard them howling from the peninsula

Bob Cary

The birch tree on
Moose Lake

On Moose Lake
(photo by Bob Cary)

ike and Julie Hillman

across the water, high two-note wails sliding into yips in the extreme upper register. The sound echoed in my dreams that night. I could understand the thrill and dread that sound has inspired in human beings down the centuries. The International Wolf Center in Ely attracts wolf biologists from all over the world intent on studying the wolves, and tourists who'd like to go out at night and hear them howl. So Iron Mike Hillman volunteered to become Leather Lungs Hillman and howl up some wolves for the tourists.

"Howling is tough business," he said. "I'm not kidding you. I practiced at home and got to be a pretty good howler. I introduced myself to the people—'Hello, I'm the Head Howler'—and that impressed them. I'd drive a van full of people out to where I thought the wolves might be and let 'er rip! Sometimes I was lucky and the wolves would howl back and the people would think I was just wonderful. Other times, I'd just get hoarse."

"Don't let him fool you," Julie Hillman said. "If he couldn't get a response from the wolves, he'd go out behind a house that had sled dogs."

Mike said, "Well, sometimes I'd feel bad for the people. There'd be kids along and they'd be really disappointed. So it might have been cheating a little bit, but as a last resort, I'd go out and howl around the bend from Don Beland's house, and his huskies always obliged! I'd try to keep the huskies howling, because if they kept it up, any wolves around would get stimulated, and the people could hear them out on the fringes of the woods, the real thing. Then I figured I'd done my job for the night."

One night after supper back at the cabin, I was sitting in the dark at my usual place by the birch tree on the shore, listening to the loons on the lake. A big orange moon was rising. Suddenly, a loud wail arose across the water that sent a chill down my spine. The wolves were back—this time very close at hand on the opposite shore. I launched the canoe as quietly as I could and paddled toward the sound. I've never seen a timberwolf in nature; I thought it would be just right to see one on a wilderness shore under a full moon. I stopped in the water a little way from where I thought the last howls had come and waited.

The only sound was the water lapping at the gunwales of the canoe. The moon rose higher. All the folklore of wolves came back to me as I sat there, the ancient evocations of the wolf at the door; the Big Bad Wolf, nemesis of the Three Little Pigs, who huffed and puffed and blew their house down; the wolf who ate Little Red Riding Hood ("My, what big teeth you have, Grandma!"); the drawings in old adventure books of wolves surrounding hapless winter travelers, baring their fangs and moving in for the kill . . .

Pure invention, they tell you at the Wolf Center. Wolves *have* devoured little pigs, no doubt, but in all the authentic history of North America, there is no record of a wolf attacking a human being. Fair enough. And I certainly had no intention of attacking a wolf. I just wanted to see one.

I waited an hour. I heard no sound except the loons and saw no movement. I finally tried a howl of my own to see if anything would happen. Nothing did. I remembered that wolves travel far and fast. In an hour, the pack could easily be twenty or thirty miles away. I paddled back to the cabin, hauled the canoe up on the bank, and went in to bed.

Just as my head hit the pillow, the wolves set up an unearthly howl. From nearby, just across the lake. Right where I had been.

"Ten years ago in Ely, somebody left a dead wolf on the steps of the Forest Service building."

Jim Brandenburg was talking about the long war human beings have waged against wolves. He is a great nature photographer. His experiences with wolves in Minnesota and on Ellesmere Island in the Canadian Arctic have resulted in haunting books like the best-seller *Brother Wolf.*

A dozen years ago, he said, he was commissioned to do ten U.S. postage stamps on wildlife. "The Postal Service rejected the wolf as one of the animals," he said. "I had to substitute the mountain lion! Mountain lions kill people. Bison kill people every year. Bears kill people. It was only the wolf, which doesn't kill people, that got rejected. That's the way everybody always felt about the wolf."

Partly because of Jim's own books on wolves, attitudes are changing, even around Ely, where wolves were detested by hunters for reducing the deer population. Jim's wolf photographs have become so popular and he has become so famous that he lives in the woods behind a gate, always closed, with a sign on it that says "No Visitors Today." He opened the gate for me and led me up to his beautiful house and studio, built on a creek above a waterfall.

"Now wolves are having their day," he said. "Really, it has gone too far. Wolves are being overstudied by the experts, with radio collars and airplanes. And they're becoming overloved by the public." I got the impression he expects to go downtown one day and find wolf aprons and wolf key rings for sale in the stores. "They're not exactly rare," he exclaimed. "There are two thousand wolves in Minnesota!" I think he fears the scholars are going to give each one of them a name.

After all his years among wolves, there was a kind of weary sadness about Jim Brandenburg. The biologists have come along and taken his animals away from him, and he seems resentful, but resigned. He's preparing to move on to another subject—perhaps, I'd guess, even to another place. He's the one person I met who seemed restless in Ely.

"My parents weren't born here, and I wasn't," Jim remarked. "So to a lot of people in Ely, I'll always be a packsacker."

Packsacker? I tried the expression on Mike Hillman the next time I saw him.

"Outsider," he said. "To tell you the truth, we're all packsackers. The Ojibwa would like to think they've been here forever, but they came from somewhere else. The French trappers and the British traders were packsackers, and so are we. It's okay to be a packsacker. But when Reserve Mining Company opened up the taconite mines in Babbitt and a lot more people moved in here, now those guys were ridge-runners."

"Ridge-runners are worse?" I asked him.

"Oh, much worse," Mike said. "See, a packsacker is usually just a guy on the run, heading up here to get away from whatever is oppressing him in the city.

But a ridge-runner, he's going to stay here. And he has enough money to buy a boat and a motor. He's going to end up being a rival fisherman!"

Mike said, "Being at the end of the road, we've always had packsackers, all kinds. In the old days, the mob in Chicago used to send guys up here to hide out until the heat was off. My dad used to take 'em fishing. People asked him, 'Aren't you afraid of these guys?' He said, 'I'm the safest one in the boat. I'm the only one who knows how to get home!'

"We still get packsackers, and we're real tolerant if they don't look too funny. Did I mention there's a two-weirdo limit in Ely?"

That one caught me with a mouthful of coffee, which I came close to sputtering onto the table.

"No, it's true. I'm serious," Mike said. "Down in the cities, you've got a lot of anonymity and there are weirdos all over the place. But Ely has a two-weirdo limit. If there's three weirdos in town, people start to worry. Then when the police come in to the coffee shop for coffee, they'll hear, 'Hey, you see that new guy in town? Yeah? What you doin' about him? Where's he from, where's his people?'

"But if there are just two weirdos in town, that's still okay."

Bob Cary, whose recollections of Ely go back forty years, says the problem in the old days was not so much odd-looking outside drifters as honest-looking homegrown scam artists.

"In the fall," he said, "the hunters would bring their deer to Elna's, where the canoe lot for Canadian Waters Outfitters is now. They had a scale right there in the middle of town, and you'd weigh out your deer there, tie him back on the car, and go for a few beers. There'd always be a couple of guys in the bar looking for some hunter who hadn't got a deer that day. They'd say, 'Well, we got an extra one, a nice ten-point buck. You can have him for fifty dollars.' They'd take the money, go out on the street and untie somebody's deer from a car, drive around the block and deliver him. Everybody was happy, except the poor guy who had worked all day for that ten-point buck. That used to happen every weekend."

In the Ojibwa language—Chippewa, some people still say—Bob Cary is *A'Kwenzie,* "Old Man." He spent two years learning Ojibwa on the Vermillion Reservation and at the community college in Ely, where it's still taught.

Bob said, "When an Ojibwa kills a deer, he kneels beside it and says, 'I'm sorry, old buck, I didn't kill you because I hate you, but because you give me meat and clothing and moccasins.' I have started doing the same thing. I think everybody ought to. Most Ojibwa hunters put tobacco in the fork of a tree before starting the hunt, not to help them get a deer but in thanks for the opportunity."

I asked Bob about the Indian casinos that are springing up everywhere.

"Well," he said, "I'll never get used to seeing a guy I met on a trapline wearing a tuxedo and dealing blackjack. But life changes, doesn't it?

"A lot of the traditions still go on, though—ricing at the end of summer, for example. Nett Lake is practically all wild rice, and it's still harvested. Outside the reservation, anybody can rice. I get mine right over here at Basswood. When the Indians are through ricing, they take two handfuls and raise their hands and let it fall through their fingers, an offering to the Spirit. The Ojibwa have a more profound idea than we do of what life is all about.

"At the same time, they accept misfortune better than we do. If you misplace your knife at your campsite, you'll curse. The Ojibwa will laugh—because the knife was moved by the *Maymayguishi,* the Little People, the tricksters who live in the spirit lakes. If you turn your back on the fire and your coffee pot falls over, you have nobody to blame but yourself. The Ojibwa laugh and say, there go the Little People again.

"I think this ability to blame the spirits and not one another is one of the things that helped families living so closely crowded together get through the hard winters without falling out. I half believe in the spirits myself. If you are camped in the woods and stay very quiet, you can hear the Little People laughing in the tops of the trees."

I smiled and said, "Sounds to me like Jackpine Bob is going native."

"It wouldn't be the worst thing that could happen," Bob said. "The Ojibwa are good people, and very honest. They say that when you die, you have to carry everything you've ever stolen on your back through eternity. A buddy of mine heard that and said, 'Damn, I better get me a pickup truck before I die!'

"But it's an Ojibwa point of honor not to be a thief. I have a friend who was in camp with an Ojibwa guide. Out of habit, he pulled his billfold out of his hip pocket and put it under his pillow before he put his head down. The guide said to him softly, 'You don't have to do that. There's not another white man within forty-five miles.' "

The Ojibwa are the best known of the canoe Indians, but they were not the first. They migrated into the northern lake country from the east at a time when the Sioux were the people of the forest. The two tribes fought over these lakes for a hundred years. Ojibwa war parties, armed with rifles obtained from the French, finally pushed the Sioux west into the plains—which is how it happened that Hiawatha, the Ojibwa, happened to be in Minnesota to inspire Longfellow's poem, and Sitting Bull, the Sioux, happened to be in Montana to take Custer's scalp.

Mike and Julie Hillman's children were away visiting relatives, and the two of them had just returned from a long wilderness canoe trip. They told me about ancient Indian paintings, predating both the Sioux and the Ojibwa, which still can be seen on cliffs above one of the distant lakes. Mike said it's a lake he always paddles across with a kind of dread.

"Most of the lakes have charm," he said. "Snowbank Lake or Burntside Lake or Argo Lake make you feel good. But Darky Lake has the Wendigo, that's the evil spirit. There's a power in that lake. The water is crystal clear, but when you look down into it, it's deep and black. The lake is just a sheer cut from one shore to the other, and the paintings are on the south cliffs. Nobody knows who did them. But everybody who goes there feels respect for those pictures and that dark water."

The Indian pictographs were already there in the days of the Voyageurs, the French-Canadian fur traders who passed along these chains of lakes as early as

1790, paddling twenty-five-foot birch canoes, each laden with a ton and a half of trade goods. To hear them tell it, the Voyageurs were jolly Gallic supermen, covering seventy-five miles a day, taking their heavy loads over the portages at a fast trot, and *singing* all the way!

I was curious about how it's done today. Mike and Julie aim their canoe into the wilderness every chance they get. They know what they're doing out there. We had a long supper over at Snowbank Lodge one night and I asked their advice. I put down the details here as a favor to aspiring Voyageurs:

"We start planning about a week ahead of time," Julie said. "For this last trip, we bought twenty pounds of family steak at Zup's and had them cut it up for beef jerky. We have our own dehydrator and we make our own jerky. The number one rule is do not take an ice cooler. We dehydrate our own fruit—apples, pears, peaches. All the drinks we take have Nutra-Sweet in them. That's because the weight in food is the sugar weight. So we take Crystal Lite instead of Kool-Aid, which weighs more. We really try to save ounces.

"We dehydrate potatoes to make hash browns. We bring packaged noodles, rice, oatmeal. And we hope to hell we catch fish."

Mike said, "We usually do all right. We don't catch a lot of fish, but we're grateful if we catch a few. We bring two fishing rods and wooden minnows and Rapalas. We fish for anything that bites. In the spring and the fall, lake trout are all over the lakes, but this time of year they're down deep, so with the Rapalas, we're going for Northern pike, walleye, and bass. But I put the Northerns back, because I don't know how to take the Y-bones out."

"We take wheat crackers," Julie said. "Hard candy. Coffee. We've learned to like powdered milk."

"We drink the water in the lakes," Mike said. "They say don't drink the water. If the water from these lakes ever makes me sick, I'll know it's time to go somewhere else."

Julie said, "We have separate colored pouches—one for breakfast, one for lunch, one for supper, so we don't have to rummage around in the pack."

"Julie is my wife and lover at home," Mike said, "but in the woods, she's my partner, which is a different thing. It's not a deeper relationship, necessarily, but a different one. It's exciting to get up early and go. We don't travel hard, we just travel steady. We carry only what we need. The Canadian Shield rears up on the border, and it separates the men from the boys. Those portages are killers. It's hard enough carrying what you need, and you want to leave everything else home."

"We do take a tent," Julie said. "We ended up with a Sierra, one of the North Face tents."

"Somebody stole my VE-25 mountain tent about six years ago," Mike said. "That was the best tent I ever had, and it broke my heart, and I haven't had the money to replace it. But this is a good tent, and it only weighs about five pounds."

"Then we carry two sleeping bags," Julie said.

"And they're good bags," Mike said. "Buy good bags. You know, people come up here with cheap sleeping bags, and yeah, they'll keep you warm at twenty degrees, but if they get wet they weigh five hundred pounds and it takes seven days to dry 'em."

"Two flashlights," Julie said, "Mini-Mags with two extra batteries. First aid kit. One big Canadian map, and a compass. And long underwear. My dad always said you should take your long underwear off on the Second of July, and go through the Fourth without it, and then put it back on again on the Fifth!"

"We carry one extra shirt for the two of us," said Mike.

I asked who gets the shirt.

Mike said, "She likes to smell better than I do if we meet somebody on a lake. We used to take two extra shirts, but I said I'd like to see if one will do it, and one does it. I don't smell too good, but the bugs don't bother me. The bugs go to the guy who smells the best. Oh, and we take insect repellent and wear long-sleeved shirts and pants the bugs can't bite through and two layers of socks.

"The old canoe guys, you'd see 'em when they came back from the woods. They'd take their shirts off and their hands and their wrists were just mahogany-colored, and their necks and their faces, but in between they were all white. They never took their shirts off in the woods. They couldn't afford a sunburn."

"And boots," Julie said.

"Wear boots," Mike said. "People come up here in those tennis shoes, and they get on a portage carrying a load they're not used to, and they get tired and twist their ankles. Wear boots, but not the big mountain boots, because then you're tearing up the country with every step you take. We wear soft-soled boots with good ankle support."

"We take a little one-burner Coleman stove," Julie said. "We start one fire a day, sometimes none. That's at night. The stove is for breakfast, for the oatmeal. We also bring a mix we've made for pancakes and pick blueberries to put in them. So if we're hungry at night and haven't caught fish, we can have pancakes."

Mike said, "We don't take an ax, we take a saw. Anybody who takes an ax up here has not made wood lately. We go for old campsites, not the ones on picturesque points, because they attract too many people and the wood's burned up. You can go across the lake and pick up dead wood all over the place. A lot of nights, building a fire isn't necessary. If we all build only one fire a day, or none, then maybe our kids will be able to find wood out there when it's their turn. Anyway, we don't spend a lot of time sitting around the fire. We go into the tent early because we're tired. And then in the morning, we're up early to see the day start and leave early and enjoy the country. It's natural country, and when we're in it, we become natural, too."

That night on Snowbank Lake, we were having our supper no more than six or seven miles south of the Canadian border. The loons and the wolves and the walleyes crisscross the border without stopping at Customs, and though it's theoretically unlawful, a lot of canoeists do, too. International boundaries look immutable on maps, but they are invisible in the wild. The dotted line between Minnesota and Ontario is nowhere to be seen. When you're in a canoe, it seems nebulous and needless.

Mike Hillman rummaged around in his hip pocket and found a poem to read me, "At the Un-National Monument Along the Canadian Border" by William Stafford:

This is the field where the battle did not happen,
where the unknown soldier did not die.
This is the field where grass joined hands,
where no monument stands,
and the only heroic thing is the sky.

Birds fly here without any sound,
unfolding their wings across the open.
No people killed—or were killed—on this ground
hallowed by neglect and an air so tame
that people celebrate it by forgetting its name.

"This last trip, we outlawed it in, to tell you the truth," Mike said. "They've closed some of the customs stations to save money, and nobody can see paddling nine or ten hours out of the way just to report in to Customs."

"Can you remember your route?" I asked Mike.

His countenance changed. He looked at the ceiling and smiled a little smile as he remembered:

"We went in at Moose River on the Echo Trail. The Moose River runs into a little tiny lake called Nina Moose Lake, and we kept going and got to American Agnes Lake, and from there we portaged into the Boulder River, and then portaged from there into LaCroix and into Iron Lake, and then into Bottle Lake and then up to Crooked Lake, then Middle Roland and Roland Lake, then into Argo Lake, then into Darky Lake and down the Darky River into Brent, and then up into Conmee Lake for a couple of days. Julie didn't want to go to Conmee because it was two more portages. The portages are brutal up there and you pay a real price for solitude, but on Conmee, we left people behind. We came down into a side bay and camped on a site that hadn't seen anybody for a long time, and we felt that we were a long way away. We left and went back into Brent, and from Brent into McIntyre, and from there into Robinson and from Robinson into Tuck, and from Tuck into Sara, and from Sara into Side, and then into Isabella, and then into North Bay on Basswood Lake, and then down home."

"We had ten great days," Julie said. "And if you leave on a trip like that with a dollar in your pocket, that's what you'll have in your pocket when you come back."

Mike said, "On the last day, we paddled right up to the landing at Winton, and I went into the general store and saw Nancy behind the counter and said, 'We've been gone ten days. What's happened while we've been gone?' She said, 'Elvis Presley's daughter married Michael Jackson!' I said well, if that's the most important news, we haven't missed a thing."

Ely is a place for getting away from it all. There aren't very many such places left.

They're building a new Holiday Inn; probably it's open by now. Since I left, one commuter plane a day has started flying in from Minneapolis, and there are other signs of progress. I'd hate to see the little town at the end of the road become too developed and refined. I'd hate to see it overrun by newcomers who never heard of Chief Black Stone or Uncle Judd or Mike Kelly, who never met Bill Magie or Dorothy Molter.

I felt at peace and at home sitting there beside the birch tree on Moose Lake, but I realize I was just a packsacker. Ely should always belong to people like Jackpine Bob Cary and Iron Mike Hillman, who realize that lakes are the eyes of the earth, people who know enough to thank the Great Spirit for the rice harvest and to tread lightly on the portages.

Boothbay Harbor, Maine

⬆

This is one of the loveliest moments of life: the moment after you have shut down the engine of a sailboat. The sudden silence always comes as a sweet surprise. You let the bow fall off the wind, feel the sails fill, feel the boat heel gently for the instant it takes the craft to recognize its new and mysterious power, and then feel it surge forward, lines taut, bow rising, sails pulling, gathering momentum now, doing its business, in control, on course.

Herb Smith shut down the engine of *Appledore V* off Spruce Point and aimed her for Ram Island on a starboard reach. I found a place to sit on the windward side of the schooner so I could watch the white houses in the hills above Boothbay Harbor sliding away behind us, and the sparse scattering of islands growing closer up ahead. Beyond those islands, there was nothing but the open Atlantic. I knew we were going to turn around and come back to Fisherman's Wharf before the sun went down, but it was exciting to think that, for the present, we were flying along toward Gibraltar.

After making adjustments to the sails, Doris Smith, Herb's wife, sat down on the cabin trunk to talk to me.

"All our boats have been *Appledore*s," she said. "It's the name of the small island off Kittery where I grew up. Herb and I built the first *Appledore* together and were married on it. We forgot to look at the tide tables. The tide went out and left the boat aground and tilting over, with all the wedding guests about to slide off the deck. So we had to wait to get married until she levelled out on the incoming tide."

We sailed past thousands of lobster buoys in the outer harbor, tidily aligned like rows of corn for easy harvest. We glided through a deep, narrow passage between Fisherman's Island and Ram Island. I admired the Ram Island lighthouse, and even more the abandoned keeper's dwelling, with an outhouse on the point which must have afforded the prettiest east-west view of any outhouse in New England.

Doris said, "We built *Appledore II* at Gamage's Shipyard in South Bristol. That was our first round-the-world boat. We sold it when we came home.

"We built *Appledore III* in our backyard in New Hampshire. We started a dairy farm but found we couldn't make a living, so we built another boat. This was the other side of Dixville Notch. That boat made quite a sensation. When we said we were going to build a boat, the farmers thought we meant a rowboat to put in the lake up there. *Appledore III* was really a great cruising boat. We made our second round-the-world trip in her."

I suffered a pang of envy. I learned to sail when I was still young enough to cross an ocean and promised myself I'd do that someday at the helm of my own boat. But promises postponed have a way of getting broken. Now I was too old, and my ability too rusty, and that particular dream, like so many others, was on the shelf for good. So it stung a little to be aboard a sixty-four-foot topsail schooner with a still-young couple who had sailed across all the oceans and around the great capes, and not once but twice, and had taken their children along for good measure!

Herb Smith said, "When we started giving day sails out of Boothbay Harbor, I listed Tommy as part of the crew. The Coast Guard inspector looked at him, and looked again, and asked, 'How old is he?' I said he's ten years old. The inspector said, 'You can't have a ten-year-old deckhand!' I said, 'Why not? He's been twice around the world.' The inspector looked it up, and found out there was no age limit in the regulations, so Tommy was legal. Good deckhand, too."

Off in the distance, I could see Damariscove Island, a place of history and legend. English cod fishermen of the 1600s found a perfect harbor there, and a four-acre freshwater pond for filling their water casks, and so made the island an outpost of theirs a long way from home. Truth to tell, whatever you have heard about Jamestown, Damariscove was the first permanent English settlement in the New World. The Plymouth Pilgrims used to sail up here to trade with the fishermen and swap news between the Old World and the New. The Nature Conservancy has returned the island to the uninhabited state in which those cod fishermen found it, a place of wild beauty. Damariscove was familiar to Rachel Carson, too. I once landed there and found a little stone cairn somebody put there in her memory.

The island slipped away to the stern. Herb Smith brought the boat about and Doris set the sails for a quiet run toward home. We fell silent. The sun settled on the horizon, growing larger and softer in the late-day mist, reddening the gaff-rigged sails of *Appledore V* as she headed obediently for her dock. We tied up quietly in the half-light of evening, with the lights coming on in town. I said my goodbyes to the Smiths and walked around to my room on the other side of the harbor.

I felt elated. To be back in Boothbay Harbor with the whole month of August ahead of me excited me so that I could hardly get to sleep that night. I lay there imagining all the ways I could see again the coves and points and islands of that infinite, indented coast—from a lobster boat, maybe, or a windjammer, or a fishing smack. In Maine, it's fun to glimpse the sea from the land, but to survey the dark forests and rocky headlands from the sea with a fair wind and a running tide is a glory to last you all your life.

It's usually also the shortest distance between two points, a straight line. On the day my friend Bob Mitchell and I went up to Pemaquid Point to look around (that's the Pemaquid Point Lighthouse over my shoulder in Bob's photograph on the jacket of this book), we drove to Boothbay proper, on through Edgecomb and North Edgecomb to Highway 1, east for a few miles and across the Damariscotta River at Newcastle, then down the Damariscotta Peninsula through Bristol, Pemaquid, and New Harbor to the Point—a distance of forty-five miles by land, I'd guess. When we got there, we could see the place we'd started from, the entrance to Boothbay Harbor, about four miles away by sea.

What's more, if you're in a boat, you have the ocean pretty much to yourself, and a galley for cooking your chowder, and an anchor for dropping in any of a thousand pretty inlets when night comes on. But if you're in a car—well, the Maine roads get crowded in August, the lobster pounds have waiting lines, and the bed-and-breakfast inns fill up with people from "away," people like me.

I suppose most vacationers do as I did—linger a day or two in Portland, exploring the cobblestone streets and interesting shops of the Old Port Exchange and enjoying its small urban surprises, the bright splash of a flower box here, a sidewalk cafe on the waterfront there, and always the smell of salt air and the cry of gulls overhead. If I were going to choose an American city to live in, Portland would be on my list.

Then, on a cloudy Saturday with rain threatening, I headed down east. *All* visitors to Maine head down east, and all on the same road. The traffic hums along out of Portland on an expansive super-highway, but everybody gets off onto a country stretch of Route 1 at Freeport to stop at L. L. Bean. I did, thinking to buy a fishing cap and some wool socks. That day, the line of traffic stretched three miles out from town, inching along toward the L. L. Bean parking lot. I'd have turned around and left, but I was hypnotized by the phenomenon. I can remember when Bean's was a little old frame building with creaking stairs up to the sales floor. It is now a vast and crowded emporium selling not only canoes, backpacks, and hunting knives, but also pottery, rugs, and lawn furniture. Bean's used to be the place where you could wander in at midnight and shop for a pair of boots. You still can, but it's better known nowadays as the catalog store that sells one hundred million dollars' worth of merchandise each year to the Japanese alone. The help is still wonderfully friendly and polite, I'll say that. After an hour or two in traffic and another twenty minutes in the cashier's line, I got my socks and my cap, and a tip from the cashier: don't come on Saturday, and don't come on a cloudy day. Cloudy days, she said, being no good at the beach, are when everybody for a hundred miles around decides to go shopping.

One other problem with Freeport is that L. L. Bean now has company. Noting Bean's success, American Tourister opened an outlet store, and Anne Klein and Banana Republic, Bass Shoe, Benetton, Brooks Brothers, Bugle Boy, Calvin Klein, Cannon Towel, Coach Bags, Corning-Revere, Crabtree & Evelyn, Countess Mara. . . . (I am giving you this list alphabetically, not chronologically, and you'll notice I'm still in the "C's.") Hundreds of such stores line the main street. From one to another slog thousands and thousands of people, far more people in Freeport, Maine, on an August Saturday than you ever see on New York's Fifth Avenue in the week before Christmas, all of them wearing shorts and eating ice cream cones and carrying shopping bags and marching along with unsmiling, determined faces, afraid of missing a bargain. I fled to my car, which I had parked in the public library parking lot in spite of stern signs warning me not to, and left Freeport vowing never to return, at least not on a cloudy Saturday.

Freeport isn't the last of the traffic jams, either. (I'm telling you, in Maine, you need a boat.) The highway's humming three-lane promise gives way to crowded two-lane anxiety, and then, at Bath, approaching the bridge over the Kennebec River, to one-lane frustration. Every beer truck and grocery truck and tanker truck transporting the bounty of America to Boothbay, Belfast, and Bar Harbor; every van full of sunburned adults and squealing children; every rental car carrying vacationers yearning for the charming and unspoiled coastal villages of Maine; every pickup, every motorcycle must cross that bridge in single file.

Luckily, there's something to watch while you wait. The giant cranes of the Bath Iron Works are always in action right beside the bridge, creating a warship or two or attaching the superstructure of a new cargo vessel. This is hard, intricate work, and fascinating to follow as you creep along in the summer traffic. I met the head of the Iron Works once, a gentlemanly lawyer named Buzz Fitzgerald, who gave up the air-conditioning in his office because there's no air-conditioning in the shop. While crossing that bridge, I always think of him down there, sweating on the job along with everybody else. And I marvel that the cranes are so much taller than the church steeples, which were meant to be the tallest structures in town. America's very first ship, a thirty-ton pinnace, was launched in Bath, Maine, in 1607, and for a while there, Bath built more ships each year than all the rest of the country combined. I hope for the sake of tradition that this old shipyard, well along into its second century now, doesn't get closed in one of those periodic Pentagon cutbacks.

There's plenty of time to think about such things at the Bath bridge. I met a man who swore that they once laid a keel at the Iron Works as he started across the bridge during rush hour, and launched the ship before he got to the other side.

There's one more river to cross if you're going where I was going. It's the Sheepscott River at Wiscasset, which declares itself Maine's prettiest village; with its collection of lovely old mansions, once home to prosperous merchants and sea captains, it may well be.

The sturdy colonial houses of Wiscasset please my eye, but the wrecks are what I always look forward to seeing. Two derelict schooners were abandoned long ago in the river just off the Wiscasset waterfront. For thirty years I have watched the great four-masted *Hesper* and *Luther Little* slowly deteriorating there. On this trip, there wasn't much left of them to be seen, two dark hulls and a forlorn spar tilted into the sky. I don't know their life story, but it may begin "Born at Bath." It ends "Died at Wiscasset."

The traffic eases after the Wiscasset bridge, and it's not far to the turn-off to Boothbay Harbor. I know the way by heart: Down Route 27, past the granite Union soldier on the hill, left on Union Street, right on Park, and along the east side of the harbor to the big wooden fisherman in his yellow foul-weather gear who marks the entrance to Brown's Wharf.

I could have chosen any of a hundred other seaside resorts and fishing villages in which to spend my August in Maine, but then Ken Brown would have heard about it and become upset with me. He built his motel in 1967 on the site of the family cannery and lobster business, and I must have stayed there for the first time that summer or the next. He doesn't remember me from those days, but I remember him, the gruff proprietor frowning his way around the premises, tidying up after his guests and his own employees. I have been back to Brown's Wharf often enough to become part of the family, almost, and it's a nice family to be part of. Ken and his wife, Joan, are always there in the lobby or the dining room to greet newcomers. (If you want a big smile with your greeting, try to be greeted by Joan.) Daughter Connie is the hotel manager, son Dennis is the chef, daughter Michelle is the bartender, son Timmy is the dockmaster. Son Larry lives nearby and is available to help out in a pinch, as is Michelle's husband, Kevin, a professional fisherman. But Kevin would rather be out on his boat, and since he occasionally brings in a four-hundred-pound tuna at twenty-five dollars a pound, everybody agrees that's where he really should be. Kevin and Michelle's son, Alexis, fifteen years old, works in the kitchen sometimes, but only after he's finished his studies for the day. Alexis is a geography whiz who has placed high in national contests. One of his awards hangs framed on the wall of the motel lobby.

If you reach up and rub an overhead beam in the Brown's Wharf bar and then lick your finger, you taste salt. In the days of the sailing ships, barks used to bring salt from Italy for curing codfish (it was too expensive to haul it overland from anywhere in the U.S.), and they stored the salt in the room that's now the bar. If you look down between the planks of the Brown's Wharf deck at low tide, you can see lobsters crawling around on the rocks; the place was built on lobsters, figuratively and literally. Brown's does not lack for authenticity.

The restaurant serves dandy blueberry muffins at breakfast and good seafood at dinner. The rooms all have space for sitting outdoors and watching the comings and goings in the harbor. And then there are the flower boxes everywhere, filled with geraniums; it seems Ken Brown was stationed in Bavaria as a G.I. and came home with a longing for flower boxes in his life.

The place has the further advantage of being on the wrong side of the harbor. The right side of the harbor is full of restaurants, shops, and people. The streets are one-way until after Labor Day, when the villagers get their village back, and there is no place to park over there. If you must go shopping, you can walk from Brown's up to the head of the harbor and cross over on a footbridge. It must be the only harbor-crossing footbridge in Maine. It provides, as Ken Brown tells his guests, a bracing walk.

I am not saying this is the best place to stay in Maine. There may be a lot of better places. I am just explaining how it happens that I have to stay there. It's all habit and affection and familiarity. And fear of what Ken Brown might say next time I saw him, if he heard I'd taken lodgings in some fancy inn in Camden or Kennebunk.

There in my room on the water, I'd stir in my bed in the mornings to hear the guttural rumble of the lobster boats leaving the harbor before sunup. That sound was the promise of a fair day, since most of the lobstermen stay in port in a storm.

Later, as I was getting dressed, I'd watch the early sunlight whitewashing the houses across the harbor; America's first light falls on Maine each morning, and a clear and lovely light it is.

Then, with no plan, I'd go out into the day, on foot down to the docks, or by car along the coast, happy just to be there. Each day I'd feel a little more of Maine soaking into my bones.

Some days I didn't have to go far. I met Stan Coffin right there on Ken Brown's pier.

Stan is a retired lobsterman who learned the skills from his father, William Albert Coffin, well-remembered around Boothbay for his seamanship. While everybody else was converting to power boats, the elder Coffin went on for a long time lobstering the classical way, in a Friendship sloop. Stan's father used to sell his lobsters to Ken Brown's father at the Brown Brothers dock, just about where Stan and I were standing.

"How old were you when you first went out with him?" I asked him.

He said, "I don't remember. I remember high seas, and trusting my father."

You can't appreciate coastal Maine without understanding the life of the lobsterman. Stan Coffin tried to help me understand:

"I got up at five A.M. and left the harbor before daylight. I used a spotlight to find my buoys. I would stay out all day, get in after dark, work until eleven o'clock at night building and repairing traps, and leave again before the sun came up the next morning. I did that week in and week out, and the year around.

"I had seventeen hundred traps, far more than the average lobsterman, and I could haul half of them in one day. I had eight-trap strings. I could haul 'em, empty out the lobsters, bait 'em and set 'em in six minutes, with the stern man doing the measuring and baiting. For bait, you need herring or porgy. Some might use mackerel, but it's no good, too oily. It physics the lobsters and they go to dying on you. If a lobster measures less than three and a quarter inches from the eye socket to the back of the body, you have to put him back, and you'll put back twenty for every one you can keep. A lot of your job is putting back shorts.

"I was known as a hard worker. If you're not willing to work hard, you shouldn't go lobstering in the first place. I had a standing order with Anderson in Yarmouth for three hundred and fifty traps a year. They were made of spruce at first, but spruce gets waterlogged and rots. The nets of the traps were hemp, which didn't last long, either. Traps today are made of vinyl-covered metal, with nylon nets. Metal traps fish better, but if you lose one, it stays down there fishing forever until the vinyl wears off and the metal rusts away, and I'm not sure the vinyl *does* wear off.

"You lose traps to storms, especially in shallow waters where I always fished, and you lose traps to other lobstermen cutting your lines. You can report that to the warden, but I never bothered with the warden. I just retaliated. If you don't react right away, you'll soon be out of business. A lobsterman might be jealous of you, think you're working too hard. He'll wait for a foggy day and go to rifling your traps. If there's one bit of fog out there, the courts will say you mightn't have seen him and throw it out. I didn't like doing dirty work in the fog, but I learned to do it. I had to, to protect myself.

"Anybody can buy a boat, build some traps, get a license, and go lobstering. But you'll never go lobstering unless you're accepted by the other men in the harbor. If I were starting now, I'd get me a string of thirty-five or forty traps, no more, and if I lost one, somebody else would lose two. If I lost them all, somebody with more than I had would lose them all. After a while, I wouldn't lose so many. And then I'd start adding traps. It's still a rough occupation. Many a lobster boat goes out with a shotgun aboard."

I said I was surprised that after all these years lobstermen hadn't developed a spirit of cooperation.

"Yes," Stan Coffin said, "it ought to be like it is on Monhegan Island. There, they only fish in winter. That's their custom. They agree what day they'll go out. And when they do leave the harbor, they all leave together. If one man is sick, they don't go, or they set his traps for him. No Monhegan lobsterman ever infringes upon another. Probably the island life has a lot to do with it. On an island, you have to learn to get along with your neighbor."

I asked why lobster boats are still made of wood in this day and age.

Stan laughed. He said, "Lobstermen think 'Glory, I don't know about that fiberglass. If I hit a rock, that fiberglass might just shatter and leave me in the water.' I guess we all feel that if God had meant for there to be fiberglass boats, he would have given us fiberglass trees."

I told Stan Coffin that I spent a day on a lobster boat in rough weather years ago and was glad when the day was over.

"You get used to it," he said. "I fished around Seguin Island my whole life. It's the mouth of the Kennebec, shallow water, and with the winds and the tides, it can be the roughest place on the coast. You're often pulling traps in breakers out there. A Coast Guardsman was watching me from shore one time. He said the only thing he could see of my boat when a breaker broke on me was the tip of my radar antenna. I called that boat *Rough Rider*. That was a good name at Seguin.

"There was only once when I stopped fishing before the day was over. That was when my son went overboard. He was twelve or thirteen and working as my stern man. We went stern-to-stern with another boat to pass over a bait box. There came a big sea and my son tried to hold onto the bait box and went right into the water. He was going down for the third time when I caught him with the gaff. That scared me so bad, I went right to shore."

It must not have scared his son so much. Now that Stan Coffin has retired, his son has taken up the family occupation. I'd seen Stan Junior's boat, *Bad Penny*, in the harbor and I asked his father about the name.

"That was his mother's idea," Stan said. "A bad penny always returns."

There's a monument on the Boothbay waterfront to the boats that didn't return, to "the proud, independent fishermen of Maine who lost their lives at sea."

John Begin told me about three of that number. They were friends of his. John is seventy-two, still lobstering, and in the words of one of his acquaintances, "a tough old baster." John had a little stroke while I was in town and was taken to the hospital. Lying there in bed, he lit up a cigar. The doctor came in, said, "Jesus, John, I can smell cigar smoke halfway down the hall. You can't smoke that thing in here!" and took his cigar away from him. At that, John Begin got out of bed, pulled on his pants and boots, walked out of the hospital, and drove home in his pickup truck. He was out in his lobster boat the next morning.

"It was in January," John said, "forty years ago. We were two boats thirty-

*Captain Gib Philbrick and Bud Brackett
(photos by Robert Mitchell)*

Afloat on Boothbay Harbor (photo by Robert Mitchell)

Ken Brown

Surprise visitors (photo by Robert Mitchell)

six miles off Monhegan, three of us on each boat. My friend Lou was skipper of our boat, the *Sandra and Earl,* and my friend Kit was skipper of the other. The wind came up, but we were out there to make money. Nobody came in just because of wind. We had a riding sail and we were riding okay. I was asleep below. I didn't think anything special was happening.

"Well, the wind came up to eighty miles an hour. One big sea moved the house back and laid the boat on its side. The boat stayed on its side a good long time. I thought it might not come back up. We had no radio, of course, and we lost touch with the other boat. We thought they'd gone off and left us. Lou needed to keep her into the wind, so he broke the stove loose from the deck and used the stove for a sea anchor.

"This was a Tuesday, I think. A Coast Guard plane finally saw us on Friday, and they sent a boat out there to tow us in. They passed us some supplies, food, and cigarettes—cigarettes were the main thing—and they towed us right into the harbor. It was late at night and I thought, well, we'll have to call a cab to get home. But when we got closer, my God, everybody in town was down there to meet us. The floats were all underwater with the weight of the people.

"That's when we found out the other boat was lost. Kit was lost, and the two hands. They never found one thing. That was the worst thing that ever happened to me on the water and, of course, it wasn't bad at all for me. But you don't expect to lose three buddies that way."

I've never met a Maine fisherman who wasn't full of confidence at sea. Maybe it's really fatalism. Anyway, in the spring in Boothbay Harbor, most of them, seeking to cover all bases, show up for the blessing of the fleet. Father Tom Lee, former pastor of the beautiful white Catholic church on the harbor, Our Lady Queen of Peace, used to perform the blessing. He showed me a photograph taken from over his shoulder as the boats sailed toward him one year, with an old one, the *Brant,* leading the procession.

"These are Yankee boats, of course," Father Tom told me, "hardly a Catholic in the lot. Some of the boys met me on the street and said they wanted to ask me about something."

The conversation, as Father Tom tells it, went this way:

"Father, you know the *Brant* sank."

"Yes."

"But you blessed her."

"Boys, let me get this straight. The *Brant* was an old tub, poorly maintained?"

"Yes."

"And we can agree she shouldn't have been out there at all?"

"Yes."

"And as I understand it, there were three boats of you coming in fully loaded, and you encountered a sea off Monhegan, and the *Brant* started leaking, and you couldn't stop the leak, and you took the *Brant* crew aboard, and you watched her go down in broad daylight?"

"Yes."

"Boys, if I hadn't blessed her, she'd have gone down with all hands in the night!"

Lobsters are expensive in restaurants, but after you find out about the hard work and hazard of bringing them to shore, you never again complain about the price.

One of the primal pleasures of Maine is to sit at an outdoor picnic table on a deck over the water with a messy toasted lobster roll dribbling on your fingers, or with a bowl of lobster stew clearing your sinuses, or with the ancient crustacean itself set boiled and steaming before you, ready to be hand-wrestled for its claws and tail. I can't pass a lobster wharf on a sunny day. I have my lobsters plain. I feel that once a human being has outgrown a highchair, he's outgrown a bib, too; therefore, I eschew the bib and always end up with melted butter on my shirt. (One of Ken Brown's waitresses told me that after a few drinks people are always walking out into the night still wearing their lobster bibs, walking advertisements for the Brown's Wharf Restaurant.)

The Lobstermen's Co-Op, next door to Brown's, serves lobsters and steamed clams, with or without bibs, from 8:00 A.M. to 8:00 P.M., in full view of the harbor. I never had an 8:00 A.M. lobster, but those are the posted hours. The Lobsterman's Wharf in East Boothbay lets you linger over your lobster on the deck while you watch the tide come in over kelp-covered rocks.

But you need no directory to such places; you can follow your instincts. In Rockport or Ogunquit or Southwest Harbor or Deer Isle, or wherever lunchtime overtakes you, just go along the water to where you think a lobster wharf ought to be—and there it is.

You cannot escape lobsters in Maine. They are on the roadside signs, on the license plates, on the menus. The McDonald's in Brunswick offers a McLobster sandwich, which I caution against. In Bar Harbor, I saw lobster ice cream, but I can offer no judgment, because after giving lobster ice cream a moment of thought, I ordered Swiss Chocolate Almond.

I have heard that lobsters once were so common in Maine that people picked them up on the beaches by the basketful. They were fed mainly to people on the poor farms and prisoners in the town jails. Now, everywhere in the country, a Maine lobster is considered an extravagant indulgence. Even lobstermen are impressed by lobsters.

"If you think about it," Bud Brackett said, "nothing else in this world can endure like a lobster."

Mr. Brackett is a thoughtful man with a kind face, and not as young as he looks. He went lobstering as a stern man when he was eleven years old, in 1929. He still goes lobstering every morning.

"A lobster can go down to two hundred fathoms and survive," he said. "You can fly him in an unpressurized plane at sixteen or seventeen thousand feet, and he'll still survive. If you keep him cold, he can live out of water for days. The little ones float for nine days when they're young. You can see them covering the surface for miles before they sink to the bottom and start feeding. I don't know how long they live after that, but as long as we do, I guess. Lobsters were on this earth before human beings were, and they will still be here when human beings are all dead and gone, that's what I think."

I realize I am making these lobstermen sound voluble, which they can be on a subject they know as well as lobsters. But the laconic State-of-Mainer is no myth.

"Have you lived here all your life?"

"Not yet."

I deserved that one from Brud Pierce. It is a standard Maine reply, which he delivered with a satisfied twinkle in his eye, grateful for being fed the classic straight line. Newbert William Alfred Pierce started out fifty years ago selling hot dogs on the streets of Boothbay Harbor from a discarded baby carriage. He has a bright orange Cushman Truckster motor scooter now, and the only peddler's license in town. It was granted by the Town Meeting of March 1981, which passed Article 65, banning pushcarts except for Brud's. He also weeds gardens, runs errands, and handles the town's packing and shipping needs. He conducts the auctions at the annual Rotary Youth Fund benefit, and plays the spoons at the Thursday night concerts on the lawn of the library. I should have known better than to ask Brud Pierce if he has lived here all his life.

The whole drift of Maine humor, in fact, is toward succinct replies to dense questions from outsiders.

"How do you get to Bangor from here?"

"Usually my brother-in-law drives me."

Or:

"How many people work here at the cannery?"

"About half."

Or:

"Does it matter which road I take from here to Eastport?"

"Doesn't matter to me."

Tim Sample is the humorist laureate of Maine, inheritor of a tradition that comes down from Artemis Ward through Josh Billings and Holman Day and Marshall Dodge. Over coffee and cake in his living room in Bath, Tom told me some good yarns, nearly all of them about the triumph of the common man over the city slicker.

"It's like a secret handshake," Tim said. "Maine humor says 'We're us, and you're from away.' "

To wit:

One of the summer people asks the country storekeeper, "What did you give your horse when he had the heaves?"

"Kerosene."

They meet again a week later.

"What did you say you gave your horse when he had the heaves?"

"Kerosene."

"Well, I tried it, and my horse died!"

"So'd mine."

Or:

"Does your dog bite?" a stranger asks.

"Nevah," says the native from his rocking chair on the porch. So the stranger gets out of his car. The dog snarls, leaps at the stranger, and sinks his teeth into his leg.

"Hey! I thought you said your dog never bites!"

"He don't," the native says, still rocking. "That ain't my dog."

Even Ken Brown, a closet sophisticate, likes to play the Yankee bumpkin for strangers. He had a message on his answering machine—"Hello, can't come to the phone now, we're all down cellar shuckin' clams"—until his wife made him take it off.

One morning, I was having my third cup of coffee with Ken and Horace Lee, the retired town banker. A gleaming white multimillion-dollar yacht, *Daybreak*, was tied up at Ken's dock.

"What's she worth, Ken?" Horace asked.

Ken replied quick as a wink. "I know exactly what she's worth," he said. "We charge two dollars a foot for the night, and she's a 104-footer, so she's worth exactly two hundred and eight dollars. If the crew comes in here for breakfast, then she's worth a little more than that!"

Horace Lee, in his quiet way, is probably Boothbay Harbor's most useful citizen. He started his bank right after World War II with $25,000 of his own money. Eventually, he was able to lend Ken Brown the money to build his first motel rooms and lend Brud Pierce the money to buy his first hot dog wagon. Horace walks around with a pocketful of quarters as a favor to people parked at expired parking meters; he feeds the meter for them and leaves his business card on the windshield. No telling how many grateful depositors he may have picked up that way over the years.

Horace, who has a wave and a nod for everybody in town, became a reliable companion on my walks around the harbor. Knowing that I love boats, he took me to see a beauty, an impeccable locally built wooden yacht named *Yorel*, back from New York for a visit, and tied up near the Tugboat Inn on the harbor. We had a word with *Yorel*'s captain, who invited us aboard for a look around, but the deck was so clean I was afraid to walk on it with my dirty shoes. I don't know how many millions *Yorel* cost her owner; I'd have settled for owning the varnished twelve-foot dinghy which rested in blocks on deck, one of the prettiest small boats I've ever seen.

"How long do you suppose it took to build a boat like that?" I wondered aloud.

Horace said, "Let's go ask Sonny. He built it."

George "Sonny" Hodgdon is retired, he says. His son, Timmy, is now president of G. I. Hodgdon Company of East Boothbay. But I noticed Sonny was knee-deep in sawdust, inspecting the keel of a big power boat, when we arrived.

"*Yorel*?" he said. "Oh, yes, *Yorel* was a job, all right."

He searched through some papers in the office and handed me a construction log of Hodgdon-built vessels going back to 1818. There I read: "1984: *Yorel*,

85' power yacht, under construction." The entry for 1985 was the same, with the notation: "6,660 total man hours." These entries followed: "1986: *Yorel,* under construction, 36,642 man hours." "1987: Ditto. 55,438 man hours." "1988: Ditto. 74,234 man hours." Then came: "1989. September. Yacht *Yorel* left for Florida."

And that's how you build a wooden boat in Maine.

"Our family came to Hingham, Massachusetts, in 1630," Sonny Hodgdon said. "The Indians drove 'em out and they kept moving north along the coast. They started a sawmill on this spot—there's the grinding stone from the mill in my driveway. This town was called Hodgdon's Mills back then.

"Caleb was my great-grandfather, and the first boat builder. He built a pinky in 1818."

(I consulted the log. It had a long list of pinks and schooners from the new Hodgdon yard: *Lena Young, Silver Moon,* and *Venice* in 1818, *Union* in 1819 . . .)

"After Caleb, there was Caleb, Jr."

(1889, *Lillian Woodruff,* 332-ton schooner, a true behemoth, which must have been a sight to see . . .)

"Then George M., my father, and my uncles."

(*Bowdoin,* the schooner that carried Admiral Donald MacMillan on his trips to the Arctic, and dozens of other big schooners, cutters, sloops, and yawls from the drawing boards of the legendary designers Owen, Alden, Herreshoff and Hand.)

"Dad practically changed my diapers here at the boat works. I remember playing in the shavings after school until it was time to go home with him. I'd whittle little sailboats and race 'em across the Damariscotta River—watch 'em until they were out of sight and come back and carve a couple more."

Sonny is still whittling, if you can use such a prosaic word for the exquisite basswood half-models he has created. They are precise representations of the hulls of more than two hundred Hodgdon-built boats. One of them, in particular, caught my eye, the model of *Clione,* a pretty schooner.

"She was built here in 1904," Sonny said.

I asked, "Is she still afloat, by any chance?"

"Yep," he said. "She's the flagship of the Key West Historical Society."

I had seen the schooner *Clione* in Key West harbor six months before. I'd had no idea she was a Maine-built boat. I was touched by the coincidence that had brought me to the birthplace of a graceful ninety-year-old with whom I had a prior acquaintance.

"It says something for the way they built boats back then," Sonny Hodgdon said. As we walked back to the construction shed, with its fresh smell of Thai teak and Brazilian mahogany, I said it appeared to me he was still building them that way today.

"Well," he said, "I leave all the work to Timmy now, the cold-molding with vacuum pressure, building this hull up in eighth-inch layers. It will take two and a half years to finish this boat. She's going to be an eighty-foot twin-screw commuter with twin eleven-hundred horsepower diesels. You can't see the laminate under this planking, but it's beautiful work under there, stronger than steel, all built up by hand."

I asked Sonny Hodgdon, "What would your father say if he could walk in here today?"

He said, "He'd approve of the woodwork, I'm sure of that. He'd probably throw up his hands at all these glasses and glues and high-technology methods. I did, too, at first. But it results in a boat that's very, very strong and very, very light."

Looking through Sonny Hodgdon's construction files, I came across a letter the great old marine architect George Owen wrote in his eighty-eighth year about Sonny's father, "gentleman and master yacht builder," and the twenty-four Owen-designed sloops and schooners that were launched at the Hodgdon yard between 1907 and 1929. It said "each and every yacht was built of the best materials obtainable in the best markets, and fabricated with the very best skill known then and now."

It occurred to me, on the way out, that from what I had seen, Professor

Owen's words could be carved over the door of Hodgdon's all these years later.

As we parted, Sonny Hodgdon said, "Of course, there's one other thing you have to learn if you run a shipyard: The owner always defeats you in the end. His wife puts a grand piano and every other damn thing in the boat you've spent years building light and fast. Nothing you can do about that."

Surpassing craftsmanship—doing it exactly right, no matter how long it takes—has always been high on my list of human virtues. I am awed by cathedral stone carvers and master gardeners and weavers of tapestries—and by boat builders who build up an eighty-foot hull in eighth-inch increments by hand. If I could have afforded it, I'd have commissioned a wooden boat from the Hodgdon yard right then and there. I went down and looked at *Yorel* again and felt sorry for myself for not having such a boat—for not having any boat at all. In Boothbay Harbor in August, it's easy to get the impression that everybody in the world has a boat but you.

I had supper with Mary Lou Teel and her husband, Peter Freundlich, old friends from the *Sunday Morning* program who have a summer house nearby; all they wanted to talk about was the fun they were having poking around their cove in their vintage skiff.

Ken Brown wanted to show off the diesel double-ender he'd just restored, so he and his son Tim took Bob Mitchell and me to lunch at Robinson's Wharf on Southport Island. It was a beautiful day, and on the way home, Ken suggested I take the tiller for a while. His boat steered like a dream, and I caught myself wondering why such a pretty little thing should be his and not mine.

As I was woolgathering in this fashion, mooning about the unfairness of life, I looked up and saw Walter Cronkite's majestic center-cockpit sailboat, *Wintje,* entering the harbor. I know that boat at a glance. I've sailed aboard it. If, to a boatless soul, life in somebody else's harbor runabout seems unfair, a glimpse of Cronkite's shining, state-of-the-art super-yacht is quite unbearable. I gave the great man a shout anyway, ran alongside, and pretended to be pleased instead of merely jealous when he invited Ken and me to come aboard and inspect his stately staterooms, and his hot tub-equipped head, and his steering station inspired by the cockpit of a Boeing 747. I love and honor Walter Cronkite and his wife, Betsy, and it was good to see their daughter and grandson out for a cruise with them. But the life I was pining for that day—voyaging to all the distant ports in a proud and seaworthy craft—is the life Cronkite actually lives. I declined his invitation to sail along to Northeast Harbor, knowing that it was a ninety-mile trip and that it would have involved a serious breach of the Tenth Commandment. I'd have been coveting all the way.

I actually considered driving up to Bass Harbor, walking into Hinckley Yacht Charters, plunking down a few thousand dollars for a week or two in a forty-two-footer, and setting sail with my crew. But I didn't have a crew. I didn't have a few thousand dollars, either. Maybe, I thought, some other time.

I didn't get over my boat dream the whole time I was in Maine. I'm not over it yet. I am drawn to shipyards and anchorages wherever I go. If there's a bit of a breeze, the sound of a halyard slapping a mast arouses a great yearning in me.

In the perfect harbor of South Brooksville one late afternoon, no less than eleven of the passenger-carrying windjammers of Maine sailed in for a rendezvous. There was the last of the three-masted schooners, *Victory Chimes,* a survivor of the days when Maine bought its groceries in the West Indies and sent to China for afternoon tea. Anchored nearby was the pilot schooner *Timberwind,* which was launched in Portland in 1931 and has never left Maine waters; if you are born in heaven, her captain once said, why go anywhere else? There was the *J. & E. Riggin,* an eighty-nine-foot oyster-dredging schooner dating to 1927; and *American Eagle,* a gorgeous ninety-two-foot fishing schooner from the 1930s; and the oldest documented American sailing vessel in continuous use, the *Stephen Taber,* launched in 1871; and there were all the others, a magnificent show. These boats are captained by happy men and women who cannot imagine what else they'd rather do with their lives. I understand them. The passengers, most of them, return year after year for the sweet passages through the coves and islands, the quiet nights at anchor, the sea chantey concerts on deck, the lobster bakes ashore. I understand them, too.

I went out to *Nathaniel Bowditch,* an eighty-two-foot topsail schooner which left the fleet in her wake in the Bermuda Race of 1923. Her captain, Gib Philbrick, is a wonderful man whose enthusiasm for what he does is written all over his face. Gib was once a fishing guide in the Rangeley Lakes. He was the basketball coach at the University of Maine. All the time, he wanted to be a schooner captain. He and his wife, Terry, took a deep breath and bought *Nathaniel Bowditch* twenty years ago.

"If a schooner owns you," he said, "it owns you all year round. In the late fall, we go over every line and block, we have new sails made if we can afford it, we care for every tiny thing. We keep her in the water where she belongs, and throw salt water on her deck every day to keep the seams tight. In the winter when I'm feeling edgy, I come down and sit aboard.

"And then—oh, man—then comes the spring!"

Among passengers and crew members on the docks in Rockland, which most of the windjammers call home, *Nathaniel Bowditch* has a reputation as a happy ship.

"Well, we have a good crew," Gib Philbrick said. "The problem is finding a good cook. I always hope one good cook will help train another, so I keep two crew members in the galley and two on deck helping me. We take about two dozen passengers on one-week sails.

"And they love it! Really, they do. I've had 'em hugging and crying when it's time to leave. I've had to shoo 'em off so we could take care of the garbage and laundry.

"See, on the Penobscot Bay, you have deep water and no ocean swell. It's a forgiving place for a sailor and a smooth ride for the passengers. I have enough Dramamine down below to anesthetize the whole state of Maine, but I never have to give it out."

Gib Philbrick looked around at the pretty harbor. The sun was going down behind steep hills.

"These islands are the tops of mountains," he said. "I never get tired of looking at them."

Then he made a remark to me that he must have made to others dozens of times. That doesn't take away from the plain truth of it. He was speaking for generations of Maine seafarers.

"They say the Gulf of Maine is one of the two greatest sailing grounds in the world," he said.

"I don't doubt it," I said. "What's the other one?"

Gib Philbrick smiled.

He said, "I haven't found that one yet."

Twin Bridges, Montana

I fell in love with Montana at first sight. I was young and all the world was beautiful to me, but Montana was a great splendor. The steep, snow-clad ranges caught my eye at first, and they are wonderful to see, but over time, my affection came to be for the welcoming valleys. And not for the valleys, exactly, but for the rivers that run through the valleys. And not for the fastest or deepest rivers, but for the smaller ones that would support a floating dry fly.

But in Montana, though you have come to fish, you walk through fields of flowers to reach the stream and get distracted by the wild roses and showy daisies and blue iris. (You learn that only one iris grows in these valleys, and that it grows only where the groundwater is close to the surface. The early stockmen dug watering ponds for their cattle wherever they found the wild iris blooming.)

And when you finally get to the river, you see the work of the beavers and share the place with muskrats and with mink. You think you're there to fish, but pretty soon you're there to see the blue heron in the shallows in the morning and glimpse the gray owl gliding noiselessly overhead at dusk and hear the coyote in the night.

I saw my first ring-necked pheasant flush from the tall grass of Montana and saw my first trumpeter swans riding the current of the Yellowstone. I had never seen wild horses until I beheld a herd of them, manes flying, galloping through a canyon in the Pryor Mountains. I saw my first antelope-covered hillside in Montana and heard my first elk bugling. I met my first grizzly bear on a trail beside the North Fork of the Flathead River. These were all startling and wonderful experiences, and I can't get them out of my head. Every time I have to leave Montana, in my dreams far away to the east, I see a golden eagle riding the thermals.

Montana clutters the mind with odd and unrelated bits of geology and paleontology. I have found huge wild rock crystals in the Big Hole Valley, produced seventy million years ago when white-hot volcanic granite rained down on the limestone hills. In Bozeman's wonderful Museum of the Rockies, I have seen petrified Montana dinosaur eggs, with petrified baby dinosaurs peeking out.

And the human history is no less spectacular. Hunters and warriors knew this land ten thousand years ago. These mountains looked down upon heroic figures, Sacagawea and Cameahwait and the great Chief Joseph and Crazy Horse and Sitting Bull. And in the parade of white explorers and settlers came some of the most astonishing characters in all the gaudy history of America, like Jim Bridger and John Bozeman and Charlie Russell and Calamity Jane, among the anonymous trappers and miners, trail blazers, homesteaders, school marms, cattle rustlers, claim jumpers, dance hall queens and flimflam men. These mountains have seen much bravery, much generosity, much cruelty and cowardice and greed—in short, much humanity.

Some of the stories are almost superhuman. Hugh Glass, the mountain man, was skinned and crippled by a grizzly bear. After days of carrying him on a litter, his companions gave up on him, took his bedroll, knife, and gun, and left him to die in a patch of gooseberries. He couldn't walk or speak—the bear had broken his legs and torn up his throat—but he could reach the berries. Day after day, that sour fruit kept him alive. After a few weeks, he was able to crawl. He crawled and limped two hundred miles to a trading post and eventually got well enough to go looking for his knife and gun. I never see a clump of gooseberries without thinking of Hugh Glass.

Even more harrowing was the adventure of Glass's friend, John Colter, taken with another trapper by a Blackfoot war party on the Jefferson River. Colter's partner was killed and dismembered on the spot. With Colter, the Indians thought they'd have a little sport. He was stripped naked and told to run for his life. This he did, in an astounding footrace across the rocky bottomland with the Indians pursuing, until flecks of blood started flying from his nostrils. He ran all the way to the Madison River, where he dived underwater and hid until dark in a beaver house. During the next two weeks, still naked, he crossed the snow-covered Absaroka Mountains to the Yellowstone River and traveled down the river to Manuel Lisa's fort on the Missouri. He knew nearly every man there. At first, not one of them recognized the naked, bloody, frozen scarecrow who showed up at the gate.

John Colter lived on to describe the geysers of the West to the good citizens of St. Louis, who ridiculed him for trying to peddle such a fantasy as truth. "Colter's Hell," they called it. We call it Yellowstone National Park.

The durable Colter had been among the forty-five men and one woman who crossed into Montana in late April 1805, following the Missouri River west. The little expedition, headed by two Virginians, trusted young friends of the Virginia President, Thomas Jefferson, proved to be the greatest American adventure of all. They say school children are bored by history. I wish they could experience the vastness of Montana as Lewis and Clark did. They could; the place hasn't changed so much. The trails are still there, and some of the very campgrounds. I would take the bored kids camping, not let them know what dangers might lie ahead next day or how far they still had to go, let them lie there on the ground listening to the sounds of the night.

In Montana, the captains reached the Three Forks of the Missouri, and named the rivers Jefferson, for the President; Madison, for the Secretary of State; and Gallatin, for the Secretary of the Treasury. ("You went pretty far west," the President observed wryly, "before you found a stream to name for me!") They followed Jefferson's river until it, too, divided into three tributaries. These, they called Wisdom, Philosophy, and Philanthropy, for the President's virtues. (Too many syllables, said the fur traders who came later. They renamed those three rivers Big Hole, Beaverhead, and Ruby. But if you ever pass through the little ranch town of Wisdom, Montana, on the Big Hole, remember it was Thomas Jefferson's wisdom that was meant by those who named it.)

Lewis and Clark deserve a Homer to tell of their Odyssey, one of the most heroic and successful treks in all of human history. They may have one someday, as their trip through the Rockies, hard reality in the pages of their maps and diaries, fades into legend in the mists of time.

The place where the Ruby, Beaverhead, and Big Hole give birth to the Jefferson, the place where Lewis and Clark paused to scout out the likeliest of these rivers to follow west, is now a little community called Twin Bridges. It's where I bought my groceries in September.

September is the perfect time to be there. The sun is slipping away to the south, lengthening the shadows of the haystacks in the fields. The green land is turning golden. Migrating birds are on the wing. The big brown trout are swimming up into the little side streams to spawn. It is time for the county fairs and the rodeos. It is time to start getting the firewood in.

This is not glamorous Montana, where the celebrities are buying up big ranches. That's off to the east, that's Bozeman and Livingston and the Paradise Valley upriver on the Yellowstone (in Montana, upriver almost always means down south) or away up near the Canadian border around Kalispell and Flathead Lake. This is working Montana, and there was a working man I wanted to spend some time with.

Delmar Rowe is a cowboy of the old school, quiet and self-assured. He knows the name and habits of everything that grows or creeps or walks or flies around here. From constant practice, his muscles remember the best way to do everything—walk a horse, mend a gate, brand a calf—so he does it all with economical grace, no wasted motion. His speech is the same, no extra words. We have been friends for many years, and all that time, Delmar would do anything for me, except talk to me for very long at a time. He is a doer, not a talker.

He and his wife, Beverly, are the only full-time employees of a good-sized ranch in the Big Hole River valley, up the river from a log cabin where I try to hide out in September to go fishing. I knew I could find out from them a lot more than I already knew about cowboying and ranch life, if only I could get Delmar to say more than one sentence at a time. This September, as it happened, the hay crop was sparse after a dry summer, and Delmar finished the haying early. So for a couple of late afternoons there, he and Beverly had time to sit on my porch with me and talk. This is the last romantic figure of American history talking, the cowboy, the real thing:

"I moved to Montana from Blackfoot, Idaho, in 1941, when I was five years old. My dad leased a ranch on the Blacktail Creek out of Dillon, and that was when I started riding horses.

"After school, I worked for a contractor in Dillon one year, but I didn't like it. So I got a job on a ranch in the Horse Prairie. I went into the army for two years, and came out, and Bev and me got married.

"We got married in Fifty-nine and spent that summer in a cow camp. It was on Thayer Creek in the Big Hole. I was twenty-three years old, taking care of two thousand, five hundred cattle for a hundred and fifty dollars a month. And we had an eighty-five-dollar car payment. And we couldn't even get the car up to the cow camp, had to park it and walk in. Right where we parked it, a moose cow was raising her calf there all summer, so we kind of had to watch out when we started walking. And we thought all this was fine!

"We have worked hard ever since, I guess you'd say. There's no end to irrigating the pastures and fencing the haystacks. But it's outdoors, out of the city, a good place to raise kids. Beverly helps me with everything. Most ranch wives work hard."

Beverly Rowe said, "Some of them do *all* the work, while their husbands sit in the bars."

"Well," Delmar said, "with any ranch job, you don't know from one morning to the next whether you'll be working, so we feel real lucky to have been here twenty-five years. I don't know where the next generation of ranch workers is going to come from, though. Our kids, Delmar and Phyllis, tried working at the ranch, but they saw it was nine o'clock at night and they were still working, so they found something else to do. Young people are not interested in this kind of work."

What I thought was that young people don't know how to do it, and haven't the patience to learn. I watched Delmar build a rail fence one time. Years later, the posts are absolutely immovable and the rails are precisely locked. It is a fence to last a hundred years. It is the accomplishment of a man who never says he is proud of his work, but is.

I fixed Delmar a cup of black coffee—he rarely takes anything stronger—and asked him to take me through his year.

"Well," he said, "in January, you're busy feeding hay, hay you harvested in the summer and hay you've had to buy if you didn't harvest enough. The calving starts about the twenty-fifth of January. You run the cattle up near the corral with your saddle horse and run the heaviest ones on into the corral.

"When you're calving, you hire an extra man to look at the cattle at night. I tell him come wake me up if anything goes wrong, and most nights, I get woke up. One time, the guy said he had a water-belly—that's a cow with a stone who can't urinate—and she was real heavy, and he thought she was going to have trouble delivering her calf. I went out to the corral in the middle of the night, and that cow he was worried about was a steer! And this guy was supposed to be good.

"Anyway, the calves start coming pretty fast. If it's real cold, you pick the calf up and carry him into the heat room. That's a stall covered with plastic. Some ranches use a stove in there. We use heat lamps. You warm him up good and then put him back with his mother.

"If a cow is having trouble with the delivery, you tie her to a post and pull the calf out. If it's real big trouble, you call the vet.

"After you have about a hundred calves—that's about the fifteenth of February—you do your first branding, and move those cows and calves out of the way. And then when you have another hundred, you have another branding, and so on.

"The worst year was the winter of Eighty-eight. It was arctic cold. We had forty-one below zero and a forty-mile-an-hour wind. Most times, when it gets that cold, it's still, but that year, the wind blew. That's what made it so bad. We were branding calves who had their tails froze off, and part of their ears. And then the diesel fuel turned to jelly and none of the machinery would run, so we had to go out and feed the cattle with a pitchfork. You'd look at the other guy and see a white spot growing on his cheek and think, there's probably a white spot on my cheek, too. It's a wonder we didn't lose our own tails and ears that winter. A rancher just over the mountains here had his cattle covered up by the snow in a fence corner and lost the whole herd. Then that summer turned to drought. . . ."

Delmar took a swallow of coffee and looked out over the ranch. I imagined he was thinking about all the things that could go wrong.

He said, "The calves don't get sick all at once, but they all get sick. They get the scours, diphtheria, pneumonia. So you're doctoring while you're calving. You give 'em sulfa pills and injections, antibiotics, penicillin. . . .

"In April, you brush the pasture with a brusher to break up the manure and clean the ditches, and then on the fifteenth of April, you turn the bulls in with the cows. Most ranchers let the bulls and cows stay together sixty days until the middle of June. That way, you know calving will only last sixty days. But Delbrook—Delbrook is the owner, and another old friend of mine—likes the little calves, too, the ones that come late, so we leave the bulls and cows together all summer.

"About the first of May, you open the gates to let the river water onto the pastures, and go to fertilizing. Fertilizing is a big expense, but it about pays for itself in hay. Through May, you're busy moving the dams, those yellow plastic things, to flood the fields the way you want.

"Around the first of June, it's time to stop feeding and get the cattle off the meadows and out to pasture on the hills. The wild grass has grown enough by then. Every day you don't have to feed cattle on the ranch is a day that you know you're probably not losing money, even if you're not making any.

"The first of July, the Forest Service permit clicks in, and you move the cattle to the forest until the first of October. We start haying in the middle of July and go for six weeks, and then spend September putting up hay. Operations with irrigation rigs usually grow alfalfa, and they'll get two hay crops a month apart, but by flood-irrigating the native grass, we only get one crop. There wasn't hardly any hay this year. That's why there's no haystacks on the ranch. The cattle have already ate it all.

"While the cattle are on the forest permit, we hire a rider to take care of them by himself. His job is to keep the fences up, keep the salt to the cattle, make sure they don't get on poison—larkspur or lupine—and doctor them when they need it. They get hoof rot, they get heart disease from the altitude. The rider is supposed to let me know when anything goes wrong, so I spend a lot of time going back and forth to the forest.

"It's hard to get a guy who will run a good cow camp all summer. He's in a little cabin up there with no electricity or plumbing, and it's a demanding job. Last year, we had the guy just shut the place down one night and go to town and get drunk. You can't hardly blame him, but you can't excuse him, either.

"Down here at the ranch, I spend the summer mending fences and getting the machinery ready. Whenever the cattle have to be moved, I ride a horse, but the rest of the time, I ride a pickup or a mowing machine. Machinery and fences have made all the difference. In the old days, the cows calved all year long, and if there was a storm, the cows would go with the storm across the range. There was nothing to stop 'em. You'd have to get on your horse and go find 'em all the time. Ranching today isn't exactly convenient, but it's more convenient than it used to be.

"In mid-October, depending on the weather, that's when the cows come home. Then you're on horseback, cutting out the strays, cutting out the dry cows, vaccinating.

"About the first of December, it's time to wean the calves. You cut 'em out and feed 'em in the corral or a feed lot—we have our own feed lot—until the first of February. We don't normally take our calves to auction. You have to pay thirteen dollars a head to sell them at auction, and pay a Beef Council fee and a brand inspection fee and so on, so we have a buyer come to the ranch. You're only going to get what the market brings, anyway. By this time, your calves weigh between five hundred and six hundred pounds. Right now, a five-hundred-pound calf brings eighty cents, right at four hundred dollars. Profit? No, there's not much profit. Ranchers don't ever want to show a profit, anyway, and it's real easy to show a loss."

Delmar stopped talking. He figured he had gone through the whole year and the story was over. I asked him if he'd ever been hurt on the job.

"No," he said, "I've never been seriously hurt."

"You got knocked out that time," Beverly said.

"Yeah," Delmar said. "We was pulling calves and we had a cow tied to a fence post and she banged into an open gate, and I was inside. The gate hit me across the face. It didn't break anything, but it did knock me out. I've had neck pain ever since."

I asked him what the doctor said about it.

"I didn't go to the doctor," Delmar said.

"He doesn't go to the doctor," Beverly said.

I once saw an unusual sight on the ranch, a moose with twin calves wading across the river. I asked about wildlife.

"Well," Delmar said, "as you know, moose on the place are always on their way somewhere else. We've had elk come through the other end of the ranch. One time a huge herd of mountain sheep came down in a real cold winter and stayed for a while. You see turkeys and pheasants and deer every day. We have geese all the time. There are the cranes and water birds in the summer, of course. I don't know how many kinds of ducks, a lot of 'em year-round. And the small animals and songbirds. You hear the coyotes at night."

"Do the coyotes do any damage?" I asked.

"They did damage when we had sheep," he said, "but I've never known them to kill a calf. They clean up the grounds after the calving. You can see them circling around the calving shed. I don't mind them."

I asked the two of them what they did on vacation.

"We never take a vacation," Delmar said.

"We did drive to Alaska that one time," Beverly said. "But Delbrook is away a lot, and he wants somebody on the ranch every night. We used to go for a ride with the kids on Sunday afternoon, just ride around and look at the country. Or go berry-picking. We have gooseberries on the ranch [the fruit that saved Hugh Glass's life]. There's a big bunch of chokecherry bushes on your place right up-river here. You just have to be there when they're ripe in August to keep the birds away from them. They make good jam and syrup. Everybody in the country used to make rose-hips jelly, but not so much any more."

"We haven't been to a movie in twenty years," Delmar said. "We fish a little. We love to fish. And I usually get one deer in the fall, but I haven't even done that for a couple of years now. And Beverly raises her flowers. . . ."

Delmar stopped right there and got up. He said, "Thanks for the coffee, Charles. Got a few things to do before dark." And the two of them were gone.

If you are looking for the true Montanans, you don't have to look any farther than Beverly and Delmar Rowe. They aren't rich, and don't expect to be. They have not lived their lives with an eye toward comfort and a pension at the end. What they have, I would guess, is worth more to them than money in the bank—the beauty of the land and the continuity of the seasons and the satisfaction that comes from doing a job that fewer and fewer human beings know how to do, and doing it as well as it can be done. Delmar found out when he was young that Dillon, Montana, population four thousand, was too big a city for him, and that a cow camp on Thayer Creek was just fine. He had the good sense to act on this discovery. Millions of people in this country doing work they hate can envy him.

Ranchers, however, are not as independent as they'd like to think they are. They are dependent on government subsidies—the Forest Service grazing permits, which ranchers regard as a birthright, are a plain giveaway—and they are dependent on the water in the rivers, which ought to belong equally to trout and trout fishermen, and they are dependent on city people to provide a market for their beef. The prices Delmar mentioned in September declined about 40 percent before the calves he was tending went to market.

But I find myself pulling for the big ranches to survive, subsidies and all. The alternative is too terrible to think about: subdivisions—time-shares and condos and twenty-acre "ranchettes"—spoiling every river valley in the state. That's what will happen if the ranchers give up and the land goes to the highest bidder.

I know some good people who are trying to prevent it. Dick Oswald, the Fish and Wildlife biologist in Dillon, is working to keep the water coming to the ranches, while trying to persuade the ranchers to leave enough in drought years for the fish. The ranchers, by way of ancient water rights, hold all the cards. But when Dick Oswald calls a meeting, they come and listen, at least. Ranchers reflexively rage against environmentalists, but the best of them *are* environmentalists, in fact, stewards of the land. You can't run a good ranch any other way.

I went to Helena to see Brian Kahn, head of the Montana Nature Conservancy. He is a forty-seven-year-old lawyer and linguist who looks fifteen years younger, a former documentary filmmaker, former boxing coach, former ranch hand, former politician, and maybe the brightest Montanan.

"My attitude toward ranchers is, first of all, to find a way to keep them in business," he said. "That preserves the wildlife right there. Eighty percent of

Forest fire on the Cheyenne Reservation

Left: Glenn Brackett
Above: Delmar Rowe

Above: Last Chance Gulch, Helena
Right: Bannack

Clint, Ruth, and Wallace McRae

Montana's birds, for example, migrate along the rivers. So when you keep the rivers out of the hands of the developers, you're doing more than preserving the landscape.

"To save these timberlands and grasslands and river corridors is worth everything we can do. In spite of the lunatic fringe, the militias and the Klan, you'll find that 99 percent of the people here are good people. They are civil and they are practical and they value the riches around them and they'll hear you out. What the Nature Conservancy says to the old Montanans is, 'We offer you a way to keep the land, to have the state you want.' To 'offer' is different from saying we have all the answers.

"What we have to offer is conservation easements. We can buy them, or Fish and Wildlife can buy them, or the Montana Land Reliance can. And if we don't have the money, we can work it out so the ranchers get the saving in taxes. They keep their ranches and stay on the land, the ranches don't get subdivided, and the public gets a heck of a bargain—the beauty and wildlife intact."

The Nature Conservancy is growing. There are five thousand members in Montana. May their tribe increase.

Montana is an empire, and imperialists from afar have always been after its resources. Right now, a Canadian gold mining company is planning to rip apart a mountain on the border of Yellowstone Park and leave behind a pool of toxic waste that is almost certain to destroy, eventually, the pure trout streams below. That corporation's executives would say, if asked, "What do you want to do, just leave all that gold in the ground?" To which the only sensible answer is, "Yes."

The first gold miners came and went a century ago. Bannack, the first territorial capital, attracted three thousand of them in a single year. Bannack is still there, with the wind blowing through the houses and sagebrush growing in the streets. It is inhabited by not a single soul. There's nothing to be seen of the gold rush except the old buildings of the ghost towns and a dredged-out moonscape in Alder Gulch.

The copper kings excavated Butte and left the city with nothing but a gigantic hole in the ground. The timber barons logged the richest forests and pulled out. Now the Californians are buying the most beautiful ranches. "Californians" is an expletive, the generic swear word for rich outsiders who wear sun glasses and drive Range Rovers, and spend their winters someplace else.

In the plains of eastern Montana, the Big Open, it's coal the exploiters are after. Huge machines are stripping it out of the land. Wallace McRae, rancher and poet, described the effect on life in "Things of Intrinsic Worth":

> Remember that sandrock on Emmells Crick
> Where Dad carved his name in 'thirteen?
> It's been blasted down into rubble
> And interred by their dragline machine.
> Where Fadhls lived, at the old Milar Place,
> Where us kids stole melons at night?
> They 'dozed it up in a funeral pyre,
> Then torched it. It's gone all right.
> The "C" on the hill, and the water tanks
> Are now classified, "reclaimed land."
> They're thinking of building a golf course
> Out there, so I understand.
> The old Egan Homestead's an ash pond
> That they say is eighty feet deep.
> The branding corral at the Douglas Camp
> Is underneath a spoil heap.
> And across the crick is a tipple, now,
> Where they load coal onto a train.
> The Mae West Rock on Hay Coulee?
> Just black and white snapshots remain.
> There's a railroad loop and a coal storage shed
> Where the bison kill site used to be.

The Guy Place is gone; Ambrose's too.
Beulah Farley's a ranch refugee.

But things are booming. We've got this new school
That's envied across the whole state.
When folks up and ask, "How's things goin' down there?"
I grin like a fool and say, "Great!"
Great God, how we're doin'! We're rollin' in dough,
As they tear and they ravage the Earth.
And nobody knows . . . or nobody cares . . .
About things of intrinsic worth.

Wally McRae, the best of the cowboy poets, lives on the rolling plains near the inelegantly named community of Colstrip. He came out into his yard and gave me a bear hug, as if he'd known me all his life. He's a big, broad-shouldered man of about my age, with a handsome moustache and the wrinkled eyes of an outdoorsman. His ranch is the Rocker Six on Rosebud Creek. Wally's grandfather, John B. McRae, came to Montana in 1882 and started ranching here just ten years after Custer followed the creek to his destruction fifty miles south and west at the Little Big Horn.

Wally put me in his blue pickup truck and gave me a tour of Colstrip. He showed me the golf course of the poem—they did build it—and the school "that's envied across the whole state," a thirteen-million-dollar high school with a theater and a swimming pool. Colstrip is a company town which benefits hugely from the taxes the coal-strippers pay. The neat community is dominated by a gigantic power plant.

Wally said, "They built it out here far enough off the Interstate so nobody could see the big stacks. They strip the coal, turn it into megawatts here, and pipe the electricity to Southern California. What they don't burn, they ship east. Here's a coal train loading. You can tell from the code on the hoppers where this coal is going, to Wisconsin Power. This all got reopened during the energy crisis in the Seventies. The power consortium sold the country a bill of goods. The operation is not profitable yet. Here's a coal-dryer they just built. They're burning natural gas to dry the coal, can you imagine that?"

I said the stripped-over land didn't look anywhere near as bad as I'd feared from his poem, nor as bad as the strip-mined ridges in the Kentucky coal country.

"We fought 'em in Helena and Washington," Wally said. "We wanted this land restored, and they've done a good job of it. But do you think that's because of the natural benevolence and public-spiritedness of the companies? Hell, no! It's because when they laughed in our faces, we went to Helena and got a 30 percent severance tax slapped on them! *Then* they were willing to negotiate. The tax is down to half that, I suppose. So they do restore the land and plant grass, but they've still messed up the water."

Wally is obviously proud of Colstrip. He has given poetry readings in the high school theater and played roles in community plays. But all of Colstrip is not proud of him. After "Things of Intrinsic Worth" came out, he said, and he helped lead the land reclamation campaign, a woman went into the community bookstore.

She said, "I see you have books by Wallace McRae."

"Why, yes," the proprietor answered.

"Well," the woman said, "I'll never do any business here again," and walked out.

Why?

"Oh," Wally said, "she probably thought I was going to lose her husband his job."

That's the Montana dilemma right there—how to guarantee the matchless beauty of the place forever without costing working people their jobs. The stubborn optimists like Wally McRae think it can be done.

Ruth McRae prepared us a good lunch of roast beef and mashed potatoes, with her own plum preserves to go with the store-bought rolls. She was a Pennsylvanian who met Wally when he was back East, serving as an officer in the Navy. It must have taken a leap of faith for her to come out to the unfamiliar plains of Montana. I meant to ask her if she'd ever read *A Bride Goes West,* Nannie Alderson's published diary of her trip from South Carolina to a ranch right here on Rosebud Creek a couple of generations before—to a house with a dirt roof and a dirt floor, one door and one window, and a privy out back that was roofless and open to the sky. Mrs. Alderson survived the new life in good spirits, as countless other ranch wives have managed to do, Ruth McRae obviously among them.

Just then, Ruth and Wally's son, Clint, arrived from his house a mile up the creek, to join us at the table. Clint is a fine pen-and-ink artist, and illustrator of his father's books. He's also his father's partner in the ranch. "We never hire anybody," Wally said, with what I thought was a little pride. "During branding time in the spring and gathering time in the fall, or whenever we need help, several ranches cooperate. They come to our place, and we go to theirs. Except for that, Clint and I do the work ourselves."

After lunch, I asked Wally McRae how it happened that a third-generation rancher became a poet.

"I liked poems when I was a kid," he said. "Bruce Kiskaddon's poems used to come in the livestock paper. My sister, Marjorie, would clip some of them with pinking shears to make them look pretty, and hang them on the wall with a blue hair ribbon. That's probably how it started. Then somewhere, I heard, 'Write about what you know.' What I knew was the ranch."

His cowboy poems, some of them, are well on their way to becoming classics that will be recited at Western poetry gatherings a century from now. This makes a pretty good argument for writing about what you know.

"A hell of a lot of kids today don't know about anything," Wally said. "They live a homogenized life, and their only experience is the TV. We don't even have TV. Well, there is one downstairs, but nothing comes in on it. We use it to look at tapes sometimes."

Soon after leaving Billings early that morning, I'd seen a column of smoke on the horizon. This turned out to be a forest fire on the Northern Cheyenne Reservation nearly a hundred miles ahead. The road east to Lame Deer took me right past it, a big, ugly blaze out of control and growing. The wind was blowing the smoke toward Wally's place, and when we went outside, we found pine bark cinders falling out of the sky.

"It's boiling up again," Wally said. "I thought they had it there a little while ago, but it has got away from them. It's been an awful dry year. Last year this time, we'd had seventeen inches of rain, and six so far this year. We probably ought to be down there fighting the fire ourselves. One of the first signs of the dissolution of a community is when they form a volunteer fire department. Hell, if there's a fire, *everybody* ought to be fighting it."

That was an expression of the neighborliness that goes way back in the sparsely settled parts of Montana. Wally had said to me, "From this ranch to Jimtown [a saloon just outside the Reservation boundary], there's only one family that hasn't been here a hundred years. I gave a graduation talk to the eighth-grade graduating class in Birney—now there's a Brigadoon, Birney. There were five in the class, one of them Indian, and all their families have been here a hundred years or more."

He looked off down the road in the general direction of Jimtown and Birney.

"So that's the sort of land this is," he said.

It is a fine land. It might have been a little luckier land if it had not been so rich in copper and coal and gold and silver. I spent that night in Billings, listening to the trains rolling through town. The train horns moaned for the crossing every half hour, and I could hear the cars rumbling along behind—coal cars, ore hoppers, tank cars, cattle cars—carrying the wealth of Montana away.

It would be a luckier land if it had more rainfall, too. The fire on the Cheyenne Reservation was the big page-one story in the *Billings Gazette* the next morning. It wasn't the only forest fire burning in the state, but it was the biggest.

It had grown to forty-eight thousand acres, with three hundred professional fire-fighters trying to stop it. They said they needed rain, but there was none in the forecast.

I took some back roads I'd never been on before, from Big Timber up to Twodot on the Musselshell River and then down the west side of the Crazy Mountains. At every cafe and gas station, they were talking about the drought and the fires. The other big topic of conversation was the spotted knapweed. At a convenience store in White Sulphur Springs, a man was shaking his head over the spread of knapweed, blaming it on the telephone and power company crews. There were anti-knapweed billboards and radio campaigns. In Livingston, high school students were giving free Saturday morning car washes, with special attention to the undercarriages of cars and trucks, to prevent the knapweed from spreading that way. It's a perennial thistle that seems to have come from Europe and the eastern states, but it has found a home on the range. Once established, knapweed is very hard to get rid of. It spreads underground, and if you ignore it, it will take over your pasture in no time. Delmar Rowe told me once that even after you've eradicated it, grass is slow to grow on the spot because of something—maybe an alkali—that the knapweed imparts to the soil. People everywhere in the world have something to wake up in the night worrying about. Here, sleeplessness is caused by Californians, drought, and spotted knapweed.

I covered a lot of miles over the next few days, wandering almost aimlessly over the gorgeous contours of Montana. I stopped near Greycliff Creek on a cool morning to visit a prairie dog town. The animals were touching noses, grooming one another, helping out with their neighbors' burrow-building—the prairie-dog equivalent of the old pioneer barn-raisings—and comporting themselves, in general, very sociably and cooperatively. Prairie-dog experts may know of flaws in prairie-dog character, but I never have observed any. Because the animals eat precious grass and dig holes in the range, ranchers have spent a lot of time shooting them or trying to poison them off. But I would say that prairie dogs, by prairie-dog nature, behave better than most human beings do by human nature.

I went to the rodeo parade in Dillon, a very appealing affair with Boy Scouts carrying the flags, the kids from the high school gymnastics club doing backflips on a moving flatbed truck, spangled cowgirls on horseback, and a column of brand-new, bright green John Deere tractors, including one with air-conditioning, FM radio, and what must have been a ten-thousand-dollar-picture window windshield. What would my grandfather, the North Carolina one who plowed with a mule, have made of that thing? And who in this crowd could afford it?

As always in a good-sized Western crowd, there were a few young cowboy drunks. One of them, plenty good-natured, recognized me from television and latched onto me on the street. "Charles," he said, "I'll be damned, it's shore good to meet you." His eyes were bleary at ten o'clock in the morning, and his breath made me take a little step back. "Charles, I'll be damned." He kept pumping my hand, and I didn't know what to do except keep smiling and tell him how glad I was to make his acquaintance, too. I finally got away from him, but an hour or two later, I had to look for a bathroom. I went into a bar—and there he was, of course. "Charles, I'll be damned," he said, reeling across the room to shake my hand again. But he never quite made it. Halfway to me, his boots got tangled up, and with a little smile, he went down like a big tree falling in the forest. One of his friends got up from the bar, picked up his buddy's cowboy hat to keep it from getting stepped on, and went back to his own drinking, with his partner out cold on the floor.

While I was in Dillon, I bought an ice cooler and some picnic supplies, marveling at the size of the weekend crowd in the supermarket. These days, people from even the most remote ranches do their provisioning at the Safeway, like everybody else. (Old cowboy verse on the wonders of evaporated milk: "No tits to pull, no hay to pitch; just punch a hole in the son of a bitch!")

With my food supply on ice in the Jeep, I was free to stay in whatever ma-and-pa motel presented itself at the end of the day. But I gave myself one night in a fancy inn, Mike and Eve Art's Chico Hot Springs Resort. It is a rambling, eccentric place, a throwback to the days when Montana's hot springs spas—there must have been a hundred of them—attracted adventurous visitors from the East. Mike Art has turned back the clock at Chico, with a rustic dining room that is surely the best in Montana; huge, haunting landscape paintings by the Montanan Russell Chatham on the walls; an agreeable saloon; and water bubbling out of the ground at 104 degrees to supply the pool. Mike's an old Clevelander, but at Chico, you know you're not in Cleveland; there's a twelve-point elk head on the wall in the sitting room and a buffalo robe spread out atop the grand piano. A modern feature is the windsock beside the main entrance. It turns out the entrance road is also an airstrip. When a pleasure-bound private pilot radios in, somebody goes out and halts traffic for a few minutes so the plane can land and taxi up to the horse barn.

All this time, I was stopping to fish wherever I saw a place to park along a river. Near Chico Hot Springs, on the Yellowstone at Emigrant, a young mule deer waded into the water a hundred yards away, regarded me with a few waggles of his giant ears, and proceeded to drink as if I weren't there. When I sat down at a picnic table beside a willow thicket to have my lunch, a woman who had come down to the river to exercise her dog walked over to say, "You'd better watch your back. A mama bear is bringing up her cubs in those bushes. She's run me away from that table twice." I said thanks and forgot about it. A few minutes later, I heard a slight rustle in the willows and a low, but unmistakable, growl. I decided to find another place to have lunch.

I walked up the narrow Boulder River in my hip waders, happening to catch it at a time when an insect hatch was on and the bright circles of rising fish appeared in every pool. I was able to hook a lively small rainbow trout on every third or fourth cast. I put each of them gently back into the stream, having taught them the difference between a bug and a Goofus Bug. These little trout are highly educable; the lesson I gave them will make it a bit harder for the next fisherman who wades that stretch of river.

Fishing has taught me lessons, too. I have learned much about the habits of old, wise trout, and of young, foolish trout, and about the ways of their stream-borne prey, mayflies, caddis flies, grasshoppers, ants, and beetles, whose lives are no less interesting for being lived in miniature.

What's more, I have learned a thing or two about human behavior on trout streams. I've discovered that patience serves better than haste, that silence is a virtue, and concentration its own reward, and that I, at least, like to fish alone; trout fishing should not become a contest.

I never string up a trout rod without wild anticipation. Often, I've been exhausted on trout streams, uncomfortable, wet, cold, briar-scarred, sunburned, mosquito-bitten, but never, with a fly rod in my hand, have I been unhappy. I can't express the joy I felt in my Montana September, driving slowly along a different river day after day, free of all obligations and open to all possibilities, with my fishing bag in the passenger seat beside me.

Let me open that bag and see what's in there: half a dozen reels in battered leather cases, at least two in need of repair; boots and waders; an old but serviceable landing net; and my well-loved and dirty fishing vest containing: plastic boxes of flies; one box all elk-hair caddises; one all Wulffs and other attractor flies in various versions and sizes; a box of big streamers; one of weighted nymphs; one of delicate imitations of mayflies at different stages of life; one of terrestrials (on certain days big brown trout can be suckers for tiny red ants); knife; scissors; bug spray; needle-nosed pliers for bending down barbs (barbless hooks take just as many fish and make it easier if you want to let them go unharmed); a bit of inner tube for straightening out leaders; a can of goo to make flies float, and another can of goo to make them sink; a pencil-light; a magnifying glass; old leaders and licenses; spare reels of floating and sinking fly line; "invisible" tippets, which always look like hawsers on the stream; a little German camera which focuses to two feet, ideal for using with one hand to photograph a trout in the other and thus prevent a memory from slipping away; and other odds and ends of gear which I never have needed, but might. Understand that I *wear* all this stuff. I once stepped off an underwater ledge in the Firehole River and the weight of that vest sent me straight to the bottom. Even after this narrow escape from drowning, I couldn't decide what to leave out.

The most important item in the arsenal is the rod. You can catch fish with a limber stick or a bamboo pole, and once upon a time, everybody did. Then rod-makers became more sophisticated, making rods out of split cane before graduating in our time to fiberglass, then graphite, the present fly rod material of choice. A precious few have returned to the subtle craftsmanship of split bamboo.

I knew that one of the great bamboo rod-makers, Glenn Brackett of the R. L. Winston Rod Company, lives in Twin Bridges. His meticulous split cane rods sell for fifteen hundred dollars and up, and the world beats a path to his door. On this trip, I worked up the nerve to pay him a visit. I needn't have worried about disturbing the master; he turned out to be a nice guy who doesn't mind talking while he works.

"The cane is Chinese," he said, "from near Canton. The Chinese supply the whole world with Tonkin cane. They used to ship it to us in beautiful rattan wrappings, then in burlap. Now it comes wrapped in plastic. That's the way the world goes, I guess. But the quality of the bamboo is still the same. We store it in a room behind the town library. It ages there for a year or two, or longer."

Glenn used to be an owner of the Winston Company, which makes fine graphite rods, but he sold his interest in order to concentrate exclusively on bamboo. There's much more art to matching, cutting, tempering, gluing, and finishing the strips of bamboo, and Glenn likes the result better.

"All Winston bamboo rods have a hollow core," he said. "I don't think any other maker will say that. It's a lot more work, but it makes them lighter and gives them better action.

"It takes most fishermen ten or fifteen years before they're ready for a bamboo rod, before they're ready to fully take part in the sport. I tell fishermen, 'You won't like it at first. You have to keep coming back to it.' It's like a relationship with a woman, maybe. After a while, the rod becomes your true companion and friend. It's good to you even though it knows your weaknesses.

"Graphite casts a fast line. It takes a good deal of time on the stream to learn the advantage of a slow line. By its nature, bamboo doesn't want to smash the fly down on the water. It wants to float it down gently. The slower line gives you more control, more precision. You want the fly *there,* it goes there. You learn to trust a fine bamboo rod, and after a while, nothing else feels right."

As he talked, Glenn's eyes were busy, concentrating on his work. He clearly wants every bamboo strip to be flawless, every finished rod to be perfect. He worked with the help of Jeff Walker and Jerry Kustich. Their eyes were busy, too.

"This is cutting and gluing day," Glenn said. "We make square rods—four-strip rods—and five-strip rods, even eight-strip, but mostly six-strip rods. These are being prepared for sale at least a year from now. They hang in this heated cabinet with the string tied tightly around them for at least a year, and four-pound weights hanging on the tip sections. You have to take the time. If you don't, the work will come back and haunt you. Cane gets better with age. You have to wait. A year from now, we take the string off, scrape them, sand them, wrap them, varnish them, put on the reel seat, and they go out the door. I hate to give each one up, but there comes a time for it to go out and meet the world."

I watched Glenn Brackett work until the end of the day. Before we parted, he, Jeff and Jerry and I sat around a packing crate, had a beer together, shelled some peanuts, and talked about fishing. I kept looking over toward the heated cabinet, where today's Glenn Brackett rods were starting the year they must wait before reaching the hands of fishermen. Someday, I thought. . . .

One morning in Montana, I turned sixty. I was rolling along on a dirt road beside a river with the sun coming up and a cup of hot Town Pump coffee in the cup holder, happy as I have ever been, and listening to the radio. Garrison Keillor's public radio almanac show came on, and I heard him say that it was my sixtieth birthday. I thought, is it? Well, I'll be damned if it isn't!

Well, all right then, I'm sixty. I thought of my father, back home in North Carolina. I'd be going to see him in a few days. He was seriously ill but still in good spirits, and he was eighty-six years old.

I'd settle for that, I thought. That would give me plenty of time to own a Glenn Brackett bamboo rod and to get the feel of it. Good for Pop. Eighty-six would be all right for me, too.

Eighty-six, if I could make it, would give me twenty-six more Septembers in Montana.

OCTOBER

Woodstock, Vermont

The first week of October in southern Vermont is the unbearably beautiful American time and place. Brilliant yellow birch-covered hills slope down to glowing green meadows. Every sugar maple along every country lane combusts in scarlet and gold. The autumn sun brightens the white church steeples in the pretty valley towns. Plump pumpkins appear in orange pyramids outside the crossroads stores, and the smell of wood smoke hangs in the air. The intensity of the season so overpowers the senses that autumn cannot be remembered from one year to the next, so its splendor always comes as a shock. When I was planning my perfect year, the one time I knew I mustn't miss was the first week of October in Vermont.

But I missed it. My father died in North Carolina during the first week of October.

He was an undemonstrative man, but he had bought a card at the drugstore the month before and written me a note. I found it when I got home from Montana: "Charles, the day you were born sixty years ago was the best day of my life." This note was moving, of course, but unlike him. It told me that he must be feeling his glass running out.

My sister, Catherine, and I cared for him, then Catherine alone, then I alone, then my brother, Wallace. Our father lay propped up by pillows on his old maroon divan with a comforter across his knees. He said less and less and ate less and less. He stoically took his pills ground up in ice cream until he was not able to do even that, or was not interested in bothering. Once, I tried to pick him up gently to move him back into a comfortable position, but he had run out of comfortable positions. He gasped in sudden pain and said, "Charlie, I swear I'll kill you!" This was the last full sentence my father spoke to me.

We buried him beside our mother in the cemetery in the pine trees. I conducted the graveside service myself, not wanting some preacher who didn't even know my father to say platitudes over him. Wallace and Catherine spoke, too. We had a moment of silence, and then everybody walked back to the house for a drink.

I liked the people who came to the funeral. Besides his friends—who really were friends—and his neighbors from up and down the road, there were the tellers at the bank, to whom he brought flowers from his garden two or three times a week; the checkout lady at the grocery store; some of the children for whom he sat out on the porch and carved toys; the waitress he used to kid around with at the cafe on the fishing pier. You could tell they all felt a good man had died.

He was a New Englander by birth, who always loved the Vermont October. After a few days, I went there for both of us.

By the time I got to Woodstock, though, the brilliant part of the fall was over. The days were misty and gray. The last leaves were falling, and I couldn't shake the sadness. The perfect year had turned far less than perfect. For a while there, I didn't know what to do with myself.

I fell back on my old habit—going for a drive. The state's dirt roads are lovingly maintained, smooth as pavement, with never a pothole or a washboard furrow, at least not in the summer and fall. (How do the Vermonters do it, when nobody else can?) They are rarely clearly marked, if at all, these back roads, but not to use them would be to miss much of the glory of Vermont. On a whim, I took such a road near Vershire, with the hope of sooner or later reaching the village of Strafford. The road took me along a brook, over a steep rise, and past a magnificent Georgian house that presided over a tidy hill farm that I couldn't have expected was there. I chose from among one-way lanes marked "Bliss's Farm Road" or "Chesterfield Hill Road," and, just following my nose, happened to make all the right choices. I came out right on the Strafford town green.

On the hill above that green stands a wooden building I love. It is an emblem of much that is fine about Vermont. Just inside the door, there's a sign that says:

> *The Old White Meeting House*
> *Built in 1799*
> *And Consecrated as a Place of Public Worship*
> *For All Denominations*
> *With No Preference for One Above Another.*
> *Since 1801, it has Also Been in Continuous Use*
> *As a Town Hall.*

I spent an inspiring day in that building once. It was on the one day in Vermont when the town carpenter lays aside his tools, the town doctor sees no patients, the shopkeeper closes his shop, and mothers tell their children that they'll have to warm up their own dinners. It was the day the people of Vermont look not to their own welfare, but to that of their towns: Town Meeting Day.

What happens at the town meeting is not representative democracy. It is pure democracy. Every citizen may have his or her say on every question. And many voices were heard that day in Strafford. For an hour, for example, they debated the question of whether to go on paying $582 a month for outside health services deemed unsatisfactory by a farmer named Brown. When the moderator, rail fence maker James Condict, couldn't tell how the voice vote had gone, he said, "I'm going to ask for a standing vote. All those in favor . . ." And here it came, the Yankee expression that originated in the town meeting and has entered into the language of free people: ". . . stand up and be counted."

By a standing vote, Strafford agreed with farmer Brown and eliminated outside health services from the town budget.

This is the way the founders of this country imagined democracy would be: citizens meeting in their own communities to decide directly on most of the questions affecting their lives and fortunes. This is the way Vermont still does it. And all voters must take an old oath: always to vote their conscience, without fear or favor of any person.

Baked beans, brown bread, and pie that had been baked by the ladies of the PTA were served to all. Then a little more wood was added to the stove and a dozen more questions were debated and voted on. Would the town turn off the one streetlight late at night to save money? Strafford decided to leave the light on. Finally came the most routine of all motions, the motion to adjourn. Moderator Condict put it to a voice vote and the verdict rang out loud and clear: *"Nay!"*

They voted it down! Democracy is heady stuff. They wanted to go on enjoying it for a while that day in Strafford.

On a weekday October afternoon, the Old White Meeting House was shut and still. But when Town Meeting Day rolls around again, it will be, again, the lively, democratic center of one town's small universe.

You could argue that Vermont is democracy's natural home, but it wasn't always. There is a maverick tradition that goes back to the Founding Maverick, Ethan Allen. For fourteen years after the Declaration of Independence, Vermont was a sovereign republic. Some residents favored union with New York, some with

New Hampshire. This wishy-washy state of affairs didn't sit well with Ethan Allen and his private band of armed bullies, the Green Mountain Boys. They hadn't fought the British for New York or for New Hampshire. They demanded that Vermont remain Vermont, and they saw to it by intimidation and violence. Allen rode into one secessionist town and blustered, "I, Ethan Allen, do declare that I will give no quarter to the man, woman, or child who shall oppose me. Unless the inhabitants of Guilford peacefully submit to the authority of Vermont, I swear that I will lay it as desolate as Sodom and Gomorrah, by God!" In 1791, not without misgivings, Congress invited Vermont to enter the union with its own name and borders. There is still a little of the independent republic about the place.

Woodstock, which I made the center of my October wanderings, is one of America's ten prettiest villages. (The other nine are also in Vermont, probably.) Woodstock's green was laid out in the 1790s, and the handsome federal houses that face it were built at about the same time, but in the preservation of the village to the present day can be detected the fine hand of Laurance S. Rockefeller.

I have never met him, not being one who moves in such circles, but I have driven on the Palisades Parkway along the Hudson River, and gone hiking in Acadia National Park in Maine, and sailed to St. John in the Virgin Islands, and appreciated the wildlife on the range in Jackson Hole, Wyoming. These, among many other places, were saved by Laurance Rockefeller. When he looks around, he must be happy with the way he has spent his money.

The most imposing house in Woodstock is Laurance Rockefeller's, the historic Billings mansion (once home of that Vermont Billings who became a railroad tycoon and left his name on the city in Montana I'd just come from). The house is on the National Register of Historic Places, along with almost all of the rest of the village. Rockefeller owns the Woodstock Inn, too, on that beautiful elliptical village green. The inn is as tasteful as lodgings can be. If you want a fireplace of your own, in a suite with a private porch, it can also become a little pricey, at five hundred dollars or so per night. Not many Vermonters could afford that, but of course, the Woodstock Inn is not there to serve Vermonters.

Even more exclusive digs are available just up the road in Barnard. The country house of Sinclair Lewis and Dorothy Thompson has been turned into a tony retreat called Twin Farms. The more desirable of the cottages there goes for fifteen hundred dollars a night. Croquet is free, and I am told they don't trouble you with a bar bill or a restaurant tab when you check out.

I made do with an inexpensive old house in the woods, where I could do my thinking and map reading and grieving for Pop without having to make small talk with other guests at breakfast. I sat on the wooden steps out there with my morning coffee and watched the chipmunks scurrying through the fallen leaves. There must have been twenty or thirty of them racing around, in a hurry to get ready for winter. When I went for my daily drives, I noticed that people everywhere were doing the same, sawing and chopping and making prodigious woodpiles in their yards, or driving to and fro in their pickup trucks, loaded with firewood. I dug down in my bag for a wool shirt and sweater. There was a chill in the air every morning now, noticeable both to chipmunks and human beings.

I took a different road each day, usually with no particular destination in mind. In Vermont, it seems to me, one road is nearly as inviting as the next. There are no billboards on any of them; Vermont restricted billboards back in the Thirties, and banned them altogether twenty-five years ago. The inns and attractions, the roadside cheese stores and antique shops, thus come into view unannounced. Even an institution as famous as the Vermont Country Store in Weston can come as a surprise, noticeable mainly for the cars parked around it. The billboard law, aside from preserving the rural views, gives every drive in the country a feeling of serendipity.

Vermont attracts entrepreneurs, and some of them have made great successes in unorthodox ways. I had one of Vermont Castings' sturdy wood stoves shipped to me once, and got invited for years after that to the annual customers' party. Ben and Jerry share the ice cream wealth with their employees. The Vermont Teddy Bear Company and Green Mountain Coffee and dozens of other start-up firms of recent years have done well. But they all have to get along without billboards.

I stopped in Newfane for a couple of hours one day. There's another of the prettiest villages in America, with its white clapboard Greek revival buildings clustered on the green: the Newfane Inn, the Four Columns Inn, the Congregational Church, the courthouse, and the meeting hall. "Stop and look at me!" Newfane murmurs to the traveler. "I haven't changed for a hundred and fifty years! Take a walk around me! Photograph me." I never have passed through Newfane without hearing and obeying.

One Sunday, I reached the Old Tavern in Grafton at lunchtime. The tavern once was a stagecoach stop on the main route between Boston and Montreal, but the main route shifted away and it's well off the beaten path today. I arrived on an unpaved road and left via a covered bridge. Inscribed above the registration desk of the tavern are the names of some bygone guests, among them Emerson, Thoreau, Hawthorne, Oliver Wendell Holmes, Daniel Webster, and Rudyard Kipling. I've never been much for Sunday brunch buffets, but this one actually was wonderfully good. I restrained myself. I had a taste of sesame chicken and wild rice, served with a free glass of good white wine, then a tiny bit of moist chocolate cake with strawberries and cream, then a wedge of the local Grafton cheddar and a good cup of coffee, all for fifteen dollars. After lunch, I rocked on the porch awhile and looked over the Sunday papers. I was tempted to check in and stay, as I did one October. Do you remember the World Series when Carlton Fisk of the Red Sox danced on the first-base line, willing that home run of his to be fair? It was that October, whenever it was. I watched that game in the Barn Room out back of the Tavern, on the only television set in the place. I suppose it's terrible to remember an elegant two-hundred-year-old inn for something you saw there on television, but that's the way modern memory goes.

I visited Plymouth, the modest mountain hamlet where that modest president, Calvin Coolidge, was born and is buried. In the summer of 1923, Vice President Coolidge was home helping his father with the haying when word came in

June and George Butler

Potter Steve Werner and Alexandra Kampmann, age five

The meetinghouse at Strafford

Justin Morgan's grave

the middle of the night that President Harding had died. By the light of a kerosene lamp, John Coolidge, the Plymouth justice of the peace, administered the presidential oath of office to his son. "How did you know that you could swear in a President?" they asked John later. He said, "I didn't know I couldn't."

I went in search of another famous Vermonter—Justin Morgan. Justin Morgan was a farmer and singing master in Randolph, Vermont, who had bought a three-year-old stallion in 1792, and used him as a saddle- and harness-horse and for work around the farm. The stallion was much admired as "the Justin Morgan horse." He was a strong and willing animal with a broad forehead, prominent and "kind" eyes, an elegant neck, a short back, a long mane and tail, and a friendly disposition. And though he was bred to a wide variety of mares, his offspring had a way of turning out just like him. All of farmer Morgan's neighbors wanted a Morgan horse to breed for themselves. By the time of the Civil War, the Vermont Cavalry rode into battle on a thousand Morgan horses. All other American breeds, the quarter horse and Standardbred and all the rest, also have in their veins the blood of this one horse, Justin Morgan, and it was the grave of the horse I went looking for, not that of the man. I found it by turning east on an unmarked dirt road south of Chelsea, taking a covered bridge across the first branch of the White River, climbing a steep hill to the right, and driving on until I thought, My God, I must have missed it. And suddenly, there it was, a modest monument in a small field of the farm where Justin Morgan was kicked to death by another horse at the age of thirty-two. I read the stone and walked around there for a few minutes. I found that I felt more keenly in the presence of greatness than I did at Coolidge's grave. In a hillside meadow across the road from Justin Morgan's monument, a couple of Morgan horses were grazing—long necks, short backs, full manes and tails, just like him.

The beauty of Vermont owes much to its livestock. Noel Perrin, the best writer about Vermont rural life, says the reason Vermont is prettier than New Hampshire, just across the river, is that New Hampshire farmers have mostly given up milking cows in favor of milking tourists, and their pastures are grown over in scrub woods. Vermont farmers, a lot of them, are still hanging on. Their cows keep the valleys open and green. I thought about this one day on a drive from Manchester up through Dorset and Pawlet in the green valley of the Mettawee River. It's as pretty as countryside gets, but it wouldn't be, I realized, without the dairy herds of Jerseys and Guernseys to keep the meadows trimmed.

Sheep are returning to Vermont, too. They far outnumbered cattle in the state once upon a time. Here and there, spinning wheels and shuttles are back in action again. You can buy Vermont weaving made with Vermont wool.

The wool comeback is too late for the old Downer's Mill at Quechee, though. Simon Pearce moved his glass and pottery factory there from Ireland, and the water that flows over the dam now powers Pearce's glass furnaces instead of Downer's looms. In Vermont, where quilts and hooked rugs and stained glass and handmade furniture are also being made everywhere, the Industrial Revolution has given way to the Craft Revival.

There's a good restaurant and an enticing shop at Pearce's, but what drew me back there a couple of times were the artisans on the factory floor. The glassblowers don't mind if you stand and watch, and their skill is amazing to see, but glassblowers are unable to chat while working. I gravitated to the pottery room, where a young man named Steve Werner sat over his wheel. He's one of the new Vermonters, drawn by the rural beauty and the chance to work at an old-fashioned job he loves.

Steve makes delicate bowls one day, sturdy pie plates the next. In fact, he makes, it seems, anything he pleases. Suddenly, on a whim, he interrupted the pie plate production and drew up a graceful tall vase instead. Watching him reminded me of my fascination with the potters at Jugtown, back in North Carolina, when I was four or five years old. My father took me there to see what they could do with the clay atop their foot-treadle wheels. It seemed magical to me.

The potter's magic still enchants children. I photographed Alexandra Kampmann, five years old, visiting with her folks from Denmark, as she got her hands wet and muddy "helping out." She loved it. Steve Werner seemed always willing to talk to kids as he worked, and even to stop working to give them the feel of the clay. He's a very good potter, and a good guy besides.

"I've been at it twenty years," he told me. "I was going to school in Madison, Wisconsin, at the university, and I ran out of money. So I went home to Racine and saw an ad for a potter—'Must have own wheel.' Well, I had a wheel. I didn't really know how to use it, but they didn't ask. They didn't even have me throw a pot for them. They just sat me down and told me to start making garden planters. So I made them. They were ugly, but nobody cared. You can look at a pot and not really see it if you don't have an eye. Working in a place like that can be depressing. The pots will sell, and you can make a living at it and never get beyond the poor form you started with.

"I was going to be a furniture maker, but my hands began to like the water and the clay. Making pots is very intuitive. I had the necessary naïveté. I kept telling myself, the next one I make, I'm going to get it right. I moved from shop to shop, and met better potters, and eventually, I did. I got it right."

As Steve and I talked, people who had come in to watch him work asked *me* to pose for pictures. Naturally this baffled Steve.

"Who are you?" he asked me.

"I used to work in television," I said.

"Oh," he said, "sorry. I never got into television."

This made me like him more.

"I don't know many people," he said, "not even many potters. Most potters seem to be introspective, and I am, too. Well, think about it—I have to relate to clay all day long! Maybe there's something to be said for the guild system, where you can go out and have a pint and talk it over when the day's finished."

I asked Steve about the clay.

"It's a mixture from all over," he said, "from the English Midlands near Stoke, from Cornwall, from Tennessee and Kentucky, all mixed together with a little feldspar, a 'glassifier.' These are twenty-pound lumps. I cut them into sixes this morning. I'm throwing them and forming them into pie plates today. Tomorrow, the plates will be a little harder, a little leathery, and I'll go through them all one by one to remove any imperfections, finish them, and put the company stamp on the bottom. Then, they'll be ready to be fired. We fire them at two thousand, three hundred degrees, give or take eight degrees. That's the little temperature window we work in. They're fired twice, first to harden them, then to glaze them. The decoration is done by hand atop the glaze."

I noticed Steve was turning out a pie plate every three or four minutes when he wasn't being interrupted.

"I can make four hundred coffee mugs in a day," he said, "maybe only six big vases, say. I've heard of a great English potter, Isaac Button, who could do two thousand small pieces in a day and glaze them all himself, and nobody could find the slightest imperfection in any of them. I'm a pretty fast worker, but not that fast."

He threw another clump of clay down on the wheel and talked me through the process:

"I wheel-wedge the clay, cone it up and down this way a couple of times just to homogenize it. Then I center it . . . spread it . . . compress the bottom—that takes a little strength, because you want the bottom to be more compressed than the sides—then I pull it . . . draw it up to the height I want . . . rib it with this little rib . . . bend my lip over . . . crust the edge if I want to . . . and there—a pie plate!" He did it almost as quickly and smoothly as he said it. With the next batch of clay, he showed off again. I was expecting another pie plate, but Steve abruptly reached inside the clay with his hand and arm, drew it up, formed it, made a spout, and said, "A pitcher!"

It is elemental stuff, the work of earth and water and fire. And it is hypnotic: the wheel turning, the hands working their magic, beautiful objects emerging one after another.

It would be nice to think that the Vermont economy could survive on farming and crafts alone, but the state always needs a few more jobs than it has. Many of its young people have to leave each year to seek their fortunes, and many of those who stay have to work at several jobs to make ends meet. The image of the frugal Yankee has a solid basis in fact. A dollar in the pocket is still worth something in Vermont.

Vermont will be all right as long as it is home to people like my old friends, George and June Butler. They bought their farm in Jacksonville in the Fifties. He was an activist Methodist preacher who looked upon the church as an instrument of social change. A good minister, George once said to me, "calls on people and raises hell!" George started raising hell with the comfortable establishment at Yale Divinity School in the Thirties. He never stopped. When I went to see the two of them on this trip, he gave me a brief sermon for free. He sat at the kitchen table with his unruly shock of white hair and his firm jaw. He fixed me with his clear eyes, and quoted to me from the Book of Amos in that stentorian preacher's voice: "Let judgment run down as waters, and righteousness as a mighty stream!" He declared, "That is the high-water mark of the Old Testament. I have tried to put it into practice."

George Butler is a man of iron principles. I'm sure the farm, as much as anything, was a place to escape from conservative parishioners and authoritarian bishops.

"Here," George said, "we settled into a life close to nature. We were influenced by Scott Nearing."

June said, "He would pick a cabbage worm off a plant and carry it carefully and drop it over the fence."

"We always loved this farm," George said.

"We *needed* this farm," June said. "If you live in a parsonage, you have no place to call home. You might have to move out of there on two weeks' notice. We wanted a place to call home."

"The farm was in disrepair," George said. "The house hadn't been occupied for several years. One room was full of spiders and the old farmer's broken-down beekeeping equipment. We bought the hundred and seventy-five acres for fifteen thousand dollars, declared it a tree farm, and harvested two thousand dollars' worth of trees the first year. So that made it affordable."

The farmhouse is now as inviting as a home can be, and the farm as tidy as any in Vermont.

"Well," George said, "we added to the house over the years. I recently built that breezeway and garage myself. And we have watched the farm grow older. That fir tree in the yard was a sapling when we came here. Now it's three times taller than the house. It's too close to the house, and it ought to come down, but the chickadees love it."

I first met the Butlers twenty-five years ago in maple-sugaring season.

"The sugaring helped us get by," George said. "We had a thousand buckets on these trees, and we started at sunup every day. Once I boiled all night. We gave attention to the quality of the syrup, and we got a good price."

A tiny brook comes rushing down out of the mountains behind the house. One day, George Butler decided that stream could help pay the bills, too.

"I built a four-and-a-half-foot dam half a mile up in the woods," he said. "For a turbine, I used a pump running backward. It turns out sixty-cycle power. We produce three times as much electricity as we can use at the house. The power company buys the excess at about five cents per kilowatt hour. We get all the power we can use for free, and some months as much as three hundred dollars to boot! All from a little brook that doesn't even have a name."

So that's how to survive in Vermont: Fix up your house by yourself, sell a little timber, do a little sugaring, generate your own electricity. And, I should add, teach music, as June did, and play the old pump organ on Sundays at the community church. And if you're qualified, as George was, do a little supply preaching and write a few freelance articles. Oh, and George's book about his boyhood is coming out this fall.

Neither of them was born in Vermont. They are Vermonters to the bone.

"We couldn't do without the seasons," George said.

"Or the neighbors," June said. "When I was laid up with my back problem, they came in and did my housework, took care of the garden, and fetched my groceries. I could never repay them, except, of course, by doing the same for somebody else."

George and June are a cosmopolitan couple by life experience, and they might have chosen to settle down anywhere. They deliberately chose Vermont, and a hardworking, old-fashioned life. I heard this attitude of Vermonters described as "preventing the future."

When you're sitting at the table with the Butlers in one of the rooms they built themselves, looking out at the fir tree the chickadees like so much; when you're crossing the covered bridge at Woodstock, or driving up Mount Equinox with its unspoiled views out across the state; when you're strolling on the common at Townshend in October, or on the Weston Green; when you're looking down on Pomfret from the Cloudland Road and noticing all the ugliness that isn't there, anywhere to be seen; and when you think about what so much of the rest of America has become, preventing the future in this one small place doesn't seem like such a bad idea.

Rio Grande Valley, New Mexico

～

New Mexico may have been "new" to the Spanish who rode north from Old Mexico, but in the unimaginable eons of history, that was just the blink of an eye ago. The place is badly named. It should be called Precambria for the sea that crashed upon its shores for tens of millions of years; or Mastodonia, for the mammals that later roamed its plains in the company of elephants and camels and saber-toothed cats; or Sandia, for the mountain where the camp of an Ice Age hunter, the earliest known American, was found in a cave. Nowhere in the United States have human beings lived as long in the same community as at Acoma, the Pueblo in the Sky, built atop a New Mexico mesa in the 1100s by the Anasazi, the "ancient ones." New Mexico is old, stupendously old and dry and brown, and wind-worn by the ages. I went to New Mexico in November to be overcome again by oldness.

And because I knew that in November I could see the cranes again.

I saw them first many Novembers ago and heard their triumphant trumpet calls, a hundred or more sandhill cranes riding south on a thermal above the Rio Grande Valley, and that day their effortless flight and their brassy music got into my soul.

They are giant birds with six-foot wingspans, graceful gliders in the air, dainty stilt dancers on the ground, each mating pair inseparable for life. I have long been acquainted with a couple of them who spend every short summer in the same secluded corner of the same Montana marsh. They arrive in late May, spiraling noisily out of the blue sky, and remain well into September, feeding and guarding their nest. Then, suddenly, around the autumnal equinox, they are gone. I have never seen them go. A morning arrives. There is silence in the marsh. They are gone.

Where they go, I think, is south and east across the Continental Divide to a vast meadow near the Henry's Fork River in Idaho, where they meet other cranes in a late-September rendezvous that may last a week or more. After stumbling upon that meadow one year, I stood with binoculars on a hill and counted a hundred socializing pairs rising restlessly into the air, settling back to earth, rising, resettling, awaiting some signal of wind or weather or intuition to tell them exactly when to rise and not return. They form at last into a shifting V-formation and climb toward the clouds above the mountains to the south. The Rocky Mountain summer goes with them.

The cranes of the Rockies belong to the oldest species of birds living on earth, one that goes back to the Eocene epoch. They have been flying south over North America for two million Novembers now, and they know the way. From the huge expanse of Montana, Wyoming, Utah, and Idaho, the great cranes pour south through a geological funnel, the San Luis Valley of Colorado. Away to the east, flocks of smaller cousins are simultaneously making their way down from Hudson's Bay and the shores of the Arctic Ocean across the Prairie Provinces and the Great Plains. At the North Platte River, some of the squadrons of these Lesser Sandhill Cranes veer southwestward down the Front Range of the Rock-

ies. By mid-November, the destination of thousands of cranes lies just ahead—
New Mexico.

Most of them are headed for Phil Norton's place.

Phil Norton is manager of the Bosque del Apache National Wildlife Refuge,
so named for the Mescalero Apaches who used to camp in the woods nearby.
The refuge straddles the Rio Grande about 175 miles north of the Mexican border, overseen by this genial Texan who worked for years in the Fish and Wildlife
bureaucracy in Washington, sometimes dreaming a simple dream of a refuge he
could call his own. They finally gave him the most spectacular refuge in the country. That's what he thinks; that's what I think, too. Phil Norton says he'll never
go back to Washington. When he's finished at the Bosque, he's finished.

Every morning when he wakes up, he thinks about the cranes. He prepares
for them all spring and summer, draining the swamps in March to promote the
growth of native plants as food for the birds, reflooding them in late summer to
make the birds feel at home when they arrive. He plants chufa, millet, smartweed,
and bulrush, which he loves like a doting gardener, and uproots invading salt
cedar, which he despises as the viper in his Eden. He cultivates cottonwoods and
willows. He plants fields of corn and bumps the cornstalks over on their sides
for easy harvesting by the birds. He toils with tractor, disc harrow, bulldozer, and
floodgate, restoring the refuge and improving on it, working always against his
autumn deadline, the day when the first cranes arrive.

He does all this with a small paid staff and an army of volunteers, mostly old
folks who migrate like the birds to spend their winters in the Southwest and who'd
rather do something more useful with their days than play bridge or golf. Phil
Norton couldn't get along without the volunteers. One of them, a retired contractor from Wisconsin, designed and built bird-watching stands in the refuge
while his wife helped out in the office. There's little to distinguish the volunteers
from the professional Fish and Wildlife staffers. They're all there shoulder to
shoulder in green uniforms, working for the birds.

Phil Norton's philosophy is one of active management: Flood that field! Plant that grain! Eradicate that tamarisk! Whatever you do, *don't* let nature take its course! "If nature took its course," he says, "this place would be a dead salt marsh." In 1941, the second year the refuge was in operation, sandhill cranes, for lack of habitat, were a severely endangered species. That year, only seventeen wintered over at the Bosque. The day I visited, with Phil Norton in charge, 13,000 cranes had already arrived for the winter, with more on the way. That is not to mention the 60,000 ducks on the ponds quacking their approval of the place, or the 45,000 snow geese feeding in the fields and drifting in long white skeins through the sky. I don't know how anybody could count the hawks and harriers and herons, the bald eagles, the pheasants and turkeys, the owls and meadowlarks and darting swallows, or the clouds of blackbirds rolling and wheeling low above the ground. I spent two long days in the Bosque and exhausted myself in the beauty of the birds.

I also saw a coyote creeping through a cornfield toward a gaggle of watchful geese, and a porcupine gnawing at a cottonwood, and a couple of mule deer ambling down a trail. I did not see—though Lord knows I searched for them—the two white whooping cranes which were said to have arrived, survivors of an apparently failing attempt to establish a migration route in the Rockies for those majestic creatures, one of several ideas being tried to help them back from the brink of extinction.

I ran four 36-exposure rolls of film through my camera while I was in the refuge. I have rarely been so disappointed by my attempts at photography. A closeup of a sandhill crane does not suggest the teeming multitude, and a wide shot of the multitude becomes a blur. I concluded that pictures cannot capture the glory of the Bosque del Apache. You have to be there. And the best time of all to be there is November. Ask the cranes.

When I left the Bosque, I headed north toward Albuquerque, Santa Fe, and Taos along the route of the Royal Road of the Spanish. It's called Interstate-25 now and the traffic moves way too fast for anybody in a moseying mood, which is the mood I was in. So I left the highway at every promising exit, even some not so promising, like the one at San Antonio, New Mexico. But somebody had said to me, "Don't miss the green-chile cheeseburger at the Owl Bar," and unlike most food tips I've collected on the road, this proved to be admirable advice. If you are looking for the bright lights of San Antonio, you will find them entirely concentrated at the Owl. For fifty years, Adolph and Rowena Baca's bar and cafe has been the only social center on a long and lonely stretch of highway. It's not a bit unusual for people to drive sixty miles west from Carrizozo or sixty miles north from Elephant Butte for a chile cheeseburger at the Owl. (In New Mexico, chili is spelled "chile"; don't ask me why.)

This is dry and dusty country, so the beer sells every bit as well as the food, and the *bar* is even older than the Bar. It comes from Gus Hilton's five-room turn-of-the-century boarding house, which used to stand about a mile away beside the railroad tracks. That's the house Conrad Hilton grew up in, the first Hilton Hotel. There's been no hotel at all in San Antonio since Gus died and Conrad moved away.

I drove off the highway thirty miles or so to visit the sleepy little village of Magdalena, too, because a tipsy old cowboy at the Owl told me that his daddy told him that Magdalena was once the rowdiest damn town in New Mexico Territory. That would have been sometime in the 1880s, when the railroad line ended at Magdalena and the cattle trails began there. This convergence gave rise to the familiar frontier town demand for saloons and bawdy houses, a demand Western entrepreneurs always seem to have appeared out of nowhere to meet. The town grew fast and lawless, and prosperous, too. In 1885, Magdalena shipped more cattle than Chicago. That's what they tell you in Magdalena. Anyway, it was a long time ago. The place has a few hundred seemingly peaceful citizens now, and a nice soda fountain.

I spent a night in Socorro and walked around the old part of town the next morning. What you learn in Socorro is that the Spanish colonizers had a streak of stubborn survival running almost as deep in them as it ran in the bloodstreams of the native tribes they encountered. In 1615, five years before the Pilgrims landed at Plymouth Rock, some Franciscan friars started building the Mission of Nuestra Señora del Socorro, "Our Lady of Help," with the usual Franciscan intention of rounding up the local Piro Indians and Christianizing the daylights out of them. The Piros and the newcomers managed to hit it off, and things were going pretty well for the settlement until about the time the mission was finished. The Apaches, the Huns of North America, came riding down out of the hills, looted the livestock, and burned down the houses. The Spanish rebuilt. The Apaches raided. After sixty years of this, the friars sighed a deep Franciscan sigh and decided they'd had enough. They abandoned Socorro and headed south toward Mexico where they had come from. The Piros, having to choose between the Spanish and the Apaches, made the choice you and I would have made: they went south with the Spanish.

Free now to destroy the mission, the Apaches did so at their leisure and went off to pillage elsewhere. The empty ruins of Socorro baked in the sun for 135 years.

But I said the Spanish were stubborn. In 1815, they came back. So did the Apaches, of course. The Spanish rebuilt the mission. The Apaches tried to destroy it again, and never stopped trying until they and their great war chief, Geronimo, finally surrendered to the U.S. Cavalry in 1886.

So Socorro survived to have an Arby's, a Pizza Hut, and a Motel 6. And a few blocks away, an old mission, still in use. I walked by there to see it and found myself thinking a little bit about ancient faith and a lot about human stubbornness.

There was one other mission I wanted to visit, or revisit, San Gregorio de Abo, in a little mountain pass to the east. But I got to daydreaming on the road along the river and missed the turnoff, so I ended up twenty miles out of my way, lost in the old railroad town of Belen. You wouldn't think to look at Belen that anybody could get lost there, but I managed it. I drove up and down the main drag trying to figure out which cross-street looked important enough to be the one that led across the railroad tracks and out of town toward Abo. I could have just stopped and asked somebody, but like most other American males, I hate having to walk up to a stranger and admit that I don't know where I am. There's a loss of manhood in it.

I finally had to forget about my manhood and ask. I pulled up to Jaramillo's barbershop and walked in. All the barbers were busy. When I reached back and noticed that my hair was beginning to grow down over my collar, I decided to put off the question and sit down and wait for a haircut first. After a few minutes with a two-year-old hunting and fishing magazine, I was motioned into an empty chair by Barney Jaramillo, who said he helps out in the shop when his father and uncle, the proprietors for the last fifty years, expect a busy day. While Barney worked on the outside of my head, I kept running his surname around in the inside, trying to remember where I had heard it before.

"Lots of Jaramillos around here?" I asked him.

"We're all over the place," he said. "We've been a long time in the country, so that's long enough to breed a whole bunch of Jaramillos, you're right about that. I probably had a great-great-great—well, I don't know how many greats I'd have to give my earliest ancestor."

When you get a Jaramillo haircut, you get your money's worth. I climbed out of the chair so closely shorn that my hat didn't fit for the next two weeks. I was almost out the door before I remembered why I'd come in the first place.

"The road to Abo?" Barney said. "You're on it. Just keep going straight and don't turn nowhere. Have a nice day, now."

On my way out of town, I saw the name Jaramillo on a lot of mailboxes and a gas station and a dry goods store. It wasn't until days later up in Taos that it came to me where I'd heard it before. When Kit Carson settled down from that dime-novel life of his and decided to get married in 1843, he presented a twelve-room adobe house in Taos to his new bride—Josefa Jaramillo. You can still visit the Carson-Jaramillo house if you want to see how the old gun-slinger lived in domesticity. It sort of pleased me to reflect that I might have had a haircut from one of his collateral descendants, the great-great-great—well, I don't know how many greats—grand-nephew of Kit Carson.

When Barney Jaramillo said go straight, he meant it literally. The road east from Belen doesn't bend an inch through twenty miles of big-time rangeland. You know it's big-time range (1) when you can't see across it, and (2) when the signs at the gates are not little home-made ones that say "Bar-J Ranch" or something like that, but big printed ones that say something like "New Mexico Cattle Company" instead. And add, as an afterthought, "Keep Out!"

After a while, the road crosses the Santa Fe tracks and turns at last up into the mountains. And a while after that, you come to Abo.

A little stream flows through a narrow valley here, as it must have flowed around the year 1150, when some Pueblo Indians found the valley an agreeable place to build their stone and adobe houses and farm their squash and bean fields. The Spanish Conquistadors, more interested in gold than in squash and beans, bypassed Abo. But naturally the Franciscans who followed found the place and, naturally, built a mission, a rather grand one with a long nave, a choir loft, a dining hall, a sacristy, a baptistery, comfortable cells for the friars, and extensive gardens outside. The Pueblo farmers sang in the church choir; they also maintained a traditional *kiva,* or underground religious chamber of their own, right on the mission grounds.

(Striking and marvelous hybrid religions can still be found all over New Mexico. Most of the Pueblo people are Catholics, but they're not quite like the Catholics of Boston. The wall of Our Lady of Guadalupe Church on the Zuni Reservation portrays Zuni spirit figures doing a rain dance—right above the cross and the picture of the Virgin Mary.)

The five-hundred-year history of Abo might have continued peaceably but for the terrible years of the mid-1600s. A dreadful drought came on. Year after year went by with almost no rainfall. The stream dried up. Natives and Spanish alike were reduced to eating hides and roots. Sometime around 1670, they all packed up and left, and, unlike Socorro, Abo was utterly forgotten. Nobody ever came back.

Except Federico Sisneros's family.

I met Federico Sisneros on my first visit to Abo in 1987. He alone took care of the San Gregorio mission ruins. It had been his responsibility as a child, when the place was part of his family's sheep ranch. His father told him to keep the sheep away from the old pueblo and the mission; this was holy ground. So Federico Sisneros kept the sheep away and took care of the mission. He continued to care for it when his family gave the land to the state of New Mexico. At first, he was paid ten dollars a month by the state. He would have stayed for nothing. Then the mission became a National Monument, and when I met him, Don Federico was the resident national park ranger. He was ninety-three years old.

"They say I am the oldest park ranger in the country," Don Federico said, in his dignified but halting English. "I don't know if that be true or not."

I told him I thought it was probably true.

He showed me around the heaped stones of the ruins. "It's too bad," he said, "but in 1905, that wall fell down on the west side." He remembered how sad he felt the day it fell. He walked me between the tall walls of the former nave, still standing. He said he thought all the time about the hundreds of people who once attended mass between those walls. "But they left here," he said, "and they never came back no more."

The whole sad history of the mission of San Gregorio seemed to live in Federico Sisneros. "And when I die," he said, shyly pointing to a small juniper tree on the corner of the mission grounds, "I have asked them if I can be buried right over there."

He died the next year. When I crossed the bridge on my return visit and parked across the road from the mission, I walked down the path straight to the juniper. It had grown a little taller over the years. Under the tree, right where he wanted it to be, there was the tidy grave of Federico Sisneros.

I made a happy discovery at the small visitors center: the name badge on the pocket of the new national park ranger said "Sisneros." She was Ernestine, Don Federico's niece. She said she lives down the road in the house in which her uncle was born. We talked about him a while, and his life of devotion. Ernestine said she is trying to do things just the way he always did them.

As we talked, a car pulled up outside, with a man and woman in it. The man hopped out with his camera and made a picture of the mission ruins. After a minute or two, the couple drove away.

"Mira-miras," Ernestine said with a smile. "That's what Federico always called them. 'Looky-lookies,' the people who never even walk through the mission, just take a look, take a picture and take off. We still get a few mira-miras every day."

I had a good talk with Ernestine Sisneros, and then took a slow stroll past the mission, through the old pueblo ruins and back again, to pay my respects one last time to the grave of the great old man who loved this place and cared for it for nearly a century. I stayed there on the mission grounds for another hour or so. In the first place, I felt like lingering, and in the second place, I didn't want Ernestine to mistake me for a mira-mira.

I meandered back to the Rio Grande in time to catch the reflections of the late afternoon sun on the brown water as I turned north toward Albuquerque. Not that there's very much water in the river at this time of year. Will Rogers said the Rio Grande was the only river he'd ever seen that needed irrigating. And Tony Hillerman, the New Mexico novelist and historian, for all his love of the Rio Grande, has acknowledged that in the late fall there are places where you can walk across the river bed and get nothing on your shoes but dust. Still, the Great River is New Mexico's aorta. Without it and its veins, the streams that rush down to it from the mountains, life of any sort would be chancy and improbable.

Without the Rio Grande, there would be no Albuquerque sprawling along the east bank. And that night, I was very glad there was an Albuquerque, a city with an embracing motel room where I could take a luxurious long shower, put on a clean shirt, and go in search of a proper martini. I found the martini at a cafe near the airport that goes by the unlikely name of the Rio Grande Yacht Club. The barroom was so congenial that I made it my headquarters for the next few nights, occupying the same table by the window, working my way through the menu with the advice of a friendly young waitress named Lisa, and occasionally exchanging rounds of drinks with the regulars. The favored beverage of the place, not bad either, was a local beer, Rio Grande Outlaw Lager, with a Georgia O'Keeffe steer skull floating above mesas and mountains on the label. "Brewed and bottled by Scott, Tom and Matt. Beer made the way it was meant to be." For a while in America, local breweries were shutting down all over. Now, from Boston to Seattle, they're springing up again. I never met Scott, Tom, and Matt there in Albuquerque, but I say long life to them.

I spent my days in Albuquerque as a contented tourist. I bought some Christmas presents in the Indian jewelry stores and antique shops of Old Town, the adobe plaza surrounding the eighteenth-century Church of San Felipe de Neri. I wandered along Central Avenue, which was Route 66, the main Chicago-Los Angeles highway, for forty glorious years. But those forty years were forty years ago; much of Central has become an avenue of broken dreams, its dance halls and pawn shops and seedy motels lending it a whiff of vice.

I stopped into the famous Central Avenue Man's Hat Shop and tried on a $300 beaver cowboy hat. It is amazing how putting on a cowboy hat makes anybody look like a cowboy. Once I read a memoir by a long-haired hippy who crossed the country on a motorcycle. He was hassled by the police and the populace at every stop. Then he bought a cowboy hat. He had no further trouble. He was no longer a long-haired hippy, he was a long-haired *cowboy,* and that made all the difference in the world. Wearing that hat, even I looked like a cowboy to myself in the mirror of the Man's Hat Shop. I have worn cowboy hats plenty of times on solitary fishing trips in the West, and the one on my head in that store was the best-looking I've ever tried on. With its tall black crown and rakish brim, it transformed me from a fat Eastern traveler into a fat Western bull

Bosque del Apache

Above: Starburst *in flight*
*Right:Slim Green (photo by
Leslie A.Woodrow)*

Left: Don Federico Sisneros's grave
Below: With Tom Smylie's falcon, Genesis (photo by Cherie Rife Smylie)

stine Sisneros

rider. It even came with a card to tuck into the sweat band: "Like Hell It's Yours. Put It Back. This Hat Belongs to . . ." Under the spell of my rough beauty in the mirror, I almost reached for my credit card. Just in time, it occurred to me that there was a big difference between wearing a cowboy hat alone on a trout river and committing deception on a city street. It made me sweat just to think about it. "Like Hell It's Yours. Put it Back." The little card spoke to me. I placed the beautiful black beaver back on the rack and sidled out the door bareheaded.

I worked out an agreeable formula for my late lunches in places like La Placita on the Old Town plaza: One (1) heaping five-dollar plate of tamales, burritos, or blue-corn enchiladas, plus one (1) gigantic five-dollar margarita, equalled one (1) hour-and-a-half nap back at the motel. By the time I woke and typed up my notes for the day, it would be almost time for dinner. I am perfectly capable of succumbing to such a satisfying routine for days at a time, and I might have, except that I am also an early riser, and in the mornings I kept seeing the balloons.

Albuquerque's cool desert mornings and light winds and open spaces make it the hot air ballooning capital of America. At about the same time of day New Yorkers go briskly out into the streets to walk their dogs, many people in Albuquerque prefer to dawdle around in the sky for a while before breakfast. Some mornings, there are so many dawdlers that it gets crowded up there. During the big international festivals, you can look up to the west from Old Town and see seven hundred brightly colored balloons gently rising and falling and softly bumping into one another. It is one of New Mexico's more flamboyant sights, and a little alarming unless you understand that these are all licensed pilots who are presumed to know what they're doing.

I went for a hot air balloon ride in the Napa Valley of California years ago, when ballooning was a new pastime and the thought had not yet occurred to anybody that flying a balloon ought to require a license. My pilot that day would have flunked his test and been grounded for life.

"I think there are some power lines around here somewhere," he said.

"Oops, there they are, right behind us. Damn if we didn't just miss 'em! Well, we *missed* 'em, that's the important thing. Have another glass of champagne."

The guy's worried-looking wife tried to follow us on the ground with a county map, a pair of binoculars, and an old station wagon. A minute or two after we bounced a few times to a hard landing in a cabernet sauvignon vineyard, she pulled up in a cloud of dust to grab a line with her husband and me to keep the balloon from flying away again on its own. This was a struggle that resulted in skinned shins and about an acre of prematurely trampled grapes. We deflated the balloon and rolled it up as fast as we could, stowed the burner and the basket and got out of there, breathing hard, before anybody could show up from the winery to survey the damage and present a bill. When I had time to think about hot air ballooning later, what I thought was, well, I did it, I'm alive, and I don't have to do it again.

But the passage of time and the beautiful sight of balloons wafting above the mists of Albuquerque's mornings finally got to me. There are plenty of balloon excursions listed in the Yellow Pages. I called the one with the cleverest name, "Hot Alternatives," and was cheerfully told to roll out of bed the next morning before dawn, take I-40 across the river to the Coors Boulevard exit, head north on Coors for a few miles, pass under the Paseo del Norte overpass, and turn left at the next stoplight into the Taco Bell parking lot. "Be there at six-thirty," the man on the phone said, "and we'll see if we can go flying."

I was there at 6:30, but we didn't go flying. A weather front was coming in, and I found Mike and Lisa Slaten and their friends Tom and Becky Reyes, all enthusiastic balloonists with their enthusiasm obviously dimming for the day. We drove their balloon-laden van a mile or two to a dirt clearing, part of the airstrip of an abandoned ranch, and stood shivering in a stiff breeze from the north, drinking coffee from a Thermos and waiting for the sun to come up. Mike said, "Sometimes when the sun comes up, the wind dies down." But when the sun peeked over the Sandia Range that morning, the wind started blowing harder than ever. "Here's what would happen to us," Mike said. He inflated a crimson toy balloon from a helium tank in the van and held it above his head. The balloon shot out of his hand and hurtled out of sight into some low clouds to the south.

"That's virga coming out of those clouds," Mike said, "moisture that evaporates before hitting the ground. Virga usually means downdrafts, and in a hot air balloon, you don't want anything to do with downdrafts."

Tom Reyes finished his cup of coffee with a thoughtful gulp and repeated what must be a balloonists' bad weather mantra: "It's lots better to be down here wishing we were up there than to be up there wishing we were down here."

I had the feeling that if Mike and Tom had been planning to fly for fun that day, they'd have inflated the balloon and taken off alone for the adventure of it. But they didn't want to subject a passenger to the same thrill. And remembering the bone-jarring thrill of bouncing through that California vineyard years before in a wind just like this one, I sort of sympathized with their point of view. We called the whole thing off for the day and went back to the Taco Bell for breakfast.

On a calmer morning later in the week, we met in the cold darkness again. This time, the garish craft known to air traffic controllers as "November 64710, Hot Air Balloon" and to the Slatens as *Starburst* was inflated and ready to go in ten minutes. Lisa Slaten handed me a paper to sign, while she explained the safety of hot air ballooning. The paper was headed, "This Document Affects Your Rights and the Rights of Your Heirs. Please Read It Carefully."

"Mike's an FAA certified commercial pilot," Lisa said. "He's supercautious."

The document said, "I know and fully understand that hot air balloon travel involves foreseeable and inherent dangers which may result in death . . ."

"The balloon is made of 1,250 yards of double rip-stop nylon," Lisa said.

". . . permanent disability," the document said, "serious injury or sickness, and I voluntarily and knowingly choose to assume any and all such risks that may attend the flight."

"The envelope is girdled with load tape," Lisa said, "the same stuff they use in car seat belts. And those two burners generate sixteen million BTU's. That's about ten thousand horsepower, enough to get you out of a jam in a hurry. Not that we ever get into a jam."

I read the rest of the document, releasing and holding harmless Lisa and Mike and their agents, lessors, and successors from any prosecution by me, my heirs, executors, or assigns. I signed the thing and hopped into the wicker basket with Mike and Tom. We lifted gently straight up into the sky.

Mike Slaten was a banker who took up ballooning as a hobby. He lost his job in one of those cyclical banking layoffs. He went to work for another bank just in time to get laid off by that one, too. He figured ballooning, for all its ups and downs, might prove a more stable line of work than banking, and could hardly fail to be more fun. He went out and got a commercial balloon license, bought a leather jacket and a white scarf, and threw away all his neckties. Now he goes around with a smile on his face, a lucky man who has found his calling.

The morning's slight breeze floated us east across the mesa toward the river. A balloon can't be steered—it goes where the wind takes it—but it can be manipulated in subtle ways by a good pilot, and I think Mike decided to show off a bit. He let the basket brush the top limbs of the cottonwood trees that line the river and brought us down to a soft landing on a tiny island in the middle of the Rio Grande. I stepped out to make a few photographs, and when I climbed back in again, Mike gave a short blast of the burners, just enough to lift us away. He had noticed, as I had not, that the breeze was blowing in a different direction along the floodplain. Now it carried us south, a mile or so downriver, with the bottom of the basket gliding no more than two inches above the muddy water, a giddy experience and surely some kind of low-altitude record, even for the skillful pilots of Albuquerque. After that, we lifted up and over the trees again, and in another altitudinal wind shift, right back north and west toward the launching field! A few horses and cows looked up at us vacantly from their farm lots. A woman waved from her kitchen window. The rising sun was beginning to burn off the ground fog over the city to the east. There was something beautiful to see in every direction below. But Mike Slaten didn't notice any of this. He was intent on bringing *Starburst* to earth only a few yards from the spot where we had taken off an hour before. And he did it. Lisa and Becky, the ground crew, always prepared in the radio-equipped van to chase the balloon over half the county, didn't even have to start the engine this time.

Once we were on the ground, Mike permitted himself a moment of smug self-congratulation. "Happens this way all the time," he said. Lisa heard him. "Once in a hundred flights," she grinned. We let the gorgeous balloon go limp, and stuffed it in its bag with champagne toasts and smiles all around. Perfect morning, perfect trip. I felt exhilarated. Mike and Tom wrote my name on the "Certificate of Flight" they give to all their patrons, dated it, and presented it to me. Above a glossy gold seal, there was an inscription:

> *The winds have welcomed you with softness.*
> *The sun has blessed you with its warm hands.*
> *You have flown so high and so well that*
> *God has joined you in your laughter*
> *And let you gently back*
> *Into the loving arms of Mother Earth.*

Very corny. But at the moment, it seemed just right.

I'd have stayed in Albuquerque another day or two if I could have found Tom Smylie, but I couldn't. The address and phone number in my wallet proved to be out of date. Too bad. I wanted to see him and his wife, Cherie, again. And their falcon, Genesis.

I thought I knew something about friendship until I met Tom Smylie and Genesis ten years ago. They were more than friends. They were bonded to each other. Tom raised Genesis, a gyrfalcon-peregrine, almost from birth. He told me, "If I just let him loose in the spring, he'll go out and catch food and bring it back to me as he would his mate in the wild, because he's imprinted to me. He is."

"Really?" I asked.

"Yep," Tom said. "He's got me trained to do just what he wants me to."

In fact, anyone who aspires to the ancient calling of falconer must do all the training, and do it over many months and years with abiding perseverance. Nearly every waking hour Tom Smylie didn't spend at his job with the Fish and Wildlife Service, he spent with his falcon. The peregrine falcon is another creature, like my well-loved cranes, that nearly reached extinction on this continent a few years ago. Caring human beings, Tom Smylie among them, by breeding falcons, are returning them to their natural place in the sky. Cherie and Tom let me hold Genesis on my own gloved fist one morning on the West Mesa and let me stare into those fierce eight-power eyes. All these years later, those eyes are locked in my memory.

Then I watched Genesis go flying. He rose so far that he was only a tiny dot overhead, until with a single shout, *"Ho!,"* the man called the bird out of the sky. With my heart pounding, I watched the most stunning power dive in nature, a falcon folding his wings and rocketing toward earth at the speed of two hundred miles an hour. The peregrine is the fastest, most perfectly developed flying organism on the planet. "Other birds flap," Tom Smylie said. "Peregrines fly."

And God help any passing horned lark or prairie chicken a flying peregrine fixes those savage eyes upon.

After I'd left New Mexico on this trip, I found that Tom and Cherie were still there after all. I hadn't looked for them hard enough.

"I retired the same time you did," Tom told me on the phone, "maybe the same day. Maybe for the same reason—because I had something else I'd always wanted to do.

"We have a six-year-old daughter now, and this year the three of us camped on a cliff on Mt. Rainier with five baby peregrines, feeding them and caring for them until they were ready to strike out on their own. Wow, what a great experience! I've dreamed of releasing falcons into the wild ever since I removed several baby peregrines from nests in New Mexico twenty-five years ago. Those birds, you know, became the foundation for the breeding recovery program at Cornell University, which has become a big success story in the East. Now, we need to restore more peregrines to the West.

"So we took these five babies from the Peregrine Fund in Boise and sat up there for eight weeks—opening the box, letting them walk around and then fly around, waiting for their hunting instincts to take over. Sure enough, after six weeks they started hunting. Finally their confidence and their wildness filled them and they flew away! Wow, what a feeling!"

I asked about Genesis.

"Genesis got to feeling so sexy that he wasn't interested in hunting any more, so he's in the breeding program in Idaho now. I have a new peregrine, Jenny. I still fly up on the West Mesa, and take Jenny along to raptor courses I teach to school children and at the University and at an elderhostel every year. People get just as excited by their new knowledge of falcons as you did when you first met Genesis."

"And what about you?" I asked Tom. "Is there anything left for you to learn about falconry?"

"It's still an art," Tom said. "The bird is always painting a different canvas for you. Jenny loves to hunt ducks, so the other day I flew her over a pond full of ducks. She went down there and landed and sat on the shore looking at them! It's still the 'art' of falconry, not the 'science.' "

"Well," I said, "I'm sorry to have missed you. Give my love to Cherie and—well, what *is* your daughter's name?"

Tom laughed. "We named her Jamelle Peregrine," he said. "That was with the thought that we know how to bring up peregrines. You have to be patient. You can't ever raise your voice or give 'em a slap when they do something wrong. You have to teach them. You have to raise them perfect and not mess up. That's the way we want to raise Jamelle."

I took the back road north to Santa Fe. Outside a tavern in the old coal-mining town of Madrid, I met a young Indian hitchhiker on his way home to Nambe

Pueblo and told him I'd take him as far as I was going. I asked him if he could speak any of the Pueblo languages I'd been reading about, Tewa or Tiwa or Tano. He said his grandmother could. I asked him about life at Nambe. He said he wanted to get into the used car business in Albuquerque. He wondered what I thought my rental car was worth. I said I didn't know. We didn't have much more to talk about, so we drove the rest of the way to Santa Fe pretty much in silence. So much for my earnest attempt at cultural exchange. I let him out at another tavern on the edge of town where he said he knew somebody.

I have loved Santa Fe since I first saw the old city bathed in the amazing clear light of its high-altitude setting. That was sometime in my youth, and I have been back fairly often. This trip, somehow, Santa Fe dissatisfied me.

It wasn't the accommodations; I treated myself to a romantic adobe *casita* in the wonderful shabby-genteel La Posada near the center of town, with lodge-pole pine beams overhead in my sitting room, a beehive fireplace in the corner, and a secluded patio outside the door.

It wasn't a shortage of Santa Fe characters; they were on hand in abundance, as always. I hadn't been in town an hour before I met a dusty personage in the bar of La Fonda on the Plaza who described himself as a cowhand, poet, sculptor, and damn good self-taught string band gutbucket player. He told me stories about his late uncle who loved to travel, never carried anything in his traveling bag but a change of underwear, a six-shooter, and a bottle of whiskey, and never took his spurs off unless he was dancing. He told me where there was going to be a hell of a wake the next afternoon and invited me to drop in.

Everything in Santa Fe was in place as before; the stoic shoulder-to-shoulder row of Indians under the portal of the Governor's Palace, with their silver and turquoise bracelets spread out on blankets for sale; the art galleries and Navajo rug shops beckoning from the side streets off the Plaza; eastern tourists gawking everywhere as they must have gawked here from the time the Santa Fe Trail brought the first of them to town.

Santa Fe was about the same; maybe I'm the one who has changed. The pastel Southwestern paintings in the galleries, which used to attract me, now seemed mannered and mundane. I did have one great meal; it was at a chic place called the SantaCafe, of which I remember roasted corn chowder with a peppery aftertaste and crisp duck breast in a sauce made of sun-dried cherries, all served in a beautiful room with bleached-white moose antlers on a white wall above a white fireplace overlooking the white tablecloths. But the food in most of the other well-publicized restaurants struck me as pretentious and overpriced.

And many people I met exuded a kind of loony New Age spirituality; they babbled about "existence issues" and "life transitions" and "crisis resolution." A woman told me she had recently moved to Santa Fe for "soul retrieval," without mentioning how far or in what direction her soul had managed to wander off.

To make things worse, the weather turned cold, and walking into the wind at Santa Fe's 7,000-foot altitude quickly wore me out. It's a great walking city, but when walking becomes more ordeal than pleasure, it's time to pile your sixty-year-old bones into the car and get out of town.

So that's what I did most days, returning to my cozy *casita* each night to read by the fireside.

I drove to Abiquiu to see once more the gray desert and red hills that inspired Georgia O'Keeffe. She lived in a converted stable there for nearly fifty years, and in a little adobe house in the nearby vastness known as Ghost Ranch. Of the landscape around Abiquiu, she said, "It looks like it's all done for you, the beautiful colors and everything. But just try to get it down on canvas." She never stopped trying until she died. She said God told her that if she painted a certain mountain long enough, she could have it. "Well," she said, "I painted it fifteen or twenty times, and it became mine." I went back to Abiquiu to see Miss O'Keefe's mountain.

I visited San Ildefonso Pueblo to pay homage to another great artist, Maria Martinez, whose revival of her people's traditional black-on-black pottery made her famous around the world. I wondered whether Maria Martinez and Georgia O'Keeffe ever met, but nobody at San Ildefonso could tell me.

I had an encounter with one living artist of New Mexico, Slim Green. I had heard of him years ago. Practically everybody with a horse has heard of Slim Green, the old master saddle-maker of Tesuque. I don't have a horse, but I met a man in Wyoming one time who was in the habit of unsaddling after a day's ride and carrying his Slim Green saddle all the way from the barn back to the house, where he kept it dusted and oiled on a rack in the living room. When that saddle wasn't serving as a saddle, it served as an object of art.

That's the way people have always felt about their Slim Green saddles, including such famous people as Errol Flynn, Gene Autry, and Robert Redford. I had known Slim Green's legendary name for so long that I assumed he surely had passed on with the other Western legends to that great tack shop in the sky. But one day, I heard on the car radio in Santa Fe that Austin Green was going to show off some of his saddles the next morning at the Maxwell Museum in Albuquerque. That was the entire announcement, but I knew it had to be Slim. I woke up early and headed back to Albuquerque.

Slim was still alive all right, and still enthusiastic and talkative at seventy-nine, and still, by the way, slim. He was still making saddles, too, but only three or four a year now, which means that most of the dozens of people on his waiting list—"I do it strictly first come, first served," he said—are going to be disappointed.

A little group of admirers came and went through the morning, studying the saddles on display, running their hands over Slim Green's handiwork, while the craftsman discoursed on his craft.

"I work maybe a hundred hours on a saddle," he said, "and these days I charge as much as seven thousand, five hundred dollars, even more if it's a real ornate saddle for a special occasion. So these days, well, figure it out, four saddles a year, that's enough to live on. I don't feel I'm cheating anybody. A saddle I sold in 1953 for three hundred dollars went for ten thousand last year. That one had my standard 'flowers,' oak leaves and acorns, so that anybody who knows saddles would know right off it's a Slim Green saddle, see. I've never stole another man's flowers, though I've had some of them try to steal mine.

"All my saddles are custom-made, meaning I take into account the height and weight of the horse and the rider, and the shape of the rider's behind. Then I start in. I carve the saddle tree out of lodgepole pine and go from there, building up the saddle with layers of shaved leather. My hides all come from the range, not the feedlot, and I take my time when I'm working. No shortcuts.

"A guy I used to know was always complaining my saddles cost too much. So he found somebody to make him one for less. Pretty soon, he came in with that saddle and asked me to repair it. He was rounding up cattle, riding hard, standing in the stirrups, when the right stirrup came right off! He almost fell and killed himself. See, inferior saddle-makers are partial to making the right stirrup out of inferior leather, since the left one is the one you always put your weight on to mount the horse. This guy had a right stirrup made from the belly, not the back. That ain't right. I've never done that in my life."

I asked Slim how he got started.

"Well," he said, "I was born in Nineteen-and-sixteen. I moved with my family from Oklahoma to Texas in a covered wagon. As a boy, I was a rodeo rider and roper, and learned the difference between a good saddle and a bad one. I could never afford a good one, so I started in repairing bad ones and trying to make them better, and I discovered I had a natural feel for leather. I apprenticed myself to a great saddle-maker, Pop Bettis, there in Lubbock. He did it right, and from him I learned to do it right, even if I ended up with a lot of wasted leather, which I do."

A wiry man in boots and blue jeans spoke up from the crowd. "Do you always make fancy saddles?" he asked. "I prefer a plain saddle, myself."

This struck me as a pretty nervy question, like asking Michelangelo why he put all those prophets and sibyls on the nice, clean ceiling of the Sistine Chapel. But Slim took it in stride.

"Well," he said, "but a plain saddle don't increase in value. One time I said to a man with a plain saddle, 'If you don't think no more of your horse than that, I'd hate to see your wife. What do you dress *her* in, burlap?' Just kidding him, of course."

The plain-saddle man looked chastened. Fearing he'd hurt his feelings, Slim added, "Of course, it's all in your taste and your background. I'm not saying I know it all. Far from it. If I thought I knowed it all, I'd just climb into that casket and shut the door. I've been making saddles for sixty years, and one of these days, I hope to learn how to make saddles."

Slim Green struck me as the model of the ideal Western man, capable and confident, but reasonable and tolerant, too, and blissfully free of the self-importance I've detected in some big-city artisans of lesser accomplishment. An Indian woman in the little circle around him, thinking to kid him, smiled and said, "On that covered wagon trip to Texas, you didn't get ambushed by Indians?"

Slim took the question seriously. "No," he said, "I've always got along with everybody. When I came to New Mexico in the Twenties, somebody said, 'Well now, you're going up there with a lot of different kinds of people with ways you don't know nothing about.' I resolved to always meet 'em halfway—and then take one more little step toward 'em after that."

Those were the words I carried away with me from my morning with Slim Green. Pretty good credo for living in New Mexico, I thought.

Or any place else.

After Slim Green, who seemed young, I went back to my study of oldness. I visited Bandelier National Monument, where the Anasazi lived in caves in a pink wall above a little creek and farmed the top of the wall, though I could not divine how they got up there to tend their crops. There I met Norman Greenberg, an anthropologist from New York City who studied with Margaret Mead long years ago, and then spent his life immersed in the history of Native Americans. Dr. Greenberg told me he has visited fifty-two countries, taught in most of them, and liked them all. He and his wife, Gilda, also an anthropologist, were managing the site that day as unpaid volunteers for the Park Service. I thought the Park Service was lucky to have them.

From Bandelier, I took a loop through the San Jemez Mountains, State Route 4, with switchbacks and icy patches and many triangular signs of foreboding: "Rocks Falling," "Trucks Turning," "Deer Crossing," "Wind Gusting." No rocks or trucks or deer or wind gusts befell me, and it was worth the drive to come out of the mountains to an immense high meadow of great beauty which a historical marker identified as Valle Grande, fifteen miles across, "the world's largest crater." It seems the meadow was once a mountain, a giant volcano perhaps 25,000 feet in height. A million years ago, the mountain exploded and sank into the earth, bad news for any creatures in the vicinity then, good news for the cattle who graze there now in the gentle bowl the catastrophe left behind.

Another day, I drove up to Taos for a good lunch of *quesadillas*. A light snow started falling as I walked around the village and tried to imagine its gaudy past. Well into the 1800s, Taos was the busiest town in New Mexico, its old Plaza alive with French trappers and Spanish traders, ecclesiastics saving souls, Indians from the Plains swapping captives for corn and beans from the Pueblos, and Yankee mountain men trespassing on foreign soil for the pure Yankee hell of it. That was before the writers and artists showed up. Taos was Kit Carson's town a long time before it was D. H. Lawrence's.

And Taos Pueblo, a couple of miles away, was there a long time before that. You can't visit the Pueblo without thinking this: Here are the real survivors of New Mexico. The Spanish came, the waves of friars, the alien trappers, the soldiers of three or four nations; the footloose adventurers came along the Santa Fe Trail, Billy the Kid and all the rest of them; the settlers came, and then the tourists on horseback, in wagons, in automobiles; the physicists came with their instruments and equations, and on a July morning when their calculations proved accurate, turned square miles of New Mexican desert into green glass. And down the centuries, from the Middle Ages to the Atomic Age to the present day, the people of Taos Pueblo have gone on living in their multi-story structures, fetching their water from wells, baking their bread in outdoor ovens, lighting their lamps at night, a people apart. "The People" is what they call themselves in their own language.

The Hispanics and Anglos to whom most of New Mexico currently belongs cannot remember when things were otherwise. But the People remember. They know that others come and go. The People endure.

New York City

〜

Nobody lives in New York City. That's what people from elsewhere in the country don't understand. They say, "I don't see how you can live in a place like New York." Well, I don't. Nobody does. We live in our neighborhoods. These are small towns just like those in Iowa or Nebraska, except that they are not surrounded by farm fields; they are surrounded by other small towns. We have our own small-town drugstores and barbershops and hardware stores and cafes, and we know the mailman by his first name, and we say hello to our neighbors on the street, including their dogs and cats. My small town runs from about Jane Street on the north to about Perry Street on the south, between Seventh Avenue and Hudson Street. Within those boundaries, I am acquainted with a lot of people, and almost nobody in the small towns next door.

In December, I came home to my village within Greenwich Village to spend Christmas.

The first stop on coming home is the Beatrice Inn, the Italian restaurant in the basement on West 12th Street, to see who's in there.

Alice McReynolds is having an early dinner with her friend, Geraldine Martin, at their table, the one just beyond the door to the kitchen. I can tell you a lot about Alice. When she was a little girl in Washington, she waved to President Wilson, who was riding down R Street in a touring car, and he waved back. How many people do you know who were waved to by President Wilson?

Alice's mother and father were married in 1894, and homesteaded a quarter-section in Montana at the turn of the century. This grew into a sheep ranch of seventeen thousand acres. Her father became a Washington lawyer but returned to the ranch in the summers, and Alice went out there as a proper young easterner in her early twenties. The place had no sheets on the beds, and an outdoor privy. How did she like it? "I blossomed and bloomed!" she told me once.

Alice is a small woman and must have been a dainty girl, but she rode her cow pony, Joker, all over the Crazy Mountains. "I can still smell the sagebrush," she said. "When you go there again, bring me back some sagebrush."

As much as Alice loved Montana, though, it was the New York life she yearned for. She came alone, in the autumn of her twenty-seventh birthday, found a job, and discovered she could go to the Metropolitan Opera for one dollar. A seat cost a dollar and a half, so Alice stood, every Saturday, up in the Buzzard's Roost at the old Met. She liked Wagner, because with Wagner, you got a lot of music for a dollar, and because Melchior and Flagstad sang. How many people do you know who heard Melchior and Flagstad?

Anyway, there's Alice with Geraldine, both of them impeccably dressed, as always. Alice must be feeling better, because I notice she has left her cane at home. It's good to see the two of them at their table.

John Simon is in the other room with Kathy Dobkin. They're here nearly every night, because, John says, now that he has discovered a restaurant that keeps the gin in the freezer, he can't stand the martinis anywhere else. If he's not home, his friends in London and San Francisco know to call him at the Beatrice. John is a good writer, and co-editor of *The Argonaut,* a new magazine of ideas and opinions. He knows a lot, and he's interesting to listen to. John always wears thick glasses and a bemused expression. He is our Beatrice intellectual.

And I see Dr. Kauth has come across the street to have his dinner. Dr. Kauth is a famous podiatrist. He worked on the feet of Katherine Cornell and Vivien Leigh. Thousands of other restaurants are serving dinner in New York City tonight, but I bet ours is the only one serving a Foot Doctor to the Stars.

The Beatrice Inn was named for Dante's beloved, of course, the Florentine teenager who inspired the greatest poems of the world; never underestimate what an Italian poet can dash off in the grip of passion. The name has adhered to this 12th Street basement for a long time. The Beatrice was a speakeasy in Prohibition days. There's still a secret bell in the front window frame, the bell the regulars used to ring for admittance. Anybody is welcome now, but I'd say the regulars are still in the majority. We are drawn by habit, by affection for the place, by the good pasta and veal, and by the historical tolerance of the management. (Smoking in New York City restaurants has been made a crime by a new generation of the tiresome prudes who outlawed drinking in the Twenties. If the small neighborhood places tried to enforce this narrow-minded idea of how life in the city must be lived, they would lose most of their old customers. The Beatrice isn't the only restaurant in the Village that survived the Twenties by becoming a speakeasy.)

In the sophisticated world of New York dining, I guess the Beatrice is not an important restaurant. But it is the center of life in my small town, my urban village. I would be lost without it. For one thing, it's only a block from the house, and I can drop in on the spur of the moment; the first definition of a neighborhood restaurant is that you don't have to make a reservation. For another, I run a tab; my wife gets the bill at the end of the month, and I have the illusion of never paying. Most important of all are Elsie and Aldo and Vivian and Bruno and Marco and Alberto.

Elsie is an elegant lady from Genoa. She is active in Italian affairs, and is entitled to sign herself "Cav. Elsie Cardia, Cavaliere de la Reppublica," an honor that came with a horse in the old days. She and her husband, Aldo, bought the restaurant back in the Fifties.

Aldo was a dashing Sardinian from a family of seafarers. As a submarine officer in World War Two, he was lucky enough to be captured at sea by a British destroyer and thus to survive the war. Late at night at the Beatrice, after the doors were locked, Aldo used to enjoy bringing out a bottle of Sardinian grappa, sitting down with the few customers who were left, and talking the night away. My wife, Petie, and I felt lucky to know him. We were in the restaurant when word came from St. Vincent's Hospital up the street that Aldo had died. There was a profound silence in the place that night, and some tears. Everybody in the neighborhood loved Aldo Cardia.

Some of Elsie's high spirits went with Aldo, but she is carrying on. So are her son, Aldo, who is tall and handsome like his father; and her daughter, Vivian, who is gorgeous and smart; and Bruno Mazza, the dignified chef—how everybody hates it when Bruno takes his summer vacation!; and my wise and observant friend, Marco Resasco, the senior waiter; and Alberto Urgiles, the other waiter, unfailingly professional and good-humored.

They have decorated the sconces above the tables with holly and they've twined lights and evergreens around the top of the walls. It's really very pretty. Christmas music is playing softly—you have to listen to be sure it's there—and the atmosphere is warm with conversation tonight. Let's see who else is here.

The trim gentleman in the tweed jacket and bow tie is William Mangold, Yale, Class of '29. He's having the osso buco; when Bruno prepares osso buco, he knows always to save a portion for William Mangold. For thirty-five years, one week after another, that quiet man in the corner put out the best magazine in the country, *The New Yorker,* under the great editors, Ross and Shawn. God, how Bill Mangold must hate the magazine *The New Yorker* has become!

Chris and Yvonne are here. Yvonne Sherwell is an actress and dancer and cabaret singer, a hell of a trouper. She has played Electra and Lady MacBeth. She's been a headliner at the Trocadero. She has danced with all the great Spanish dance companies. For a long time, for good measure, she was the hat-check girl at the Algonquin; a columnist once wrote about the charm she lent to the famous old lobby. You name it—dramatic lead, torch song, flamenco solo— Yvonne can do it. I'm surprised she's not on a stage somewhere tonight.

And there's Janet Berry over there, Doctor of Science from Purdue, Doctor of Jurisprudence from New York University. Those are the Ph.D.'s I know about. There could very well be others. Blackstone the Magician took a rabbit out of a hat on a stage in Washington, Indiana, and handed it to Janet when she was seven. That may be where her love of animals began. She kept that rabbit in a comfortable hutch in the basement until she went away to college. Now she's a trustee of the Animal Medical Center in New York and says her best friend is her little schnauzer, Juliet, who understands sixty or seventy spoken phrases. Janet knows this because of the way Juliet wiggles her ears when she understands.

At Vincennes University, Janet studied chemistry because she had a crush on the chemistry teacher. That led to chemical engineering at Purdue, where she was the only woman in the class, and the only one to graduate with honors. Next thing she knew, she was separating uranium isotopes for the Manhattan Project.

Janet's life story jumps around a little. "The world outside Indiana appealed to me," she told me. "I listened to Lindbergh's New York ticker-tape parade on my dad's Atwater Kent radio, and I was enamored with the idea of New York. I couldn't wait to come on out here. [New Yorkers go "out" to California. Indianans come "out" to New York.] And when I got here, I thought I was in heaven."

She came to New York to be a chemist and decided she wanted also to be a patent attorney, so that meant law school at N.Y.U. "There were five girls in the class. Two flunked out, one got pregnant, the other one helped me find an apartment in the Village. I ended up writing the patents for butyl rubber, for polyethylene. I wrote a thousand of 'em. I'm still a consulting attorney on patents and trademarks. I'm just as excited about New York today as the day I got here.

"I was married twice. My last husband had two dumb wives. With me, he finally got a smart one and decided dumb was better, after all. So it was good-bye to him. But I could never say goodbye to New York."

I know. We are in the pounding urban heart of America! It is Christmas time! The Rockefeller Center tree is glowing and the Fifth Avenue shops are beckoning! And I haven't left this basement on 12th Street yet. It's just that I thought I could tell you more about New York City from a corner of one neighborhood restaurant than by chasing all over town. If you understand this, you understand everything: certain kinds of people are drawn to this city when they are young. New York calls to them if they want to be writers or painters, or actors or singers or dancers, or if they want to make careers in advertising or broadcasting or finance, or journalism or publishing or law. Even if the idea of the big city frightens them, they have to come, because New York is the place where they can test themselves against the best.

The young people keep coming. Some of them decide it's not worth it and go home. Some of the others, having stayed and experienced New York greatly, are having dinner at the Beatrice Inn tonight.

There's Jackie Bonnet, at the window table. Jackie says the luckiest thing in her life was that she didn't know how to type. So when she went to work for the director John Houseman, and he gave her something to type, it took her hours of hunting and pecking. He moved her to the stage crew, and she became his stage manager for all those great plays of the Theater Group, *Murder in the*

Cathedral, Three Sisters, Six Characters in Search of an Author. Jackie is an heiress, the only heiress I know. Her grandfather was a Sephardic Jew, Morris Schinasi, who lived in a mansion on Riverside Drive and imported Turkish tobacco to the United States in the Twenties—*all* the Turkish tobacco that was imported. The trust fund from her grandfather came down to her. "I've never been a consumer," Jackie told me. "I had this income, and thought I should do something with it." So she started the Donnet Foundation. The Donnet Foundation is just Jackie—no Board of Directors to consult, no office, no telephone. She supports struggling filmmakers with emergency grants to help them finish their films. So now, old Schinasi's Turkish tobacco money is paying for such movies as *Oreos With Attitude,* by a young black director, Larry Carty. Jackie is finishing her own film, *Paving the Way,* about women of her generation who made great strides before Gloria Steinem came along. Thanks to Jackie, I now know how heiresses dress for dinner, in old tweed jackets and blue jeans.

Susan Pettibone is here. She collects paintings. The walls of her apartment are covered with them, mostly by painters she knows, like the very good Village impressionist John Dean. Susan is a graduate of the Police Academy who investigates police corruption. When her work gets her down, she can come home to her art, which lifts her up.

Dr. Jack Chadbourn is over there, having dinner with some of the nuns from St. Vincent's. They are the kind of nuns who wear slacks and sweaters instead of habits. I think Jack likes them because they laugh at his jokes. Several times a year, Jack brings all his young cardiology interns to the Beatrice for a night off from the terrible pressures of the hospital. Those are always happy nights, with much loud talk at their long table.

Jane Jacobs, the great writer about cities, used to take her meals here when she lived in Manhattan. So did Arnold Gingrich, the *Esquire* editor, and Domenico Facci, the sculptor, and Paul Sann, the gruff old editor of *The New York Post.* Paul Draper, one of the most elegant dancers who ever put on a pair of tap shoes, used to do a little five-second dance on his way through the door sometimes to announce to Aldo that he was here.

But my favorite of the old customers was the Professor. His name was Howard McParlin Davis. I can see him now entering the restaurant, gravely removing his topcoat, his gloves, and his beret, handing them to Alberto, and quietly taking his seat at one of the tables for two along the left wall. Everybody at the Beatrice always treated the Professor with great respect, and I did, too. I had dinner with him once or twice when we both were alone and made a visit to him at his house on Perry Street. He had been chairman of the Department of Art History at Columbia University. He loved to talk about Giotto, the Florentine master who must have been acquainted with Dante and Beatrice. When he was younger, the Professor once spent a summer commuting from Venice to Padua to study Giotto's frescoes in the Arena Chapel. I asked him how he studied them. He said, "I went every day, and just looked at them." But he was looking with a sharp eye. For forty years at Columbia, the Professor caused his students to see Giotto and Van Eyck and the other great painters of the Northern European and Italian Renaissance through that educated eye of his. From what I've heard, he was one of the most inspiring teachers in Columbia's history.

The Professor lived alone. His wife had died, and his daughter, Alison, was away in Los Angeles. I asked what Alison did for a living.

"She's an exotic dancer," he said.

"Your daughter is a stripper?" I blurted out.

"Well," he said, "she doesn't just stand there naked. I know it isn't ballroom dancing, but she does dance. I am very proud of her. I hope you can meet her one day."

Before long, the day came. The Professor developed congestive heart failure, and Alison came back from Los Angeles to take care of him. She would call from the house and come by the Beatrice to take home a plate of lasagna, or whatever her father felt up to eating that night. The Professor had told me once that he began his classes with a comparison of a Byzantine Madonna, stiff and stylized, with a Titian Madonna, voluptuous, warm, and human. Alison turned out to be a Titian Madonna.

I went over to the house on Perry Street to make a photograph. The Professor put on his beret and posed with his daughter, the stripper. I learned that Alison was a Barnard graduate who had taken her father's art history courses and had traveled to the art centers of Europe with her parents. Along the way, she became a classical pianist and guitarist.

"But I loved being on the stage at Thirsty's in Van Nuys," she said. "Dancing is empowering and enlightening. I talked more than I danced, really, talked to these men about their families. It was poignant. I thought of myself as a therapist, a sort of healer. I got so interested that I'm studying counseling now."

I told her I'd never thought of a connection between stripping and counseling before.

She smiled her Madonna smile. "Well," she said, "dancing was fulfilling a fantasy, too. It's naughty, it's fun, it's a turn-on. I was tired of being appreciated just for my mind."

Professor Davis died in late summer. Now, at Christmastime, Alison comes to the Beatrice alone, sometimes sitting at the Professor's old table on the left wall. I think she is wonderful. She has stayed on at the house, putting her father's papers in order, commuting to Los Angeles for her counseling classes, and working on a book about her own life. She has a title: *The Naked Ballerina, Diary of a Professional Tease.*

You see? They say there are a million great stories in the city. You can go out and look for them all, or you can sit here in this basement on 12th Street with the Christmas music playing softly, and wait for them all to come to you.

But I did venture out into some of the other Manhattan principalities, because it was Christmastime. New York puts garlands in her hair at Christmas and looks her best, partly because of Lou Dorfsman. He is the brilliant designer who gave CBS its style, back when CBS was noted for its style. One December in the Sixties, Lou had the idea of decorating the bare trees outside Black Rock, the

Alison Davis and the Professor

*Christmas Eve blessing
of the animals at Central Presbyterian Church*

CBS building at Sixth Avenue and Fifty-second Street. He bought hundreds of thousands of tiny white lights and outlined every trunk and branch and twig. At night, that corner became a setting from a fairy tale. Everybody who passed by was enchanted, and the idea caught on. As I made my way around the city in this December, it was hard to find a block without a shimmering row of lighted street trees. They must look especially pretty to Lou Dorfsman.

New York is the true City of Light in any season. At Christmas the candle-power doubles and redoubles. Times Square in December is blinding after dark, with the decorations augmenting the gigantic advertising signs. As I walked down Broadway one night on my way to hear my friend Roo Brown sing a set at Judy's Supper Club, I had to make my way around clumps of out-of-towners standing in the middle of the sidewalk, just taking in the spectacle. Who was it who once observed that Times Square would be *truly* beautiful to someone who couldn't read?

From my neighborhood, I inched through the heavy holiday traffic by taxi-cab, and up to the considerably more sumptuous neighborhood of St. Thomas Church on Fifth Avenue. I wanted to hear the *Messiah.* Actually, it takes a little effort *not* to hear the *Messiah* at Christmas time in New York. In the morning paper, I counted advertised performances in nineteen places, including sing-along *Messiah*s and a swinging *Messiah,* "Too Hot to Handel!" But the full-length, three-hour version at St. Thomas had what the others did not—the otherworldly voices of the St. Thomas Boys Choir.

The boys are fifth-to-eighth-graders, and children of privilege—students at the only church-related residential choir school in the country. They study English, Latin, French, math, history, science, art, and music theory. On Saturdays, they distribute food to the homeless. And they sing—four hundred pieces of sacred music each year in the five weekly choral services of the church and in concerts around the world. You'd hardly think they'd need a rehearsal for the *Messiah,* but Gerre Hancock said they did. He has a grand title—"Mus. Doc.,

Organist and Master of Choristers"—and he says he's never quite sure what he's going to hear from the choir from one day to the next. "These voices are always in a state of flux. This morning, the choir will not sound the same as it did last week."

Dr. Hancock has a longer-range worry, too. "In northern, urban places, boys' voices are changing earlier and earlier. This is true of our choir, and it's true in Europe, including Scandinavia. But it is not true in the Southern Hemisphere. Everybody knows this is happening, and nobody can explain it. It used to be common for us to have fourteen-year-olds in the choir. Now, it's very rare."

Dr. Hancock let me come to a rehearsal. The boys sang with the men's choir and a thirty-seven-piece orchestra of period instruments, practicing their endings and intervals, and their standings and sittings, against the soaring background of alabaster saints behind the altar—High Baroque music in a High Gothic setting. St. Thomas was built entirely of stone, exactly the way the churches of the Middle Ages were built. The vault of the nave rises nearly a hundred feet above the floor, but for all its vast spaces, the church is an acoustical marvel, anyway. The music sounded flawless to me. Gerre Hancock found flaws:

"Clean octaves! Hold those long, long, eight-beat notes! It's not clean! Clean it up, please, gentlemen!"

He walked a third of the way up the aisle, still conducting, to listen from there, and walked back to say to the orchestra: "Sounds a little flippant. I think we're all getting a little tired. Try it again. Think of the nature of the work." And sure enough, on playing it again, a majesty appeared in the music that wasn't quite there before. I could see the difference a good conductor makes, the difference between perfectly okay and terrific.

On the night of the performance, the music sounded even better than it had in rehearsal. I can't imagine any of the other ensembles in New York singing "For unto us a Child is born, unto us a Son is given" with beauty as great as this choir sang it, ending with those powerful words, emphasized by the horns: "Wonderful! Counsellor! The mighty God! The everlasting Father! The Prince of Peace!"

And the boys achieved a fabulous treble sound in "All we, like sheep, have gone astray." It was pretty hard to imagine these particular singers going astray. They were all innocence, heavenly voices coming out of cherubic faces poking out of poinsettia-colored robes. And they sang clean octaves, and held the long eight-beat notes. I left exhilarated.

For me, it's not Christmas without the *Messiah*. Handel already had forty-six operas and thirty-two oratorios under his belt when he dashed off this music in three weeks in 1741. He kept fiddling with it for years, rewriting the songs for different voices, changing the meter and the rhythm. He knew Londoners loved massive sound, so he stayed busy assembling louder orchestras and choruses. He, himself, played the organ, loudly.

After Handel's death, the thing got bigger and bigger. In 1857, the "Hallelujah Chorus" was performed at the Crystal Palace in Norwood, England, by a chorus of two thousand, an orchestra of four hundred, and a twenty-ton organ. I'd love to have heard it. Even New York has never tried to top that.

In my first December as a New Yorker of leisure, I wanted to do some things I hadn't done before. So one afternoon I went to the circus.

The Big Apple Circus is a one-ring show under a big blue tent. Its performers live for thirteen weeks each winter in trailers parked in Damrosch Park, right under the windows of the Metropolitan Opera House, and so do its elephants and horses and pigs and ducks. Yes, there's a pig and duck act; it needs a little work, maybe, but it knocked out a big crowd of school kids under the big top, devouring hot dogs, popcorn, and cotton candy. They cheered their heads off for the jugglers and aerialists and bareback riders, too. I don't know what circus performers get paid, but if I were a clown or a tightrope walker or a trapeze artist, the laughs and gasps and cheers of a tentful of kids like that would almost be wages enough.

By good luck, I got a seat on the front row next to Frank D. Robie, president of the Circus Fans Association of America. Frank is an old-timer with a nice smile and stars in his eyes. He said he was brought up in Woodville, New Hampshire, on the Connecticut River, and lived for the day when the circus came to town. As a kid, he used to help set up the tent, watch the circus parade roll down Main Street, go to the show, and even visit the empty lot after the circus had left.

"All that glamour and tinsel gone," he remembered, "only the sawdust left behind. I used to feel like crying. I found a clown's shoe in the sawdust one time and thought, what good is one shoe? I have thousands of circus souvenirs now. How I'd love to have that shoe!"

Frank sat through the show transfixed and smiling. He's seen pretty much every variation of every act, but when he's at the circus, he can't keep that smile off his face.

There would be no long-running circus in Manhattan if it weren't for a Brooklyn boy, Paul Binder, who worked as an actor with the Dartmouth Players, stage-managed Julia Child's French Chef television show in Boston, mastered juggling with the San Francisco Mime Troupe, traveled through Europe earning his living by juggling on street corners, and came back to New York to found the Big Apple Circus nearly twenty years ago. He made a lot of kids happy one afternoon in December, I'll tell you that. Also a couple of old guys, Frank Robie and me.

Then Harvey Phillips came to town, spreading the tuba gospel. Harvey Phillips is to the tuba what Fritz Kreisler was to the violin, the great performer and popularizer. We had an early morning cup of coffee together and he bragged about the tuba: "We go off the end of the piano keyboard on the left. The keyboard stops with A. A good tuba player can go down another fifth. And at the other end of the keyboard, the tuba can play an octave above middle-C. I can't imagine any other instrument sounding as noble. This afternoon, in

Rockefeller Center, we'll have ten-year-olds playing next to tubists from the New York Philharmonic. The kids get pulled along that way. They play over their heads."

The occasion was the twenty-first annual TubaChristmas, a celebration Harvey puts on all over the country. Any tuba player is welcome to show up and play. Against my better judgment, I let Harvey talk me into conducting "Silent Night." I put on a red TubaChristmas stocking cap, wrapped a red TubaChristmas scarf around my neck, walked out there in front of the crowd, held my breath, and gave four hundred tubas a downbeat. What a feeling of power! Halfway through the piece, feeling like Rostropovich or Ozawa, I was tempted to do some directorial showing off, but the band was playing together and I figured I'd better keep it that way. "Silent Night" is in three-quarter time, so to be safe, I just kept making emphatic triangles in the air. I held the last note an extra beat or two, and those tuba players, bless them, held it on cue and ended in unison. In the wave of relief that swept over me, the smattering of applause sounded like an ovation. I started my conducting career by leading the kindergarten rhythm band in Washington, North Carolina, and ended it fifty-five years later in Rockefeller Center, with no performances in the interim. I am now retired.

I don't know much about music, but I love hanging around musicians, and Bob Kindred and Anne Phillips gave me a good excuse to do that for a couple of days. Bob is a swell jazz saxophone player. He plays without squawks. In his hands, a slow song in a minor key in the lower register becomes a poem, and the saxophone becomes a lyrical instrument. Anne is his wife, a conductor and composer. The two of them wrote a Jazz Nativity, "Bending Toward the Light," which has become a regular holiday event in New York. It was always performed in churches (one year in a synagogue!), but this December, the pageant was graduating to Avery Fisher Hall at Lincoln Center for two performances.

Bob and Anne signed me up as "host," which meant that in return for coming out on stage and giving a two-minute introduction, I got to hang out in the dressing room for the rest of the evening with the likes of Clark Terry, Lionel Hampton, Al Grey, Jon Faddis, Dave Brubeck, Tito Puente, Jackie Cain and Roy Kral, Gene Bertoncini, tap dancer Jimmy Slyde, and singer Gail Wynters. This would have been a big thrill for me even if there hadn't also been a thirty-voice choir to listen to, and a jazz singing group, and a big band led by Bob Kindred.

Swinging "We Three Kings of Orient Are" may not sound like a great idea in theory, but when Clark Terry, Al Grey, and Jimmy Slyde came down the aisle dressed as the kings in robes, turbans, and plumes, the full house stood and cheered. Each of them took a solo on stage, Clark playing that trumpet of his with his world-famous wit and imagination, Al making his trombone sound like an angel's golden horn, and Jimmy stopping the show with his dance. Afterwards, the Three Kings approached the manger and left the two horns and the tap shoes as their gifts to the Christ Child. You never know what form a religious experience might come in. When the final jam session was done, for all the blaring horns and the dancing, the evening had a feeling of great reverence about it. Outside Lincoln Center afterwards, a smiling woman said, "My husband and I come from Phoenix for this every year." To feel the way I felt after the curtain came down that night, I'd cross a continent, too.

In all my years as a reporter, I realized, I had let the joy of Christmas get away from me. I had been too busy working in those Decembers past to let the season sink in. I took down *A Christmas Carol* from the shelf, and was surprised to recognize myself, a bit, in Dickens's description of Scrooge: "Oh, but he was a tight-fisted hand at the grindstone . . . secret, and self-contained, and solitary as an oyster." I was glad to have given up the working grindstone, and to have time, now, as Scrooge had in the end, to take a more generous view of the world. A year of wandering on my own, meeting good people and hearing good stories, had lifted my spirits. Some of the joy of life had come back to me. " 'God bless us every one!' said Tiny Tim."

Christmas Eve arrived with a poignance I hadn't expected. I suppose I had thought I would always spend my free Christmas Eves at the old home place in North Carolina, but Papa was gone, the house was dark and empty for the first time at Christmas, and my sister and brother were staying home with their families this year. Petie and I made our way through a light rain to a Christmas Eve church service.

"But ask now the beasts, and they shall teach thee; and the birds of the air, and they shall tell thee; or speak to the earth, and it shall teach thee; and the fishes of the sea shall declare unto thee . . . In the Lord's hand is the soul of every living thing." The Reverend William H. Pindar chose that beautiful passage from the Book of Job for a reason. Christmas Eve at Central Presbyterian Church on Park Avenue is the night of the Blessing of the Animals.

"There were two sets of footprints at the manger," Mr. Pindar said in his sermon, "those of human beings and of animals. God put them there so we could learn to love ourselves better, and love all the creatures of creation. Be a better animal yourself in this season. Walk in the rain. Sing, even if you are alone." He quoted Gertrude Stein: "I am, because my little dog knows me."

People came down the aisle with their dogs and cats to be blessed. A little girl said to the minister, "My dog would try to eat every dog in sight, so I brought my turtle." A little boy brought his gerbils, one in each hand, and held them up for Bill Pindar's benediction. One of the choir girls, Casey Kimura, nine years old, brought her kitten, Topsfield. Elderly women waited in line with their companion dogs, a dachshund, a collie, a pair of young huskies. At least two people brought fishbowls, with fish swimming serenely therein.

Several children came with their teddy bears. A little boy stood in line gravely holding his yellow rubber duck. Andrew Fullmer, six years old, came with a plastic dish containing three worms. He said, "They are Blackie Number One, Blackie Number Two, and Wiggly. I found them in Riverside Park this fall. They are my only pets."

All were duly blessed. An impassive hound looked down upon the proceedings from the first row of the balcony, his face appearing among those of the other parishioners above an evergreen decoration and a red bow. During Mr. Pindar's closing prayer, dogs barked and canaries sang.

Then we all sang: "Joy to the world! The Lord is come!" And everybody walked out into the rain of Christmas Eve. God bless us every one.

ABOUT THE AUTHOR

In thirty-seven years with CBS News, Charles Kuralt won a host of honors, including thirteen Emmys and three Peabody Awards, for his work both "on the road" and on *Sunday Morning*. He is the author of five previous books, including the bestselling *A Life on the Road* and *On the Road with Charles Kuralt*. He makes his home in New York City.